Weight Loss Surgery Cookbook

for
dummies®
A Wiley Brand

Weight Loss Surgery Cookbook

2nd edition

by Brian K. Davidson and Sarah Krieger, MPH, RDN, LDN

Weight Loss Surgery Cookbook For Dummies®, 2nd Edition

Published by: **John Wiley & Sons, Inc.,** 111 River Street, Hoboken, NJ 07030-5774, www.wiley.com

Copyright © 2017 by John Wiley & Sons, Inc., Hoboken, New Jersey

Published simultaneously in Canada

No part of this publication may be reproduced, stored in a retrieval system or transmitted in any form or by any means, electronic, mechanical, photocopying, recording, scanning or otherwise, except as permitted under Sections 107 or 108 of the 1976 United States Copyright Act, without the prior written permission of the Publisher. Requests to the Publisher for permission should be addressed to the Permissions Department, John Wiley & Sons, Inc., 111 River Street, Hoboken, NJ 07030, (201) 748-6011, fax (201) 748-6008, or online at http://www.wiley.com/go/permissions.

Trademarks: Wiley, For Dummies, the Dummies Man logo, Dummies.com, Making Everything Easier, and related trade dress are trademarks or registered trademarks of John Wiley & Sons, Inc., and may not be used without written permission. All other trademarks are the property of their respective owners. John Wiley & Sons, Inc., is not associated with any product or vendor mentioned in this book.

LIMIT OF LIABILITY/DISCLAIMER OF WARRANTY: THE CONTENTS OF THIS WORK ARE INTENDED TO FURTHER GENERAL SCIENTIFIC RESEARCH, UNDERSTANDING, AND DISCUSSION ONLY AND ARE NOT INTENDED AND SHOULD NOT BE RELIED UPON AS RECOMMENDING OR PROMOTING A SPECIFIC METHOD, DIAGNOSIS, OR TREATMENT BY PHYSICIANS FOR ANY PARTICULAR PATIENT. THE PUBLISHER AND THE AUTHOR MAKE NO REPRESENTATIONS OR WARRANTIES WITH RESPECT TO THE ACCURACY OR COMPLETENESS OF THE CONTENTS OF THIS WORK AND SPECIFICALLY DISCLAIM ALL WARRANTIES, INCLUDING WITHOUT LIMITATION ANY IMPLIED WARRANTIES OF FITNESS FOR A PARTICULAR PURPOSE. IN VIEW OF ONGOING RESEARCH, EQUIPMENT MODIFICATIONS, CHANGES IN GOVERNMENTAL REGULATIONS, AND THE CONSTANT FLOW OF INFORMATION, THE READER IS URGED TO REVIEW AND EVALUATE THE INFORMATION PROVIDED IN THE PACKAGE INSERT OR INSTRUCTIONS FOR EACH MEDICINE, EQUIPMENT, OR DEVICE FOR, AMONG OTHER THINGS, ANY CHANGES IN THE INSTRUCTIONS OR INDICATION OF USAGE AND FOR ADDED WARNINGS AND PRECAUTIONS. READERS SHOULD CONSULT WITH A SPECIALIST WHERE APPROPRIATE. NEITHER THE PUBLISHER NOR THE AUTHOR SHALL BE LIABLE FOR ANY DAMAGES ARISING HEREFROM.

For general information on our other products and services, please contact our Customer Care Department within the U.S. at 877-762-2974, outside the U.S. at 317-572-3993, or fax 317-572-4002. For technical support, please visit https://hub.wiley.com/community/support/dummies.

Wiley publishes in a variety of print and electronic formats and by print-on-demand. Some material included with standard print versions of this book may not be included in e-books or in print-on-demand. If this book refers to media such as a CD or DVD that is not included in the version you purchased, you may download this material at http://booksupport.wiley.com. For more information about Wiley products, visit www.wiley.com.

Library of Congress Control Number: 2016956166

ISBN 978-1-119-28615-8 (pbk); ISBN 978-1-119-28617-2 (ebk); ISBN 978-1-119-28616-5 (ebk)

Manufactured in the United States of America

10 9 8 7 6 5 4 3 2 1

Contents at a Glance

Recipes at a Glance

Breakfasts

Lunches and Brunches

Appetizers

Poultry Entrées

Beef and Pork Entrées

Lamb and Other Meat Entrées

Fish and Seafood Entrées

Vegetarian Entrées

Meals for One or Two

Side Dishes

Soups and Stews

Snacks

Smoothies

Desserts

Table of Contents

Introduction

I f you're reading this, odds are you've made the very important decision to improve your health by having weight loss surgery. You most likely made this choice after years of struggling to live a healthier lifestyle by trying other methods to lose weight. You probably spent countless hours researching procedures on the Internet, reading books, interviewing doctors, talking to weight loss surgery patients, and speaking with other healthcare professionals, putting in the necessary time and effort to make sure this procedure was the right decision for you.

Your surgeon provides you with a tool — your surgery — to assist you in losing weight and leading a healthier life. Making that tool work is up to you, and a big component of your success will be your long-term eating plan.

Now is the time to use good nutrition to maximize not only your weight loss, but also your health, vitality, and renewed sense of well being. *Weight Loss Surgery Cookbook For Dummies* is an invaluable resource as you embark on this new chapter of your life — your weight loss journey — and we wish you all the success in the world.

About This Book

This book is all about eating well after weight loss surgery. (If you're looking for information on the types of surgery available, check out *Weight Loss Surgery For Dummies.*) At the beginning of this book we walk you through the four stages of your postsurgery diet and provide plenty of advice about living with and caring for your new pouch. Because life after weight loss surgery is an ongoing journey, we focus most of the book on what to do once you can eat "real food" again. We show you how to plan, shop for, and cook delicious and healthy meals that you and your family will love.

You receive cooking guidance from Chef David Fouts, who is known as the world's premier culinary expert for weight loss surgery. And he is also a weight loss surgery patient, so you know the recipes and cooking advice come from someone who understands what gastric bypass patients go through. You find a compilation of imaginative, inventive recipes to suit every palate, specifically designed to meet the unique needs of people who have had weight loss surgery and people just wanting to eat healthier. So that you can stay informed of what you're eating, each recipe lists the stage of the postsurgery diet it can safely be tried, the serving size, and the nutritional information. You can eat with confidence, knowing you're eating healthfully, helping manage your weight, and maintaining your overall well being.

If you're familiar with a *For Dummies* book (*Weight Loss Surgery For Dummies*, perhaps?), you know they're divided into parts and chapters. The editors and authors designed this book in a nonlinear fashion so you can read it cover to cover or skip around to the areas that interest you the most. For those of you who are accustomed to the post-op lifestyle and handy in the kitchen, you may want to want to dig right in to Chef Dave's delicious recipes (which have been tested by a professional recipe tester).

The following are a few conventions that you find in this book and that you should be aware of:

>> All eggs are large.

>> All butter is salted. Don't substitute margarine unless specifically noted.

>> Mushrooms are white button unless otherwise specified.

>> All sugar is granulated unless otherwise specified.

>> Pepper is freshly ground black pepper unless otherwise specified.

>> All salt is table salt unless otherwise specified.

>> All herbs are fresh unless dried herbs are specified.

>> When a recipe calls for sugar substitute, any sugar substitute that contains no sugar is acceptable. Some are sweeter than others, and personal preferences vary, so you may want to experiment by starting with a smaller amount than the recipe calls for and increasing the amount if needed.

>> Water used for boiling is not listed in the ingredients.

>> Nonstick cooking spray is not included in ingredient lists but should be kept on hand.

>> All temperatures are Fahrenheit.

>> Nutrition information that appears at the end of each recipe is per serving. Keep in mind that substituting ingredients or changing the serving size will alter the nutrition information.

>> All nutrition analysis is based on the weight of volume of the ingredient. For example, if a recipe calls for 8 ounces boneless, skinless chicken breast, raw weight was used. If the recipe calls for 8 ounces cooked chicken breast, weight after cooking is used.

>> ℧ This symbol indicates a vegetarian recipe. Note that these recipes may still include eggs and dairy.

Foolish Assumptions

In writing this book, we made the following assumptions about you:

>> You or someone you care about is considering or has had weight loss surgery.

>> You want to improve your skills in the kitchen and learn how to make delicious weight loss surgery–friendly recipes.

>> You want to give yourself and the surgery the best opportunity for success.

>> You want to continue on your journey for a healthier, happier life.

>> Or, you are a professional who works with weight loss surgery patients. You want to understand more and provide a trusted resource for your patients.

Icons Used in This Book

As you read through the chapters of this book, you find the following friendly icons that are designed to draw your attention to different nuggets of information and useful tidbits:

REMEMBER

Be sure to pay attention to the information next to this icon. This advice can help you make good choices, eliminate risks, and improve your skills in the kitchen.

TIP

When you see this icon, you're sure to find good ideas that will help you along on your journey.

WARNING

Pay close attention to this icon. It will help you avoid common pitfalls and mistakes.

Beyond the Book

In addition to the material in the print or e-book you're reading right now, this product also comes with some access-anywhere goodies on the web. Check out the free Cheat Sheet for a quick guide to what to eat after weight loss surgery, info on portion sizes, and more. To get this Cheat Sheet, simply go to www.dummies.com and type **Weight Loss Surgery Cookbook For Dummies Cheat Sheet** in the Search box.

Where to Go from Here

Weight Loss Surgery Cookbook For Dummies is written so you can start wherever you like. This may depend on where you are in your weight loss surgery journey and your skill set in the kitchen. If you are considering but haven't had the surgery, you may want to read this book cover to cover in a linear fashion to gain a clear understanding of your post-op restrictions and lifestyle changes. If you have already had weight loss surgery and are beyond the transition phase to solid foods, you may want to start at Chapter 3.

If you're a novice and want to learn how to prepare your kitchen, what tools you need, and what items to have on hand to cook like a pro, start with Chapter 5. If you're an experienced cook and are looking to dig right in to some new and delicious recipes, feel free to start at Chapter 7.

1

Eating Right with Every Bite

Get step-by-step dietary guidelines for the transition from clear liquids to solid foods, starting with day one after surgery.

Find out about portion sizes, your new nutritional requirements, and the benefits of meal planning.

See what you need for a well-stocked fridge, freezer, and cupboards.

Get tips on caring for fresh and raw foods, cooking methods, choosing the right temperature, and measuring common ingredients.

Chapter **1**

Fueling the New You: Ingredients for Success

In order to make the most of your surgery, you need to change your lifestyle after you have your procedure. This doesn't have to be a chore — in fact, when you see how good you feel when you give your body all the nutrients it needs, you'll want to continue doing it.

Establishing new eating and exercise habits is an essential part of achieving and maintaining a healthier weight. Each patient is expected to change the foods eaten, the amount of food eaten, and how that food is eaten, in order to provide the body with the nutrition it needs and to promote weight loss. These dietary changes and nutritional guidelines are meant to be followed for the rest of your life.

In this chapter and throughout this book, we start at the beginning, from your first day at the hospital, through your transition to solid foods, to sticking with a healthy eating plan for life. We outline portion sizes and general guidelines to assist in making your transition as easy as possible.

A weight loss surgery lifestyle includes planning and preparing small, high-protein meals, chewing every bite thoroughly, exercising, keeping a diet and exercise diary, and more. Your bariatric team will provide nutrition and fitness guidance and help you develop plans that will work best for you.

When it comes to food, different people have different tastes and schedules. Listen to your body and your surgeon's directions, and call your bariatric team if you have a question about your specific situation.

Are you frightened of the kitchen? The amazing thing about cooking is that you can make it as easy or difficult as you want. We show you how to organize your kitchen like a pro and guide you through the shopping aisles. (Here's a hint — buy foods that are healthy, convenient, and good.) You find out the best way to prepare and cook your meals. We also assist you in understanding nutrition and your food intake so that you can maintain your weight long after surgery. We think you'll find you have more energy and just feel better in general.

Understanding the Bariatric Surgery Diet

The diet after weight loss surgery gradually progresses from liquids to purées to solid foods. Because the size of your stomach is effectively reduced to about the size of 1 cup or less, your meals are smaller. You have to eat more frequently throughout the day, and you need to make sure you chew your food slowly and thoroughly, so it doesn't become stuck and so it's properly digested. You need more time to eat than you used to, but you'll notice you feel fuller with less food. You eat and absorb fewer nutrients than you did before surgery, so to prevent deficiencies, you need to commit to a regimen of vitamin supplements for the rest of your life.

After surgery, your pouch is swollen and your diet has to progress gradually from clear liquids to solid food to prevent discomfort and the premature stretching of your pouch. This is done in the four main stages described as follows. In Chapter 2 we cover each stage in greater detail, including specific foods, daily menus, and helpful tips.

>> **Stage 1, Clear Liquids:** This stage starts the day after surgery and includes any liquids you can see through — excluding alcohol.

>> **Stage 2, Full Liquids:** When you're able to tolerate clear fluids and have your surgeon's blessing, you get to add full liquids to your eating plan. These are identified as foods that are liquid or semiliquid at room temperature.

>> **Stage 3, Smooth Foods:** These foods are mixed in a blender until they're very soft and smooth in consistency. This stage is also known as *puréed foods*.

>> **Stage 4, Soft Foods:** In this final stage before regular eating, you add solid but soft foods.

REMEMBER

Specific dietary guidelines vary for each procedure and each patient. What we discuss are some of the general dietary changes weight loss surgery patients can expect after weight loss surgery.

Making Healthy Choices

By understanding a little about nutrition and applying what you know, you will feel healthier, look better, and have more energy.

Getting what you need in smaller portions

A typical meal in a bariatric surgery diet includes protein-rich foods such as lean meat, eggs, and lowfat dairy products as well as starches and whole grains, fruits, and vegetables. Eating protein helps you feel fuller longer. You'll be able to eat a variety of foods — in smaller portions, of course. Check out Chapter 3 for details on portion sizes.

REMEMBER

Since you are only eating small portions of food, choosing foods that are healthy is very important. Nutrient-rich foods deliver the most nutrition for the least amount of calories. To find nutrient-rich foods you need to check out the food labels to find out what a portion of the food is and how many calories and which nutrients are in a portion.

Drinking enough water at the right time

Water is important because it flushes toxins from your liver and kidneys, regulates body temperature, and reduces the risk of many cancers. It also helps with digestion, lubricates your joints, allows you to use glycogen in your muscles, which provides you with energy, and helps eliminate hunger by taking up space in your pouch.

Prior to surgery you received a great deal of water from the foods you ate. After surgery you don't have the same capacity to eat, which is why many post-op patients are prone to dehydration.

REMEMBER

You need to ensure you're drinking enough water. However, you also need to avoid eating and drinking at the same time because your new pouch is too small to allow both liquid and solid foods.

Checking out eating guidelines

After you make the transition to solid foods, follow these dietary guidelines:

>> Plan your meals.

>> Eat three meals a day.

>> Start each meal with a protein source.

>> Chew, chew, chew each bite.

>> Don't overeat — stop before you feel full.

>> Drink between each meal, not with your meals.

>> Don't eat in front of the TV, in the car, or while you're reading.

>> Keep healthy foods available and get tempting unhealthy foods out of the house.

>> If you're going to a party, offer to bring a healthy food item to ensure you'll have something there you can eat.

>> Pay attention to the taste of your food.

>> Try not to eat late in the day.

>> Use a food diary to keep track of what and when you eat and how you feel.

Finding out what foods your new pouch will tolerate after surgery is a matter of trial and error. *Dumping syndrome,* a common condition for gastric bypass surgery patients, occurs after you eat foods that are high in sugar, fat, or sometimes dairy, or high-calorie liquids. It can cause nausea, diarrhea, light headedness, cold sweats, abdominal cramping, weakness, and a fast heartbeat. (We talk more about dumping syndrome in Chapter 2.) Many people who experience dumping find it good incentive to avoid the foods that triggered the reaction for a while.

Keeping a food diary

A food diary is a useful tool not only when you're losing weight but also when you're trying to maintain your weight. A diary helps you be aware of what you're eating and whether you're veering from your healthy eating plan. Diaries can also help you to increase your awareness of why you're eating. If you write down any emotions you feel when you think you're hungry, you may discover that the feeling is something else — maybe thirst, fatigue, or stress.

TIP

Check out Chapter 3 for more information on how a food diary can help you achieve and maintain your weight loss goals.

Organizing and Readying Your Kitchen

Before starting on your cooking adventure, make sure you have your kitchen in order. Nothing is more frustrating than starting a recipe and being unable to find your favorite cookware or utensils or realizing you don't have the necessary ingredients on hand.

The first step to getting organized is to assess what you have, edit down to what you really need, and arrange it in an efficient setup, the primary goal of which should be accessibility. In Chapter 5 we help you organize your kitchen, stock your cupboards, and introduce you to essential equipment. By laying this groundwork you can make your cooking experience more efficient and enjoyable, which will help you stay on track with healthy meal preparation.

Planning to Eat Well

By taking the time to plan meals ahead of time, you're more likely to stick with your eating plan, stay within your budget, and find ways to use up what you already have on hand.

To take out all of the guesswork and free up time every day, take a little time one day a week and plan your meals for the week. You can extract a grocery list from your menu choices and do the week's shopping in one trip, which prevents frantic dashes to the grocery store for a forgotten ingredient. Cooking will be more enjoyable because you're more prepared.

TIP

Smart shopping is the name of the game. This means purchasing foods that are healthy, convenient, and good. Here are some smart shopping tips:

>> Buy the least-processed foods (closest to their original form) you can find.

>> Shop with a list.

>> Don't shop when you're hungry.

>> If possible, shop alone so it's easier to focus on healthy foods and buy just what you need.

>> Read labels carefully.

Practicing Food Safety in the Kitchen

REMEMBER

Fresh fruits, vegetables, and raw meats are always better than processed, but "safety first" is the rule.

It's upsetting to think about, but the foods you eat to stay healthy can make you sick. Fortunately, you can do many things to protect yourself and your family from foodborne illness. At the grocery store, avoid cans that are bulging and jars that have cracks or loose lids. At home, follow these tips from the Food and Drug Administration:

>> Be sure that your refrigerator and freezer are the right temperature for storing food.

>> Refrigerate or freeze perishable foods right away.

>> Throw away anything that looks or smells suspicious. If you think a food might be bad, don't taste it!

>> Wash your hands well before preparing food.

>> Keep your work area, wash rags, and utensils clean.

>> Cook meats thoroughly.

Check out Chapter 6 for more tips and tricks to ensure all your meals are safe to eat.

Chapter **2**

Dietary Guidelines for the First Few Months After Surgery

Chances are, before your surgery you got a lot of information from your doctor about what to expect afterwards. You probably also sat in your surgeon's office with a registered dietitian who painstakingly explained the diet you have to follow for the few weeks following surgery until you're able to eat "real" food again. The facts, guidelines, and warnings probably made perfect sense at the time, until you left the office and it all suddenly became very overwhelming. Don't feel bad — you're not alone!

Be reassured, your period of healing and adjustment will come to an end and you *will* be able to eat regular food again. You need to be conscientious of what you eat and the portion sizes, but having weight loss surgery certainly doesn't mean that life as you knew it has come to an end. You'll be able to go to a restaurant and have a lovely meal with friends. You just may want to split an entrée or take some home!

In this chapter we explain what to expect from your new pouch and some of the new sensations and symptoms you may experience. We show you what you can eat in the days and weeks after your weight loss surgery, and walk you through each of the four initial stages of foods. We also clue you in on food preparation tips and provide some sample menus to get you started in the right direction.

Here are a few things to remember as you recover:

>> **Every person is different, and every surgery is different.** You may have friends or family members who had weight loss surgery, and they all have stories about their experiences. Remember that this is your own unique journey and they may experience things you don't and vice versa. For example, some people can't tolerate rice, but you may do just fine with it. If you have a question about whether something is normal, call you surgeon's office, not your next-door neighbor.

>> **Keep in mind your surgeon's directions as well as your own specific tolerances.** The guidelines we provide in this chapter are suggestions based on clinical nutrition guidelines from the American Society for Metabolic and Bariatric Surgery and the American Dietetic Association. However, you and your surgeon know the details of your particular situation, so be sure to follow doctor's orders, and listen to your body! Again, call your surgeon or dietitian if you have a question about your specific situation.

>> **Your bariatric team is just that — your team.** Your surgeon, dietitian, bariatric coordinator, and psychologist are all committed to helping you make this the best experience possible so you achieve the success you deserve. Don't hesitate to call on them if you have any question or concerns.

>> **Get support!** Research shows that people who attend support groups are more successful at weight loss than those who don't, so regularly attend and participate in a support group. Face it, if you knew everything you needed to know, you wouldn't be reading this book. A support group is a great place to talk to others, share experiences and ideas, and get information resources, and they can be a lot of fun! Take your spouse or family members, because they're in this for the long haul, too. Your hospital may have a support group, or you can find groups online. A note of caution: Not everything you read on the Internet is absolutely true. Use reputable websites, and if you have questions, ask your bariatric team.

Say Hello to My Little Friend: Treating Your New Pouch Well

Your pouch is about the size of an egg and holds one to two ounces. You know how gently you have to handle an egg? Well, the pouch also requires special care, which begins in the hospital and continues throughout your life.

After surgery, the pouch is swollen for anywhere from a week or so (if you had sleeve gastrectomy, also known as gastric sleeve) to a few weeks (if you had adjust-able gastric banding [AGB]) to a few months (if you had Roux-en-Y gastric bypass

[RYGB], also called simply gastric bypass [GBP], or biliopancreatic diversion with or without duodenal switch [BPD/DS]). This in itself makes it difficult to eat much food at all. As time goes on, you're able to eat more. Some hunger is normal, so you may also *want* to eat more. At this point, it can be helpful to use smaller plates and utensils so it looks as if you're eating more and to help guide you in taking small bites. Forming good eating habits now (this means watching portion sizes) is important so you don't return to old eating habits and stretch the pouch.

TIP

Foods may taste a little different after surgery, especially if you had gastric bypass. If it tastes metallic, which is common, you can use plastic forks and spoons to minimize the taste. Cold foods tend to have less aroma, so eating chilled foods may also help unusual tastes. This side effect usually passes with time.

REMEMBER

Keep in mind that no matter how closely you follow your surgeon's instructions, you are probably going to experience side effects at some time. By following instructions closely, however, you can minimize the frequency and severity of the symptoms. The following sections describe common side effects you may experience and how to deal with them. Keep in mind that in addition to increased severity of these side effects, not following your surgeon's instructions can result in not achieving your weight loss goals, nutritional deficiencies, decreased energy, and just not feeling well.

Staving off nausea and vomiting

Common complaints after surgery are nausea and vomiting. If you feel pressure or fullness in the center of your abdomen, *stop eating!* Nausea and vomiting may occur during the first few months after surgery as you get used to your new pouch.

If you experience nausea and vomiting, chances are you have done one (or more) of the following:

>> **Not chewed your food well enough.** Chew each bite of food 25 to 30 times until it has a puréed consistency.

>> **Eaten too quickly.** Put your fork down between bites. Don't be rushed by others. Take 20 to 30 minutes to eat a meal.

>> **Eaten too much at one time.** Measure all foods. Take pencil-eraser-size bites. Stop when you are physically satisfied — not full.

>> **Eaten a food that's hard to digest.** Avoid fibrous foods such as celery, popcorn, and tough meats.

>> **Eaten a food you don't tolerate well.** Introduce new foods one at a time so if you don't feel well after, you know which food you didn't tolerate.

>> **Consumed fluids with a meal.** *Do not eat and drink at the same time!* Stop drinking about five to ten minutes before you eat to make sure the pouch is empty and wait about 30 minutes after you eat to begin drinking again. If your pouch is full of fluids, you won't be able to eat. Drinking too soon after a meal overfills the pouch and may make you nauseated.

WARNING

Vomiting is more than simply a nuisance and discomfort. Unresolved vomiting can lead to complications such as:

>> Obstruction of the opening to your pouch due to swelling of the lining of the stomach

>> Development of a hernia (an abnormal opening in the abdominal wall that allows the contents of the abdomen to protrude through) at the incision site

>> Dehydration, which can result in symptoms such as fatigue and headache, or more serious consequences such as decreased kidney function and electrolyte imbalances

>> Breakdown or tearing apart of the staple line in the stomach or incision

>> Nutritional deficiencies that can cause other health problems

If you experience nausea and vomiting, stop eating until it passes. If you have any question about whether your symptoms are normal, or you cannot keep water down, consult your surgeon immediately.

Staying regular

Surgery itself can affect your digestive system, but the lifestyle changes that come with a pouch can also cause you to experience irregularities. The following sections provide tips to help you get back on track.

Don't assume that any sudden change in bowel habits is a result of your surgery. If the symptoms (diarrhea or constipation) don't subside with treatment, see your surgeon to rule out other causes.

Curing constipation

Constipation is a common complaint after surgery. Right after surgery you're sore and that's probably the last thing you want to think about, but it happens. Usually it means you need to drink more fluids — the more, the better.

Immediately after surgery, you may be constipated due to the effect of the anesthesia or pain medication, which slows bowel function. Keep sipping fluids and move around as much as possible to move things along.

If you experience constipation later, it's most likely due to insufficient fluid intake. Some supplements, like calcium and iron, can also contribute to constipation. Don't stop taking your supplements, just keep drinking!

Another reason for constipation is lack of fiber, which can happen easily when your intake of fruits and veggies is restricted. If you're in Stage 2 of the eating plan, be sure you're drinking 48 to 64 ounces of fluid a day. In Stage 3 you can try soft cooked fruits and vegetables. In Stage 4 you're free to try fresh fruits and vegetables. Later, high-fiber cereals are a really good option.

Suppositories, stool softeners, fiber supplements, and enemas can also help, but talk to your surgeon about the problem first and find out what she advises.

Just remember, if you add fiber to your diet, you need to add more water, too. And don't forget to get up and move around! Exercise (even just walking) can often get things going.

Dealing with diarrhea

On the other end of the spectrum is another common complaint: loose stools, or what we typically call diarrhea. If you have diarrhea or are having more than four or five bowel movements a day, call your surgeon. And be sure to drink plenty of water, because you can become dehydrated quickly.

You're more likely to experience diarrhea if you have had GBP or BPD/DS than if you have had AGB. Diarrhea is often due to the following causes:

>> Unabsorbed fat from eating fatty foods

>> Sugar alcohols like sorbitol or mannitol that are found in sugar-free foods and tend to cause gas, bloating, and diarrhea

>> Intolerance to lactose (found in dairy foods), which can cause gas, bloating, and diarrhea

>> Eating foods you don't tolerate well

Your surgeon may prescribe medication or probiotics to treat the diarrhea. Probiotics are supplements that can be used to change or improve the natural bacterial balance of intestinal tract.

Keeping properly hydrated

If you remember one thing from the pre-op information you received from the dietitian, it's probably how important fluids are. Fluids are necessary for almost every bodily process as well as fighting off fatigue — not to mention helping your metabolism to encourage weight loss. We recommend you get 48 to 64 ounces of fluid a day. Because you can't drink very much at one time, this means you need to have something with you *at all times* so you can be sipping.

A really good way to gauge if you're getting enough fluids is by the color of your urine. If it's pale yellow or clear, good job! If it's gold, drink more.

In addition to dark urine, other signs of dehydration include

>> Parched mouth

>> Dry skin

>> Fatigue

Water is certainly the best thing to drink. If you don't like the taste of water, try adding some lemon or lime juice or a sugar-free flavoring packet. Try to stay away from fruit juice because it can lead to *dumping syndrome,* which is discussed later in this section. Juice can also sabotage weight loss because it contains a lot of sugar and calories. If you must drink fruit juice, limit yourself to about four ounces a day and dilute it 50/50 with water.

If you love coffee, tea, or carbonated beverages, you're going to have to make some changes. The caffeine in coffee, tea, and colas can be dehydrating, and it will be challenging enough to stay hydrated as it is. Go for decaffeinated tea or coffee, and don't add calorie-laden cream and sugar. A little skim milk and artificial sweetener should be fine. Carbonated beverages are not recommended because they can distend your pouch and lead to uncomfortable gas and bloating.

Just a word about alcohol — *don't.* Like the drinks mentioned earlier, alcohol is a diuretic, meaning it has a dehydrating effect on your body. You may also metabolize alcohol differently than you did before surgery. Always check with your surgeon before introducing alcohol into your diet.

Sip fluids *slowly* and don't use straws. Drinking too quickly can lead to nausea and a feeling of fullness and even vomiting. Straws can introduce air into your pouch and lead to gas and bloating. (Chewing gum does the same thing.)

Avoiding the dreaded dumping syndrome

Dumping syndrome is a miserable condition that may happen to those of you who have gastric bypass surgery. Symptoms can range from mild to severe and may include

>> Nausea

>> Diarrhea

>> Light headedness

>> Cold sweats

>> Abdominal cramping

>> Weakness

>> Fast heartbeat

Dumping syndrome occurs after you eat foods that are high in sugar, fat, or sometimes dairy, or consume high-calorie liquids. These kinds of foods travel quickly through your pouch and are "dumped" into your small intestine. Doctors believe this triggers a series of hormonal responses that cause you to experience symptoms, sometimes right after eating and sometimes hours later.

Dumping syndrome can last from ten minutes to four hours depending on what and how much you have eaten. Unfortunately, time is the only cure; you can't take anything to get rid of it. The best suggestion is just to go to bed and ride it out.

Some people may experience less dumping syndrome as time passes. For others, it may be a chronic condition.

REMEMBER

If you had GBP, your surgeon can give you recommendations about how much added sugar (as opposed to natural sugar in fruit and dairy) you can safely eat at one time. The following additional guidelines may also help you avoid dumping syndrome:

>> Avoid foods high in sugar.

>> Avoid foods high in fat.

>> Have small, frequent meals.

>> Increase protein intake.

>> Increase fiber.

>> Increase complex carbohydrates.

Most people who experience dumping find it good incentive to follow these guidelines for a while. If these measures don't help you, let your surgeon and dietitian know.

Figuring out food intolerances

Anyone who has had weight loss surgery has some experience with food intolerances. Unfortunately, there's no rhyme or reason for who has what intolerances. For some people it's dairy, for some it's beef, for some it's applesauce. You may suddenly be nauseated by something you have eaten all your life. The following foods are commonly not tolerated well:

>> Meat

>> Pasta

>> Doughy bread

>> Rice

>> Potatoes

A food intolerance is not a food allergy. It happens when your pouch is not ready to accept a new consistency or is irritated by the offending food. The most mysterious part of food intolerances is that they often subside — a week or two later you may be able to eat problem foods again. If you discover an intolerance, wait a while and try it again. However, some people find that certain intolerances are more or less permanent.

TIP

After surgery, reintroduce yourself to foods one at a time so you may be able to identify what doesn't sit well. Also, when introducing a new food, eat a very small amount of it. The best way to avoid intolerances is to take it slow and stick to the phases of your diet as instructed by your dietician.

Easing Back into Eating after Your Weight Loss Surgery

No matter what kind of weight loss surgery you have had, the size of your new pouch limits the amount of food you can eat at one time. Before surgery, your stomach was approximately the size of your fist, with the ability to expand and stretch. After surgery, your pouch is much smaller and may only hold a few ounces of food at one time. If you have had GBP, your pouch is about the size of an egg. It cannot stretch like your old stomach, so because your food intake is limited, the food that enters your pouch needs to be nutritious.

Since you have just had stomach surgery, you need to let your insides heal. In order to facilitate this healing, you progress through four stages of a recommended postsurgery diet. The diet stages give your pouch time to heal and adjust without putting strain on it. You don't want to get food stuck that would cause you to vomit and run the risk of tearing the sutures your surgeon has made. Although no diet rules are set in stone, there are general nutrition recommendations written by bariatric medical professionals that most surgeons follow. The length of time you're instructed to follow each stage of the diet depends on the type of weight loss surgery you had and your surgeon's specific instructions.

You may also find that you don't have much of an appetite at first. If you had AGB surgery, you may find yourself getting hungry by about two weeks after surgery. This is because the swelling around the band has gone down. If you had GBP surgery, it may be weeks or months before you start to feel hunger.

Following your surgeon's guidelines

Every surgeon's schedule for getting you back to "real" food may be a little different. Their instructions are based on research, best practices, and personal experience. Although this book and other sources can give you good guidelines, it's important that you follow the directions *your* surgeon gives you.

Why is this important? You probably have heard over and over that your surgery is a *tool* in your weight loss journey. Hopefully, you wouldn't try to build a house without the right tools and a blueprint to show you how to complete your project. Your surgery is the tool you need, and the surgeon's guidelines are like the blueprint to success. They work together to help you achieve your goal without banging your thumb too many times!

Your surgeon's guidelines will have very specific instructions regarding the kinds and textures of liquids or foods you're allowed at each stage of your recovery, based on what kind of surgery you had. Remember, your body is healing for the first six to eight weeks after surgery. Some of the very good reasons for paying attention to these directions are to

>> Lessen the chance of an obstruction caused by eating food you're not ready for or too large a particle

>> Decrease your chances of nausea, vomiting, diarrhea, and dumping syndrome

>> Keep you well hydrated

>> Prevent vitamin and mineral deficiencies

>> Reduce your risk of developing protein calorie malnutrition

>> Ensure you lose weight and look and feel great!

Your surgeon will probably require you to return to his office for a series of postoperative visits (no, not just one) during the first year and then annually after that.

Keeping these appointments is important even if you think you're doing fine. You need to have ongoing monitoring of your weight loss, lab values to detect possible vitamin or mineral deficiencies and nutrition intake, and have a chance to address other medical concerns you or your surgeon may have.

Eating and adding foods step by step

REMEMBER

Different types of foods and liquids empty from your pouch at different rates. One of the most important things to remember from now on is the more solid the food, the longer it stays in your pouch, and the longer the food stays in your pouch, the longer you feel full. Even though your head may tell you that you're ready for solids, your pouch can't handle the strain until enough time has passed. Your dietitian can help you with the guidelines and make your transition through each stage of the diet easier.

Following is a quick rundown of the four dietary stages (we go into more specifics on each stage in the remaining sections of this chapter):

>> **Stage 1, Clear Liquids:** In this context, a *clear liquid* is one you can see through, without added sugar, carbonation, or caffeine. You're in this stage for the first few days after surgery. Gastric sleeve patients may stay at this stage for up to a week.

Your surgeon lets you know when you can move to the next stage.

>> **Stage 2, Full Liquids:** A *full liquid* diet consists of food that pours off a spoon and has no added sugar, is lowfat, and has no lumps.

You usually follow this stage for one to two weeks or as directed by your surgeon.

>> **Stage 3, Smooth Foods:** *Smooth foods,* also called *puréed foods,* have no lumps but sit on the plate without running all over. You want foods with no sugar added and lowfat.

The length of time you're on this stage varies greatly among surgeons. Always follow your doctor's orders since she knows best for your circumstances. If you have complications from the surgery, you may be on this stage longer than usual.

>> **Stage 4, Soft Foods:** *Soft foods* are solid foods that you can mash with a fork. You still don't want to run the risk of getting too-solid pieces of food stuck or have problems with vomiting, so these foods are well cooked, not too chewy, and in small pieces, like ground meat instead of a chunk of meat. The same rules apply to this stage as the others: no added sugar, and lowfat.

You eat soft foods for at least two weeks. This amount of time depends on the kind of surgery you have had (GBP patients may stay on this stage a little longer) and how well you tolerated what you ate in the previous stage.

WARNING

Don't push through the diet stages too fast. Your pouch and head need time to adjust. You will have fewer problems like nausea, vomiting, and food sticking if you take your time. Some people are anxious to eat normally again, but you need to develop a new normal.

REMEMBER

Even with the same type of surgery, some people are able to move to the next diet stage sooner than others, so try not to compare yourself to someone else who had surgery. Remember to always follow your doctor's orders.

Stage 1: Clear Liquids

Initially, while you're recovering in the hospital, you're fed ice chips and possibly clear liquids. You may be a little nauseated, and the liquids minimize the risk of vomiting (which you definitely want to avoid at this point). Generally, you're on clear liquids only a day or two.

What you can eat

Basically, clear liquids are just liquids you can see through. Water immediately comes to mind, but several other liquids qualify as well:

- » Thin, pulp-free juices that have been diluted 50/50 with water (orange juice and tomato juice are *not* allowed at this stage)
- » Clear beef, chicken, or vegetable broth (look for high-protein broth)
- » Clear sugar-free gelatin
- » Sugar-free ice pops
- » Decaf coffee and tea (even though you can't see through coffee, it's allowed)
- » Sugar-free, noncarbonated fruit drinks
- » Flavored sugar-free, noncarbonated waters
- » Clear liquid sugar-free supplements

Clear liquid tips

Clear liquids tend to be better tolerated either at room temperature or warm. Remember, sip, sip, sip! Try to drink 2 or 3 ounces every 30 minutes. Strive for 48 to 64 ounces of liquid each day.

Measuring liquids is easy if you ask your nurse to give you a cup with measurements marked. The hospital staff tracks how much you drink as well and will have measuring cups on hand. Take a cup home and use it until your diet is advanced. If you feel nauseated while drinking, stop and let a nurse know.

Sample menu for a clear-liquid diet

The following sample menu shows what you may consume in a day during Stage 1:

>> **Breakfast**

- Apple juice diluted 50/50 with water
- Chicken broth
- Sugar-free gelatin
- Decaf coffee

>> **Snack**

- Clear liquid sugar-free supplement

>> **Lunch**

- Beef broth
- Sugar-free gelatin
- Decaf tea
- Sugar-free ice pop

>> **Snack**

- Clear liquid sugar-free supplement

>> **Dinner**

- Chicken broth
- Sugar-free flavored water
- Sugar-free ice pop
- Sugar-free gelatin

>> **Snack**

- Clear liquid sugar-free supplement

BEING SUGAR SAVVY

We mention sugar-free food numerous times in the diet guidelines, but it can be difficult to determine if a food is truly sugar free. Always check ingredient labels, and in addition to the word *sugar*, be on the lookout for sugar's many aliases:

- Honey
- Dextrin/dextrose
- High fructose corn syrup
- Fructose
- Glucose
- Sucrose
- Galactose
- Fruit juice concentrate
- Cane syrup
- Lactose
- Maltose
- Turbinado
- Brown sugar
- Molasses

Some sweeteners known as *sugar alcohols* have fewer calories than sugar but may produce gas, bloating, and diarrhea. They may be listed as

- Mannitol
- Sorbitol
- Xylitol
- Maltitol
- Isomalt

(continued)

(continued)

Using sugar substitutes in moderation is perfectly okay. They tend to be low in calories, but remember that just because a food has a sugar substitute doesn't mean it's lower in calories than foods that contain sugar. If sugar is taken out of a product, it's often replaced with fat, so make sure you read nutrition labels carefully. Some popular sugar substitutes include

- Acesulfame-K
- Aspartame
- Saccharin
- Sucralose
- Tagatose
- Stevia

Watch out for the terms *sugar free* and *no added sugar*. There's a *big* difference! *Sugar free* means just that — it has no sugar. Think diet soda or diet (sugar-free) gelatin. *No added sugar* doesn't necessarily mean it has no sugar. Some foods, like fruit, have natural sugar, which is why you have to dilute fruit juice 50/50 with water, particularly if you are a bypass patient (though it's a good idea for everyone in terms of calories avoided).

REMEMBER

You won't have much of an appetite after surgery, but don't worry if a nurse brings you a tray with a lot of liquids on it. It's just to give you some variety; you're not meant to drink all of them. As long as you stay hydrated, just drink what you comfortably can.

In this stage, your focus is on staying hydrated. It may seem strange not to be receiving food, but you'll only be in this stage a day or two. Your surgeon will let you know when to progress to the next stage.

Stage 2: Full Liquids

Full liquids are foods that are liquid or semi-liquid at room temperature and you can't see through. These foods should pour off a spoon (not just fall off in a lump). If you're tolerating clear liquids, your surgeon may approve full liquids as soon as the second day after surgery.

REMEMBER

Eat slowly, listen to your body, and stop eating *before* you are full. Eating past this point may result in nausea and/or vomiting. Remember that it typically takes 20 minutes for your brain to register that your stomach is full. The quicker you eat, the less opportunity it has to register in your brain that you're satisfied.

How long you remain on full liquids varies among surgeons, but generally it's one to three weeks. Remember to follow your surgeon's and dietitian's instructions.

What you can eat

Following are some foods you can eat when you're in the full-liquid stage:

>> All liquids from the clear-liquid phase. Get half of your fluid intake from clear liquids.

>> Lowfat strained or puréed soups.

>> Cooked cereals that have been thinned and are a soupy consistency.

>> All juices (remember to dilute fruit juice 50/50 with water).

>> Skim or 1 percent milk; plain, lowfat soy milk; or buttermilk (or lactose-free milk if you're lactose intolerant).

>> Sugar-free custards or puddings.

>> Sugar-free hot chocolate.

>> Protein shakes and powder with at least 10 grams of protein per 100 calories, fewer than 3 grams of fat per 100 calories, and fewer than 12 grams of carbohydrate per serving.

>> Light yogurt with no added sugar (no fruit on the bottom).

Full liquid tips

At this stage, reinstate mealtime. Even if you don't consider full liquids real food, make mealtime special. Sit down at the table with your family, turn off the television, and really be mindful of what you're eating.

REMEMBER

Your pouch is able to tolerate about 2 ounces of full-liquid foods at each meal in this stage. Remember, this is 2 ounces by volume, not by weight! Little medicine cups work great to help you portion your meal. Take 20 to 30 minutes to finish your 2-ounce liquid meal. Keep in mind that you may need to consume a lot of small meals a day and constantly sip clear liquids between meals to get enough fluids (48 to 64 ounces a day).

Following are tips to help keep you healthy and feeling good in the full-liquid stage:

>> **Eat (well, drink) slowly.** Take about 30 minutes to finish your meal.

>> **Liquids at room temperature or warm may be easier to tolerate.**

>> **Use a cup with measurements to track your intake, and don't use straws.**

>> **Use a baby spoon and put it down between bites of food to help you eat slowly.**

>> **To fortify the protein content of full liquids, mix in a small amount of powdered nonfat milk or protein powder.**

   You can even fortify milk with powdered nonfat milk. Mix ⅓ cup powdered skim milk into 8 ounces of nonfat milk before drinking or using in soups or pudding.

>> **Prepare any puddings, soups, and so on with nonfat milk to maximize protein and minimize fat and calories.**

>> **Use only protein powder or shakes containing fewer than 3 grams of fat, fewer than 12 grams of carbohydrate, and at least 10 grams of protein per 100 calories.**

>> **Get in the habit now of keeping a food diary.** (See the sidebar "Food diary = weight loss success.")

>> **Take your multivitamin and any other supplements your surgeon or dietitian has recommended.** Make this a lifelong habit.

TIP

Another habit to begin: protein supplements. As you consume fluids in between your meals, focus on meeting your protein needs. Your dietitian will help you establish a daily protein goal based on your specific needs. You can also find out more about protein supplements in Chapter 4.

Sample menu for a full-liquid diet

Your top priority right now is to stay hydrated. Make sure you get 48 to 64 ounces of fluid each day, 24 to 32 ounces of clear liquid and the remaining 24 to 32 ounces of full liquids. Your meals should not measure more than 2 ounces of food.

>> **Breakfast**

   • Cooked wheat cereal made with skim milk

   • Sugar-free light yogurt (no fruit on bottom)

>> **Snack**

- Low-carb protein supplement

>> **Lunch**

- Cream of tomato soup made with nonfat milk
- Light yogurt with no added sugar (no fruit on bottom)

>> **Snack**

- Low-carb protein supplement

>> **Dinner**

- Strained cream of mushroom soup made with nonfat milk
- Mashed potatoes thinned with nonfat milk

>> **Snack**

- Low-carb protein supplement (if needed to meet protein needs)

FOOD DIARY = WEIGHT LOSS SUCCESS

Food diaries are a great tool for weight loss and weight loss surgery recovery for the following reasons:

- Food diaries make you more aware of what you eat and the quantity of food you eat. If you get in the habit of writing down every morsel, you're less likely to mindlessly graze.

- Food diaries can be important in figuring out which foods you're not tolerating well. If you note any symptoms, you can check out your diary and find trends ("Oh yes, I felt bad the last time I ate cauliflower, too").

- Food diaries make it easy to show your surgeon and dietitian what you've been eating if you reach a plateau or begin to lose weight too rapidly.

- The best reason of all? Research shows that people who write down what they eat lose more weight than people who don't.

Your diary doesn't have to be anything fancy; it can be a little notebook or you can purchase a food diary from a bookstore. You can also choose from many online tracking programs as well as applications for smartphones (check out Chapter 3 for more details). Just find what works for you and make it a habit.

Stage 3: Smooth Foods

Congratulations, you're on your way to "real" food! If you're at this stage, your surgeon has determined you're healing well and tolerating the full–liquid phase of your recovery plan. Smooth foods (also known as puréed foods) are foods that have been put through the blender or food processor to smooth them out. You may follow this phase for up to four weeks depending on your surgeon's recommendations.

What you can eat

You can enjoy some very soft normal foods again. In addition to the liquids you have enjoyed up until now, you can add things like

>> Blended lowfat cottage cheese (great source of protein!)

>> Blended scrambled eggs

>> Blended cooked vegetables

>> Mashed or blended bananas

>> Mashed potatoes made with skim milk

>> Silken tofu

>> Sugar-free applesauce

>> Blended meats

>> Lowfat ricotta cheese

REMEMBER

You still can't consume large amounts of food. More than likely, you can only eat about ¼ cup at once if you had gastric bypass, or ¼ to ½ cup if you have a band.

Make sure your stomach is ready for this volume increase by increasing portions slowly. Listen to your body!

Preparing puréed meals

You need to blend or food process most of your smooth foods to make them the right consistency. This is a bit of an art, and you may experience difficulty getting the right consistency at first. Should you need to thicken foods, you can add things like

>> 1 tablespoon mashed potato flakes

>> 1 tablespoon nonfat powdered milk

>> 1 tablespoon instant grits

>> 1 tablespoon instant rice cereal

>> 1 to 1½ tablespoons unflavored gelatin or sugar-free gelatin

>> Commercial thickeners (ask your pharmacist or support-group friends about the commercial thickeners they recommend)

If the consistency is too thick, you can thin with

>> Nonfat milk

>> Water

>> Vegetable juice

>> Broth

TIP

Invest in a food processor for smooth foods. You'll enjoy a much nicer result.

Smooth food tips

As you begin to introduce more foods, *how* you eat is just as important as what you eat. The following tips help you eat well and achieve your weight loss goals.

>> **Skip the baby food.** It often has added water, thickeners, and sugar. You deserve (and will enjoy) real food, so take a few minutes to try some of the recipes in this book.

>> **Use standardized measuring cups and spoons to measure what you eat.**

>> **Introduce one new food at a time and only every couple of days.**

>> **Continue to keep your food diary, including any unusual symptoms you may experience.**

>> **Listen to your body and stop eating *before* you are full.**

>> **You may need to eat four to six times a day to get all of the nutrients you need.**

>> **Eat your protein foods first and use protein supplements between meals.** You need to aim for 60 to 80 grams of protein a day, so you will probably need supplements to help you meet your needs, especially early on.

>> **Eat slowly and take small bites.**

>> **Don't drink beverages with your meals, and wait 30 minutes after your meal to begin drinking again.**

HOW TO FREEZE SMOOTH FOODS FOR LATER USE

Freezing smooth foods in ice cube trays is a simple way to make your life a lot easier for the time you are in the smooth phase. When preparing your food, make extra and then follow these directions to freeze some for later:

1. **Be sure your ice cube tray is clean and dry.**

2. **Coat the ice cube tray with nonstick pan spray.**

3. **Place your smooth food in each cube of the tray, leaving ¼ inch space at the top for expansion.**

4. **Wrap the filled tray with plastic wrap and freeze.**

5. **When it's frozen solid, remove food from the ice cube tray and place in air-tight container. Keep frozen.**

6. **To reheat, simply heat one or two cubes in the microwave until completely heated.**

Note: Each slot in a standard ice cube tray yields about 2 tablespoons of food.

» **Remember to get 48 to 64 ounces of fluid a day.** Supplements can also help you meet your fluid requirements.

» **Because you're able to eat only limited amounts, you need to eat nutrient-rich foods.** In other words, you want to get the most nutritional bang for your calorie buck.

» **Continue to stick with foods that are lowfat and sugar free.**

» **Use small plates and utensils to control portions.**

» **Take your multivitamins and any other supplements your surgeon or dietitian has recommended.**

Sample menu for a smooth-food diet

You have many more options in this stage, which means it's easier to meet your nutritional needs (especially protein). Focus on using foods to meet your needs and only use supplements to fill in the gaps. The following sample menu shows what you may eat in a typical day:

>> **Breakfast**

- No-sugar-added yogurt
- Unsweetened applesauce

>> **Snack**

- Low-carb protein supplement

>> **Lunch**

- Cream of tomato soup made with nonfat milk
- Blended chicken moistened with chicken broth
- Blended green beans
- Sugar-free pudding

>> **Snack**

- Low-carb protein supplement

>> **Dinner**

- Blended meatballs with beef broth
- Mashed potatoes made with nonfat milk
- Fat-free gravy
- Blended carrots
- Sugar-free applesauce

>> **Snack**

- Sugar-free pudding made with fortified nonfat milk or low-carb protein supplement (if needed to meet protein needs)

WHAT CAN I EAT BETWEEN MEALS?

You may feel hungry between meals, but eating all day long will sabotage your weight-loss efforts, even if you only eat a little at one time. People often think they're hungry when they're actually thirsty. Since you're not drinking with meals, between meals is the perfect time to be sipping liquids, which may keep hunger pangs at bay. If you're lacking enough protein for the day, having a small amount of protein supplement between meals may be your answer. (Just remember to wait 30 minutes after drinking a supplement before you begin sipping other liquids.) You can also indulge in some sugar-free gelatin, a sugar-free ice pop, or sugar-free pudding.

Stage 4: Soft Foods

Soft foods — finally! (Some surgeons consider this part of the puréed phase, so be sure to check your personal instructions.) By now you're probably feeling and looking pretty good but are a little tired of the liquids and smooth foods and ready to kick things up a bit. Be patient. This fourth stage may last two to three weeks, but remember, the slow progression your surgeon has prescribed is for the best. The last thing you want to do is get a piece of food stuck. We've seen it happen, and trust us, it is not pleasant!

TIP

If you're bored with your diet, look at what you're eating. Is it the same thing over and over? Get creative! Use some of the recipes in this book. You can make each stage more interesting and satisfying by using a little creativity.

What you can eat

This is a good time to begin to think about how to meet your nutritional needs without the use of supplements. As you eat, ask yourself "Is this a healthy food for me that will help me reach my health goals?" A well-balanced diet can provide all the vitamins and minerals you need. This means lean protein, lowfat or fat-free dairy, fruits, vegetables, whole grains, and small amounts of healthy fats. Variety is key! Keep healthy foods handy and get unhealthy foods out of the house.

In this stage you'll find it a little easier to get your protein requirements without using supplements. You can add in the following soft foods, some of which are high in protein:

>> Finely ground or minced tuna, shrimp, scallops, and whitefish

>> Finely ground or minced chicken, turkey, veal, pork, and beef

>> Eggs

>> Lowfat soft cheese

>> Lowfat cottage cheese

>> Beans

>> Soft cooked vegetables

>> Canned fruit packed in its own juice or water

>> Whole-grain crackers

WARNING

Some foods may still irritate your pouch and cause you discomfort. Following are some foods you still need to avoid:

>> Dry, tough, grisly meats

>> Raw vegetables

>> Fresh fruit with skins and seeds

>> Doughy breads

>> Rice and pasta

>> Coconut

>> Peanut butter

>> Dried fruit

>> Greasy, high-fat foods

>> Nuts

>> Popcorn

>> High-sugar foods

Soft foods tips

REMEMBER

When your surgeon tells you you're finally able to eat foods with some texture again, you will probably be very excited. Don't go overboard just yet. Keep meals to about 5 ounces and add new foods and textures slowly to give your pouch time to adjust. Following are some tips for a smooth transition:

>> **Eat protein foods first.** Hunger is normal, and protein will help you feel more satisfied.

>> **Don't drink beverages with meals, and wait 30 minutes after your meal to begin again.**

>> **Continue to drink 48 to 64 ounces of fluid a day in addition to your meals.**

>> **Take small (pencil eraser size) bites and chew, chew, chew.**

>> **Eat slowly.** Take 20 to 30 minutes to complete a meal.

>> **Introduce one new food at a time and don't try more than one new food every couple of days.**

>> Continue to keep your food diary, including notes of any unusual symptoms that may indicate you are not tolerating a food.

>> Use small plates and utensils to help control portions.

>> Use fat-free gravy, light mayo, and broth to moisten food.

Sample menu for a soft-food diet

With fewer restrictions, you'll probably really like this stage! Use this sample menu as a guide to help you eat well. You can add low-carb protein supplements as needed to meet your protein goals.

>> **Breakfast**
- ½ banana
- One scrambled egg

>> **Lunch**
- Ground beef patty with fat-free gravy
- Soft-cooked broccoli
- Fruit cocktail in its own juice

>> **Snack**
- Plain fat-free yogurt with artificial sweetener or low-carb protein supplement (if needed to meet protein needs)

>> **Dinner**
- Chicken and vegetable soup
- Whole-grain crackers
- Pears canned in water

>> **Snack**
- Sugar-free pudding or low-carb protein supplement (if needed to meet protein needs)

Chapter **3**

Keeping the Weight Off: Healthy Eating for Life

By having weight loss surgery, you have made a lifelong commitment to taking very good care of yourself. This may not be something you're accustomed to doing. Not only does your diet affect what goes on the outside, it also definitely affects what is going on inside, and because you can't eat as much as before, what you do eat is much more important. Making sure you get all the nutrients you need takes some work. By understanding a little about nutrition and applying what you know, you'll feel better, look better, have more energy, and perhaps get off some of those medications you have been on for years. No one said it's easy, but following a nutrition plan can make a world of difference in how you feel about yourself.

Everyone who has had weight loss surgery is different, and what affects one person may not affect the next. And unfortunately, sometimes finding the best plan is a matter of trial and error. If you find you have questions (as you most certainly will), call your surgeon, bariatric coordinator, or dietitian, even if your question arises long after your surgery. The bariatric team is there to support you successfully through this process. And if your surgeon requires you do to things a little differently than what we say in this book, always follow her instructions.

This chapter has all the nitty-gritty of what you need to know about eating a well-balanced diet in the correct portions. It also tells you about some of the tools you need to help you achieve your goals. If you're like us, you lead a very busy life and need to know how to make good choices and even eat at a fast food place occasionally. Because this is a lifelong commitment, you need to know how to eat for the rest of your life. So let's get going!

Following the Cardinal Rule: Your Pouch Rules

So you're back to eating "real" food again. Think it will be like it was before surgery? Think again! You're going to find that you frequently answer to your pouch, even now that it has healed. Eat too much and your pouch will rebel. Eat too fast and your pouch will let you know. Don't chew your food thoroughly and woe be to you! You had the surgery to create this new phenomenon called your pouch, and it demands your respect.

While that may sound harsh, your pouch is also the tool that will help you finally reach your weight loss goals. If you take good care of it and treat it right, it will be your new best friend!

REMEMBER

If you had adjustable gastric banding, your weight loss will be somewhat slower than for someone who had gastric bypass or gastric sleeve. Don't blame your pouch; it's just the nature of the surgery. In some ways, if you have a band you have to work a little harder than someone who had bypass surgery. You won't experience dumping syndrome (discussed in Chapter 2) when you eat something too sugary or fatty, and you can pretty much continue to eat the foods you ate before surgery, just in smaller amounts, more frequently. Hence, without the physical limitations of someone with gastric bypass, it becomes very important that you stay focused on your goals and be diligent about tracking the calories you put into your body each and every day.

Keeping your pouch from overstretching

Immediately after surgery, your pouch is about the size of an egg and holds about one to two ounces of food, but it does stretch over time. The key is not to stretch it so much that you sabotage your weight loss efforts. To make sure you don't stretch it out too much or too fast, you need to

>> **Eat only three small meals a day and one to two snacks.** You'll find your energy level is higher and you won't be so ravenous at dinner if you have an afternoon snack. Be sure to read the Chapter 18 on snacking and making good choices.

>> **Eat slowly so you don't overfill the pouch.** Try to take 20 to 30 minutes to eat your meals (remember, it takes 20 minutes for your brain to register that you have had your fill!).

>> **Remember that constant snacking even in small amounts (otherwise known as grazing) may not stretch out the pouch but certainly can inhibit weight loss.** Those calories add up quickly!

Avoiding angering your pouch

Ever heard the expression "try to fit a square peg into a round hole"? When you find yourself nauseated or vomit after eating, you've tried to do the same thing. You may have committed one of the following no-no's:

>> **Eaten too much.** We discuss portion sizes in the later section "Keeping an Eye on Portion Sizes."

>> **Eaten too fast.** Put your utensil down between bites. Learn to savor your food and don't be rushed. Take 20 to 30 minutes to eat a meal.

>> **Not chewed your food thoroughly enough.** Chew each bite 25 to 30 times to a puréed consistency. Otherwise, chunks of food can get stuck. Trust us, this is *very* uncomfortable!

>> **Continued drinking with meals.** Stop drinking 5 to 10 minutes before you eat to make sure the pouch is empty and wait about 30 minutes after you eat to begin again. If your pouch is full of liquids, you won't be able to eat. Drinking too soon after a meal may overfill the pouch.

>> **Experienced a food intolerance.** This is very individual and can be frustrating. Introduce each new food one at a time so you know which food you didn't tolerate if you don't feel well later. Wait a few weeks and reintroduce the food. The following foods may give you a problem:

- Stringy or dry meat

- Bread or biscuits, especially if made from white flour

- Pasta, especially if made from white flour

- Rice, especially white rice

- Peanut butter

- Membranes of citrus fruits and vegetables

- Peels, seeds, cores, and skins of fruits

- Fibrous vegetables such as corn, celery, spaghetti squash

- Nuts

- Popcorn

- Coconut

- Greasy or fried foods

- High-fat meats such as sausage, bacon, bologna

- Carbonated beverages

Texture can be an issue with intolerances. You may be able to tolerate finely chopped celery in a recipe but munching on a celery stick causes problems. Be sure to follow recipe directions in this book closely.

WARNING

What if you do experience nausea or vomiting? Stop eating and drinking until the feeling passes. If you're vomiting to the point where you can't keep down water, call your surgeon immediately.

Keeping an Eye on Portion Sizes

Portion size is key to your weight loss efforts. We often find that people basically know *what* to eat but just eat too much of it. For example, you probably know that olive oil is much healthier than lard. But did you know that each has the same number of calories — about 135 calories per tablespoon? So more isn't better just because something is good for you!

The advantage you now have is that your pouch will let you know when you have eaten too much (of course, by then it may be too late and you may feel nauseated). By having to slow down your eating, you will tend to eat less. To help you eat slowly, try the following tips:

>> Take pencil-eraser-size bites of food.

>> Use smaller utensils, such as infant spoons and forks and salad plates to help control portions.

As you learn to savor your food and are more aware of your eating, really listen to your body and stop when you are satisfied. You may need to relearn how to do this. While you're eating, ask yourself frequently, "Am I still hungry?" By eating more slowly, you reach the point of satisfaction and are able to recognize it before you get too full. Do *not* keep eating until you are stuffed.

Your dietitian may provide you with menu suggestions. You may want to follow these for a while until you get the hang of meal planning, at which time you can get creative with foods you like. Many foods can be adapted to lower fat or lower sugar versions that promote weight loss *if* consumed in the correct portions. This book provides many easy, tasty, healthy recipes that you will want to try.

Use the bariatric food guide pyramid (shown in Figure 3–1) to help you design your own menus in the recommended portion size. Remember, the portion sizes are recommended as the limit. Listen to your body and stop when you are satisfied!

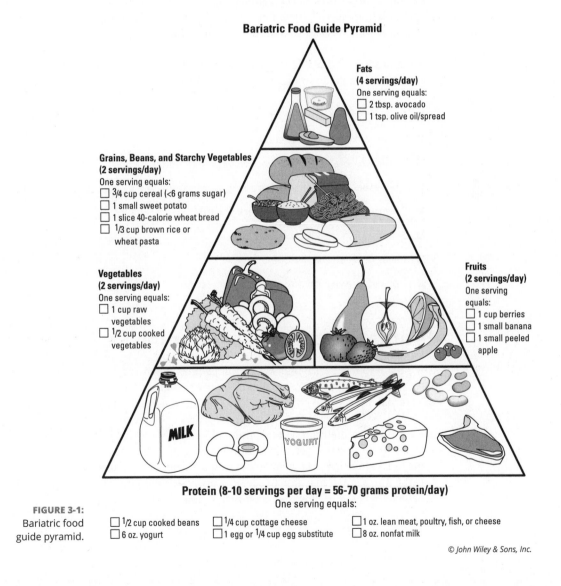

Bariatric Food Guide Pyramid

Fats
(4 servings/day)
One serving equals:
☐ 2 tbsp. avocado
☐ 1 tsp. olive oil/spread

Grains, Beans, and Starchy Vegetables
(2 servings/day)
One serving equals:
☐ 3/4 cup cereal (<6 grams sugar)
☐ 1 small sweet potato
☐ 1 slice 40-calorie wheat bread
☐ 1/3 cup brown rice or wheat pasta

Vegetables
(2 servings/day)
One serving equals:
☐ 1 cup raw vegetables
☐ 1/2 cup cooked vegetables

Fruits
(2 servings/day)
One serving equals:
☐ 1 cup berries
☐ 1 small banana
☐ 1 small peeled apple

Protein (8-10 servings per day = 56-70 grams protein/day)
One serving equals:
☐ 1/2 cup cooked beans
☐ 6 oz. yogurt
☐ 1/4 cup cottage cheese
☐ 1 egg or 1/4 cup egg substitute
☐ 1 oz. lean meat, poultry, fish, or cheese
☐ 8 oz. nonfat milk

© *John Wiley & Sons, Inc.*

FIGURE 3-1:
Bariatric food guide pyramid.

Determining an accurate portion

Initially you need to weigh or measure all of your food in order to learn how to take care of your pouch. But as time goes on, measuring is still important. Researchers estimate that most people underestimate their portion sizes by as much as 25 percent, which can really add up. Stay honest with yourself about the calories you take in. A time will come when you think you know what ¾ cup of cereal looks like in your bowl and you don't have to measure each time. We strongly recommend measuring every time you can. However, should you become that confident, at least check yourself periodically to make sure you're not experiencing the dreaded "portion creep." And if you eat from a bowl that measures one cup, it will be easier to monitor portion sizes.

Sometimes it isn't feasible to measure or weigh your foods (like when you go out to eat). Here's a guide so that you can visualize what a portion looks like:

» 1 cup cereal = a baseball

» ½ cup cooked or raw vegetables = a baseball

» 1 ounce or 2 tablespoons avocado or peanut butter = a golf ball

» 1 tablespoon olive oil, salad dressing, or mayonnaise = a poker chip

» 3 ounces chicken or meat = a deck of cards

» 3 ounces fish = a checkbook

» 1 slice of bread = an iPhone

» 1 baked or sweet potato = a computer mouse

Estimating the size of your meals

The Japanese have a saying: *hara hachi bunme,* which means "eat until you are 80 percent full." If you take smaller bites, eat slower, and use internal cues instead of external ones, you'll enjoy your food more and feel satisfied sooner.

Your surgeon or dietitian will recommend a calorie level for you to adhere to, and it varies from practitioner to practitioner. Men may be put on a general level of 1,300 to 1,500 calories and women at 1,200 to 1,400, or your surgeon may have you breathe into a small machine to see how many calories you actually require a day. Whatever the case, follow the recommendation.

You may also be given a meal plan to follow. While some plans require only three meals a day, some include two or three small snacks. A typical menu with three snacks may look something like this:

>> Breakfast

- ½ small banana
- 1 scrambled egg
- ½ slice whole-grain toast
- 1 teaspoon margarine

>> Midmorning snack

- Protein shake or 1 cup skim milk

>> Lunch

- 2 ounces baked fish
- 1 small sweet potato
- ½ cup green beans
- ½ apple

>> Midafternoon snack

- Protein shake or ½ cup sugar-free, fat-free pudding

>> Dinner

- 3 ounces chicken
- ⅓ cup brown rice
- ½ cup stir-fry vegetables prepared with 1 teaspoon olive oil
- ½ cup berries

>> Evening snack

- 6 ounces sugar-free, fat-free yogurt

Some plans don't allow any pasta, rice, bread, or potatoes — ever. Again, please follow your surgeon and dietitian's recommendations.

REMEMBER

No liquids are included in the meals. To keep from overfilling your pouch, you need to continue to observe the "no drinking with meals" rule. Stop at least 5 to 10 minutes before you eat, and do not drink for 30 minutes after you finish.

You may also have noticed there is no junk food in the menu. Remember, because you can't eat as much, it is very important that the foods you eat are nutrient rich. Foods like the ones in the menu above give you more nutrition bang for your calorie buck!

TIP

You are not required to finish your meals. Listen to your body, and don't eat until you feel pressure or fullness in your chest or abdomen, signaling you may be ready to vomit.

REMEMBER

You may have times when you simply aren't hungry (and you may really enjoy that feeling), but don't skip meals or forget to eat. You need to get enough nutrients so you stay healthy. And believe it or not, not eating enough can also slow down your weight loss. When you don't eat enough calories, your body goes into self-preservation mode and becomes much more efficient at hanging on to the fat it already has.

Making Wise Food Choices

By now you're realizing that you're limited in the amount of food you can eat. To be able to eat well without overeating, select *nutrient-rich foods,* including fruits, vegetables, whole grains, lean protein, and lowfat or fat-free dairy, which deliver the most nutrition for the fewest calories. To do this, you *must* read labels. You need to know what a portion (or serving) of the food is (no, it is not the whole bag in most cases) and how many calories and which nutrients there are in a portion.

After all, which is going to be better for you: a 60-calorie apple or 60 calories worth of jelly beans? Before you eat something, just ask yourself the following questions:

>> Is this particular food going to move me toward my weight loss goal?

>> Is this food good for my body?

Consider your personal financial budget. You have a limited amount of money, just like you have an optimal amount of calories you consume a day. Everyone wants to get the most for their money. Same thing with calories — you want the most nutrition you can get for the calories you have to "spend" each day. Your weight loss success and good health depends on how much nutrition you can get for your calorie dollar.

On the opposite end of the health spectrum from nutrient-rich foods are foods and beverages that are considered *empty calories.* These foods include things like chips, candy, cookies, pastries, and high-calorie beverages, including alcohol. Besides the fact that you don't get many nutrients (but a lot of calories) from these foods, they're likely to contribute to dumping syndrome (go back to Chapter 2 for more on dumping syndrome).

REMEMBER

Another concept you need to consider when making menu choices is variety. When thinking about meeting your nutritional needs, select different foods each day, because different foods provide different nutrients. You may drink milk for calcium and protein but be neglecting meat, which is high in iron (and milk is not). Strawberries are high in vitamin C, but apricots are high in vitamin A. Remember, variety is the spice of life!

When putting together a healthy, varied diet, you need to know some basic food facts. The following sections give you need-to-know info on protein, carbohydrates, and fats, the core breakdown of any diet. We also discuss fiber, a key ingredient in the recipe for health and weight loss.

The building blocks of nutrition

The foundation of your diet comes from protein, carbohydrates (carbs), and fats. These are known as *macronutrients* and provide the calories in your diet. Each of the macronutrients contributes to health in its own way. Keep in mind, many foods contain combinations of protein, carbs, and fats, so you may see some of the same foods discussed in each of the following sections.

There has been a lot of discussion in recent years about diet. Are carbs bad? Should we eat more protein? Less protein? Is fat good or bad? The truth of the matter is that we need all three — protein, carbs, and fats.

In light of the surgery you have had, it's vital that you have a basic understanding of nutrition and apply it to your daily life in order to decrease risk of malnutrition, feel good, look good, and have lots of energy. In this section we discuss the nuts and bolts of good nutrition so that you know *what* to choose to eat, and not just how much.

Eating protein first

In your pre-op surgery class or visit with the surgeon you heard all the reasons protein is important. Probably all you recall at this point is "If I don't eat enough protein, I'll lose my hair!" (Hair loss can also occur as a result of the surgery.) Protein is important for many other reasons, though — so important that it's the base of the bariatric food guide pyramid (refer to Figure 3-1 earlier in this chapter). Protein-containing food contributes nutrients such as zinc, B vitamins, phosphorous, selenium, thiamine, iron, and magnesium, and helps your body do the following things:

>> Heal after surgery

>> Build muscle

>> Contract your muscles

>> Maintain healthy blood

>> Maintain a healthy immune system

>> Have more energy

>> Feel full longer

WARNING

Without adequate protein, your body will develop a deficiency called *protein malnutrition* (PM). This results in your body breaking down its own muscle for energy (not a good thing), weakness, anemia, and of course hair loss.

Your surgeon and dietitian will give you a level of protein they want you to strive for each day. In general, this is anywhere from 60 to 80 grams a day. Some people tolerate protein better than others after surgery. While getting your nutrients from real food is best, using protein supplements will likely be necessary, especially if you don't tolerate protein foods well. (We discuss protein supplements in the later section "Meeting your protein goal with supplements.")

GOOD SOURCES OF PROTEIN

So what do you eat to get this all-important protein? Well, you get protein from a variety of foods, the best sources being animal products. The protein in plants is found in smaller amounts and isn't as high quality. The following list shows you sources of protein and the amount of protein you can expect to get. For packaged goods, comparison shop to find the option with the highest amount of protein.

>> Meat, fish, and poultry* (7 grams per ounce)

>> Cheese (be sure it is lowfat or fat free)* (7 grams per ounce)

>> Eggs* (7 grams each)

>> Yogurt (again, lowfat or fat free and no added sugar)* (12 grams per cup)

>> 1 percent or fat-free milk* (12 grams per cup)

>> Tofu* (7 grams per ounce)

>> Legumes (beans) (7 grams per ½ cup)

>> Nuts and seeds (4 grams per ¼ cup)

>> Soy milk* (12 grams per cup)

>> Vegetables (2 grams per ½ cup cooked)

>> Whole grains (3 grams per serving)

>> Cottage cheese* (7 grams per ¼ cup)

>> Nut butters (7 grams per 2 tablespoons)

Sources of high-quality protein

PROTEIN TIPS

Protein is so important that half of your plate at each meal should be protein and you should *eat it first.*

Eat 15 to 20 grams of protein at each meal, which is about 2 to 3 ounces. Your protein for the day should equal about 30 percent of your daily calories.

When eating proteins like meat, be sure you take very small bites, and chew, chew, chew! Make sure the meat is very moist and not stringy. Dry, stringy, inadequately chewed food can stick causing problems.

Make sure you know what the correct portion size is for the food you're eating and look at the nutrition facts to see how many grams of protein are in that serving. If there's no nutrition label, you can look up the information on the Internet. Then record the amount of protein you consume at each meal or snack in your food diary.

PROTEIN-FILLED SNACK IDEAS

Of all of the macronutrients (protein, carbs, and fats), protein is the most satiating and will make you feel full longer. Pretty good reason to eat your protein, isn't it? Include some source of protein at each meal *and* snack. A snack may consist of:

- String cheese and an apple
- Peanut butter and whole-grain crackers
- Cottage cheese and fruit
- Whole-grain cereal and lowfat or fat-free milk

Be sure to check out Chapter 18 for good snacking ideas.

Checking out carbs

Are carbs good or bad? Well, they can be either. The right kinds are definitely good for you. Many people have the misconception that all carbs make you gain weight. Too much of *anything* can contribute to weight gain, but carbs like soda pop, candy, and cookies are particularly bad. These empty calorie foods provide calories but few nutrients.

GOING FOR HEALTHY CARBS

Carbs are necessary for energy for both the body and brain. Without adequate carbs, your thinking may be fuzzy and you may feel sluggish and tired. Healthy carbs are good sources of vitamins A and C, potassium, folate, iron, magnesium, selenium, calcium, and B vitamins like thiamine and riboflavin. Carbs also provide fiber, antioxidants, and phytochemicals necessary for good health. Healthy carbs include the following foods:

>> 100 percent whole-grain bread

>> Brown rice

>> Fruits

>> Vegetables

>> Lowfat or fat-free dairy

>> Beans

>> Whole-grain cereals

>> Whole-wheat pasta

WARNING

Carbs should equal about 40 to 50 percent of your daily calories. Your goal is to consume a minimum of 100 grams a day.

STAYING AWAY FROM ADDED SUGARS

When you read labels you see the category *Sugars*. These sugars count as carbs, and they may include natural sugars found in healthy carbs (like the lactose in milk and fructose in fruit) as well as added or simple sugars. You need to look at the ingredient label to see if the food has added sugar, in which case, avoid it. Check out Chapter 2 for all of sugar's aliases.

Interestingly, many foods you wouldn't suspect, such as ketchup, barbeque sauce, pasta sauce, and bread, have added sugar in them. The next time you go to the grocery store, inspect ingredient labels for added sugar before adding foods to your cart.

Besides increasing your calorie intake, eating too much sugar may cause the dreaded dumping syndrome. While not everyone experiences dumping syndrome (generally only gastric bypass patients), the resulting diarrhea, nausea, and shakiness will make an anti-added-sugar believer out of you. (Refer back to Chapter 2 for a refresher on dumping syndrome.)

Getting the skinny on fats

Like carbs, fat has been given a bad name. In fact, we need some healthy fat in our diet. Too much fat, though, especially saturated and trans fats, not only sabotages your weight loss but also can increase your risk for chronic disease.

Without adequate fat in your diet you'll experience the following outcomes:

>> Your hair and nails will be brittle and dry.

>> Your skin will be dry.

>> You may develop deficiencies of some of the fat-soluble vitamins.

>> You may develop deficiencies of essential fatty acids (ones you have to ingest through food).

>> You'll have less energy when you need it.

The key is too eat enough of the right fats. What do we mean by "the right fats"? You may have heard terms like *monounsaturated*, *polyunsaturated*, *saturated*, and *trans* fats. These terms have to do with the chemical makeup of the fat, which affects how your body uses it. Saturated and trans fats are not good for you, but monounsaturated and polyunsaturated are considered "heart healthy" fats. Read on to find out how and why to incorporate healthy fats into your diet.

SOURCES OF HEALTHY FATS

The following foods are good sources of healthy monounsaturated and polyunsaturated fats:

>> Olive oil

>> Canola oil

>> Peanut oil

>> Avocados

>> Vegetable oils (safflower, sesame, soybean, corn, and sunflower)

>> Nuts and seeds, especially walnuts and ground flaxseed

>> Fatty fish, such as sardines, salmon, and mackerel

These fats help prevent heart disease by decreasing total cholesterol and LDL (the unhealthy kind of cholesterol in the blood) and increasing HDL (the healthy cholesterol in the blood).

REMEMBER

Getting the benefit from heart-healthy fats is not a case of adding them to your current diet. Instead, exchange unhealthy fats already in your diet for some of these heart-healthy fats. It's also definitely not a case of "if a little will do a little good, a lot will do a lot of good." Fat is a much more concentrated source of calories than either protein or carbs. Compare the numbers:

>> Protein has 4 calories per gram.

>> Carbs have 4 calories per gram.

>> Fat has 9 calories per gram.

So even with healthy fats you have to watch portion size (particularly if you're prone to dumping syndrome) and count the calories. Olive oil, a healthy fat, has the same number of calories as lard, which as most people know is not a healthy fat. (Both have 135 calories per tablespoon.) Stick to about 1 teaspoon healthy fat at each meal.

IDENTIFYING UNHEALTHY FATS

You may be asking "How do I know what unhealthy fats are in my diet?" After all, you may or may not be able to see and identify fats in some foods. The types you want to avoid are saturated and trans fats.

Saturated fats are often implicated in increasing your LDL (bad cholesterol) and increase your risk of heart disease. Fats from animal sources are the main sources of saturated fats.

Note: Small amounts of butter are used in some of the recipes in this book. This contributes significantly to the flavor, and per serving it is a very small amount. As with anything, it is important to practice moderation.

Trans fats are predominantly found in processed foods like cookies, crackers, doughnuts, and fried foods. These unhealthy fats come from *hydrogenated oils,* liquid oils that have been turned solid in order to extend the shelf life of processed foods. It's the reason why cake-type snacks stay good in your pantry for a very long time. Many manufacturers are now required to list trans fats on nutrition labels. The problem is that a food product can have up to ½ a gram of trans fat per serving and still be called *trans fat free.* In order to completely avoid trans fats, you have to read ingredient labels and avoid foods with anything *fully hydrogenated* or *partially hydrogenated.*

The following list is some general guideline for trimming unhealthy fats from your diet:

» Don't use fat as a primary seasoning. Learn to use herbs and spices instead.

» Trim visible fats.

» Use 1 percent or fat-free dairy products.

» Replace high-fat foods with lower-fat alternatives (but remember they can still have just as many calories!).

» Avoid cream sauces.

» Avoid fried foods.

» Avoid pastries, cookies, and cakes.

» Focus on whole grains, fruits, vegetables, lean protein, lowfat or fat-free dairy, and healthy fats in moderation.

Fiber facts

Fiber is found in plant-derived foods such as whole grains, vegetables, fruits, nuts and seeds, and legumes (beans) and cannot be broken down by the body. As a result, these fibers pass through the body and carry other things off with them. Fiber helps to protect against heart disease, diabetes, and contributes to gastrointestinal (GI) health by preventing constipation and helping to prevent diseases of the GI tract like diverticular disease and colon cancer.

Many people don't get the 25 to 30 grams of fiber a day recommended by the American Cancer Society. Getting enough fiber is even more difficult after weight loss surgery because you're eating much smaller amounts of higher-fiber foods. You can find the fiber content (in grams per serving) of a food by looking under *Total Carbohydrate* on the nutrition label.

Keeping things moving

Fiber is sorted into two categories: soluble and insoluble. Soluble fiber forms a gel in water and helps to protect against heart disease by binding cholesterol and moving it through the body. These fibers also help lower glucose levels.

Soluble fibers are found in the following foods:

» Whole grains like oatmeal and barley

» Oat bran

>> Beans and peas

>> Citrus fruits and apples

>> Nuts

Insoluble fiber does not form a gel in water. It promotes bowel movements and prevent constipation, which can lead to diverticular disease and hemorrhoids. Insoluble fibers are found in the following foods:

>> Whole grains

>> Vegetables

>> Fruit skins

>> Wheat and corn bran

>> Seeds and nuts

Most foods are a combination of both kinds of fiber. An apple is a great example. The skin is a source of insoluble fiber and the inside is loaded with soluble fiber. No wonder the old saying advises you to "eat an apple a day" (just chew it well)!

TIP

Besides protecting against heart disease and helping bowel movements, another benefit of fiber is that it can make you feel full longer. Foods with fiber tend to stay in the stomach a little longer, which is why oatmeal makes a hearty breakfast that staves off hunger for hours. Because you don't feel hungry as often, fiber is a great weight loss tool as well.

You may have trouble with fiber for a while after surgery, and may actually be told to not include fiber in your diet for a while. Let your surgeon and dietitian's specific recommendations regarding fiber be your guide.

If you suspect you would benefit from a fiber supplement, several supplements are available on the market. Some are flavorless and can be mixed into a food or beverage. Others may be flavored and get mixed into water. Call your surgeon for his or her recommendation in terms of brand and dosage.

Checking out fiber-filled foods

Follow these fiber tips for the best results:

>> Eat at least five portions of fruits and vegetables per day. You can increase your intake by adding vegetables to pasta sauces and soups and having fruit for dessert or a snack.

- » Look for breakfast cereals with at least 5 grams of fiber per serving.

- » Swap white bread for 100 percent whole-grain bread. Avoid breads with the word *enriched* in the ingredient list.

- » Try brown rice instead of white rice.

- » Experiment with less-popular whole grains like quinoa, barley, and bulgur.

- » Give up white pasta for whole wheat.

- » Include beans in soup and salads.

REMEMBER

When trying to increase your fiber intake, remember that refined processed and refined foods are low in fiber. Consider an apple: A medium apple has 3.3 grams of fiber, a half cup of applesauce has 1.5 grams of fiber, and a half cup of apple juice has a mere 0.1 grams. Whole foods or foods that are closer to their natural state are higher in fiber as well as many other nutrients that are stripped out by the refining process.

TIP

A couple of words about increasing the fiber in your diet:

- » Do it slowly. Increase gradually to allow your GI tract to adjust. Increasing fiber quickly results in gas, cramping, and bloating. Very unpleasant!

- » Make sure you stay well hydrated because fiber absorbs water.

Keeping a Food Diary to Stay On Track

Earlier in the chapter we discuss how your calorie budget is similar to your financial budget. How do you know when you're out of money (or calories) if you don't keep track of them? Just a few days of being "overdrawn" on your daily calories can mean the difference between gaining or losing weight.

Research tells us that people who keep track of their calories lose twice as much weight as people who don't. Seems like a small thing to do, right?

Don't stop keeping your diary after you have achieved your desired weight loss. Just like the surgery is a tool you have committed to for life, the food diary should also be a lifelong tool to help you maintain the weight loss.

Finding out what's in it for you

Tracking calories is definitely an important tool for weight loss and maintenance. By writing down what and how much you eat, you are able to stay aware of your food intake and whether or not you tend to graze. Food diaries can also help you to increase your awareness of *why* you're eating. If you write down any emotions you feel when you just want "something to nibble on," you may decide that rather than a cookie, what you really need is a short nap.

Food diaries also help you to plan what you are going to eat each day. Some people write down what they're going to eat each day first thing in the morning. After all, if you fail to plan, you plan to fail.

TIP

If you experience nausea or vomiting, it can be due to a food intolerance. By tracking what you eat, as well as any symptoms you may be experiencing, you may be able to identify trends. It may be that the last couple of times you drank milk, you became nauseated. If this is the case, wait a couple of weeks and try milk again.

And tracking calories isn't just for your benefit. If you aren't achieving optimal weight loss, your surgeon or dietitian will want to see your food diary to see where you may be off track or whether or not you need another fill if you have an adjustable gastric band.

Choosing and using a food diary

Ideally, a food diary for someone who had weight loss surgery should have the following components:

>> Time of day

>> How you feel, both mentally and physically

>> What food you're eating

>> How much food you're eating

>> Number of calories

>> Number of grams of protein

>> Ounces of water consumed each day

You may also want to include other information, such as if you've taken your supplements or exercised.

There are a variety of sources for food diaries. Your surgeon or dietitian may give you a form you can download and print yourself. You can find many logs and journals available at bookstores. Or, if you're really resourceful, you can customize and create your own. It can be a simple as a small notepad you keep in your purse or pocket.

In addition, there are now many online food diaries and apps for those of you who are computer savvy. Many of them can be customized to meet your individual needs and are really handy, particularly if you use a smartphone or carry a laptop with you throughout the day. Many of these tools are totally free, and others let you try out the tools on a trial basis before paying a monthly fee. Some of the more popular websites are:

> www.fitday.com

> www.sparkpeople.com

> www.calorieking.com

> www.thedailyplate.com

> www.obesityhelp.com

TIP

If you have had adjustable gastric banding with a LapBand or Realize band, you have access to terrific online monitoring tools through Web sites developed specifically for their patients.

Any of these tools can be effective. The bottom line is to find the tool that works for you — the one that you will use.

Eating Out

Like most people, you likely lead a very busy life. Between errands, work, and carting kids around, it's probably inevitable that most of us will find ourselves at the mercy of fast food at some point.

Don't panic!

Healthy eating is all about making good choices, watching portion sizes, and knowing what's in the food you're eating (watch out for sugar and fried foods!). Fortunately, more and more fast food establishments are making it easier to eat more healthfully.

Many fast-food restaurants are making nutritional information available in brochures or on their Web sites. (And as for the ones that don't make this information available, what are they hiding? It's up to you to patronize restaurants that will support your weight loss goals with healthy foods choices.) In the meantime, you can go to your local bookstore or take to the Internet to find calorie, carbohydrate, protein, and fat contents of commonly consumed foods. Many of these books (such as *The Calorie Counter For Dummies* [Wiley]) list chain restaurants by name and are small enough to keep in your purse or car so you have the information at hand.

Most surgeons have a card they can give you identifying you as someone who has had weight loss surgery. By showing the card to restaurant employees, you can order off the kid's menu or receive smaller portions of entrées.

General tips for surviving the fast-food menu board

TIP

Now, what happens if you find yourself standing in line at a fast-food restaurant without nutrition information available? Here are some guidelines you should consider when making good fast-food choices:

>> **Pay attention to the descriptions of foods.** Avoid foods that have the words *deep fried, creamy, breaded, crispy,* and similar words in their descriptions.

>> **The plainer you can eat your food, the better off you will be.** Don't be afraid to ask to have something prepared the way you want it.

  • Have them leave off the "special sauce," full-fat cheese, and mayo.

  • Get your salad dressing on the side and dip your lettuce or fork into the dressing.

  • Leave toppings like bacon, cheese, and croutons off salad.

  • Drink water instead of high-calorie beverages like sweet tea, sodas, or juices. Remember not to drink with meals.

>> **Avoid the value meal.** Face it, if it's in front of you, you'll be tempted to eat it. Even better, ask for the kid's meal (the card we discussed above could come in handy). Or, of course, you can share something with someone else.

>> **There is nothing wrong with just eating the meat out of a sandwich.** You can always discard one (or both) pieces of bread.

>> **Eat just until you are satisfied.** One of the authors has a friend who pours salt (lots of salt!) on her food after she has reached the point where she is satisfied so she won't eat anymore.

Good choices for a variety of restaurants

At some point, you're going to find yourself at a restaurant wondering what you can eat. This section gives you some ideas of foods to look for that will be healthier and good for weight control.

Burger joints

A typical burger chain meal for most people is a hamburger, french fries, and a soda. Instead of the meal you might have once had, eat one of the following:

» Regular single patty burger

» Grilled chicken sandwich

» Veggie burger

» Grilled chicken salad with lowfat or fat-free dressing

» Egg on English muffin with lean ham or Canadian bacon

» Grilled chicken strips

Chicken restaurants

What if you're off to a fried chicken restaurant? Skip anything that has the words *fried, original,* or *extra crispy* in its description and go for

» Skinless chicken without the crunchy stuff

» Grilled chicken without the skin

» Grilled chicken salad with dressing on the side and without croutons, cheese, or bacon

» Side salad (not coleslaw — it's loaded with fat and sugar!)

Quick Mexican restaurants

More and more quick Mexican restaurants are out there. You can make better choices when going to one of these by sticking to healthier basic dishes like rice, whole (not refried) or black beans, and salsa or pico. Watch out for the extras like sour cream, queso, and tortilla chips. Some of these restaurants advertise healthier menu options. Opt for:

» Veggie burritos

» Chicken soft tacos

>> Rice and beans

>> Lighter versions of menu items

Quick Italian restaurants

Quick Italian restaurants often serve pizza. Generally, you can have a healthier pizza meal by following these easy tips:

>> Opt for thin crust instead of thick or stuffed.

>> Ask for half the cheese and skip greasy meats like sausage and pepperoni. For more protein, ask for Canadian bacon.

>> Ask for extra vegetables on the pizza.

>> A side salad with dressing on the side is a great way to fill up on veggies and go lighter on the pizza.

>> Or instead of greasy pizza, order pasta (preferably whole wheat) with a red (not creamy) sauce. If you indulge in meat sauce or a meatball, understand that these are often made of high-fat meat and may not agree with you.

Quick Asian restaurants

Quick Asian meals can be tricky even though they tend to be better sources of veggies. Ever noticed how shiny the dishes can be? That shine is fat, and it can wreak havoc with dumping syndrome. Look for dishes that are steamed, roasted, or broiled. Stick to the following options:

>> Clear broth soups like egg drop, wonton, hot and sour, or miso, without the crunchy noodles.

>> Steamed veggies and meat or seafood.

>> Brown rice instead of fried or white rice.

>> Clear sauces like soy sauce on the side.

>> Try eating with chop sticks! It will slow you down so you can't eat too much at one time.

Restaurant salads

While salads may seem like the perfect choice when eating out, be very careful! Some salads can pack on a whole day's worth of calories. To stay on plan, really pay attention to the add-ons and follow these tips:

- » Request lowfat dressing on the side and either dip your fork into the dressing and then pick up the lettuce or dip the lettuce lightly into the dressing. Vinaigrettes are usually a better choice than creamy dressings.

- » Avoid croutons and bacon and add just a sprinkling of cheese.

- » Add lean protein like chopped ham, egg, tofu, or beans. You will feel full longer.

- » Add nutritious vegetables to the salad. Look for beets, tomatoes, sugar snap peas, and green beans.

Frozen dinners

Not going out but still need fast food? Many of us rely on frozen dinners from time to time. Not all frozen meals are created equal, so carefully read nutrition facts labels. You may have to take a little extra time in the frozen food aisle to find a frozen dinner you like that meets your nutritional requirements. Many frozen dinners, though considered "healthy," rely heavily on starches like pasta and are light on protein. They can be very high in sodium, as well.

Keep these tips in mind when shopping for frozen dinners:

- » Watch calories. Limit calories to 250 to 350.

- » Make sure the meal has at least 15 grams of protein.

- » Choose meals with less than 600 milligrams of sodium.

- » Make certain the meal has 3 to 5 grams of fiber.

- » Look for entrées that include lots of vegetables. They'll be lower in calories and fill you up more.

- » Choose meals with whole grains or brown rice.

- » Look for meals with 0 grams trans fat and limit saturated fat to 4 grams.

You can also round out the meal with a side salad or piece of fruit.

Hydration Motivation

Before beginning this section, go pour yourself a glass of water. In a few minutes, you'll be glad you did!

Water is an essential nutrient, meaning you must take it in through your diet. Many foods also are made up of water. Because you aren't able to eat as much as before, that water must be replaced. You need more water than any other nutrient, and without water you wouldn't survive more than a few days. In your body, water does the following jobs:

>> Carries nutrients through the body

>> Carries waste products out of the body

>> Participates in metabolic reactions

>> Serves as a lubricant and cushion around joints

>> Regulates blood volume, body temperature, and blood pressure

No wonder it's so important! Your body is made up of about 60 percent water and you're constantly losing it through sweat, urine, feces, and breathing. Replacing the water you lose is essential.

Just like you can't eat too much food at one time, you also can't take big gulps of water. People are accustomed to drinking when they're thirsty, but by the time you realize you're thirsty, you're already a little dehydrated. Getting hydrated again is very hard when you can't take large drinks, so you need to have water or other approved liquids available at all times and sip every couple of minutes.

WARNING

You can recognize dehydration from the following signs:

>> Parched mouth

>> Dry skin

>> Fatigue

>> Dark urine (if you're well hydrated, your urine is pale yellow or clear)

One of the major reasons for readmission to the hospital after weight loss surgery is dehydration. Getting into the habit of drinking more than you're used to is hard, but you can get accustomed to it.

Adequate fluids are the key to preventing dehydration. In general, you need about 48 to 64 ounces of fluid a day (more if you're physically active or the weather is hot). Your surgeon or dietitian may have a more specific recommendation for you.

Water works

Your beverage of choice should be water. Not everyone likes plain water — some people pick up a metallic or different taste, and other people dislike that it has no taste. You can do several things to help you meet your fluid needs:

>> Add a squirt or slice of lemon or lime to your water

>> Add a sugar-free flavoring packet for water

>> Dilute your favorite sugar-free beverage 50/50 with water

>> Dilute fruit juice 50/50 with water and limit juice to 4 ounces a day (especially important if you're a gastric bypass patient to prevent dumping syndrome)

>> Drink decaffeinated, unsweetened tea or coffee

>> Drink other sugar-free, decaffeinated drinks

Beverage do's and don'ts

Drinking enough liquids is important, but how you drink is just as important to your success (and feeling good). Following are some recommendations that should help you meet your fluid needs:

>> **Don't drink carbonated beverages.** The bubbles can cause gas and bloating, which is very uncomfortable. We always get the question, "Can I drink flat cola?" Sorry, no. The heat of your body will make the flat pop release more carbonation.

>> **Don't use straws.** These, too, introduce air into the pouch. People tend to take bigger drinks with straws and drink faster. This could mean you drink more than your pouch is equipped to hold and cause nausea.

>> **Don't drink caffeine.** It's generally discouraged because it can be dehydrating, and after all, that's what you're trying to avoid.

>> **Do dilute fruit juice 50/50 with water.** Limit the amount of juice to 4 ounces a day to avoid dumping syndrome and excess calories.

>> **Don't eat and drink at the same time.** Stop at least 5 to 10 minutes before you eat and wait 30 minutes after you eat to begin again. If your pouch is full of liquids, you won't be able to eat. Drinking too soon after a meal may overfill the pouch.

>> **Don't add calorie-laden cream or sweeteners to tea or coffee.**

>> **Do track your water intake.** An easy method is to put 64 ounces of water in a jug first thing in the morning. Throughout the day, drink directly from the jug or pour out the same amount if you drink something else. Do whatever works for you to be sure you get in the amount of fluid you need to stay hydrated.

>> **Do drink before, during, and after exercising.** Aim for at least 64 ounces of water if not more each day if you're exercising (and we hope you are!).

WARNING

>> **Don't drink alcohol.** A couple of reasons why not to imbibe are

- Alcohol is a diuretic, which means it's dehydrating.

- Alcohol affects some people who have had gastric bypass surgery very differently than most people. The limited capacity of your pouch means alcohol moves into your small intestine more quickly where it is absorbed faster. It may only take a little alcohol to make you inebriated.

If you really want to enjoy a drink, check with your physician beforehand. Also, never drive after a drink. You may think you feel okay, but your blood alcohol level will tell otherwise. No one wants a DUI!

Supplementing Your Diet

We repeatedly bring to your attention the fact that you cannot eat as much as you were able to before (like you didn't know that, right?). Because of this, the foods you do eat should be nutrient-rich foods to keep you from developing some nutritional deficiencies. Even if you do everything you can to eat a healthy diet, deficiencies may still occur. Generally, this is more likely to occur in patients who had surgeries that affect the absorption of nutrients, such as gastric bypass. However, they can occur in anyone who's not eating wisely, not eating enough, or not taking supplements.

Even with a well-balanced diet, taking a supplement like a multivitamin is necessary. Others supplements may be required as well based on your own particular needs. Keeping your follow-up appointments is vital so that your surgeon has a chance to monitor your nutrient levels and determine what your changing needs are. Deficiencies aren't obvious until they're severe enough to manifest physically, so by keeping your appointments and getting your lab work done as ordered, they can be identified early and treated.

Any supplements your surgeon prescribes are a requirement, not a recommendation. After all, you went through all the trouble of having the surgery to feel better, so why not feel the best you can?

Discovering what vitamins and minerals can do for you

Vitamins and minerals play a huge role in your health. They regulate the following body functions:

- » Appetite
- » Nutrient absorption
- » Hunger
- » Metabolic rate
- » Fat and sugar metabolism
- » Energy storage

You can see that vitamins and minerals are necessary not only for good health, but also for weight loss.

Vitamins and minerals must be taken in through diet or supplementation. Getting as many nutrients as you can in your food is preferable, but getting them through supplements is much better than nothing. The nutrients in foods are used more efficiently by your body. Supplements often consist of binders and fillers that your body doesn't need or use. And food tastes better!

Multivitamins

When looking for a multivitamin, it's essential that you read labels carefully and consider the following points:

- » Time-release and enteric coated vitamins are not recommended for weight loss surgery patients.
- » Children's vitamins are not recommended because they don't have all the vitamins and minerals you need.
- » Several specialized bariatric formulas are available, and your surgeon may have a brand preference.

For about the first month after surgery, chewable or liquid vitamins are recommended no matter what kind of surgery you had. After the first month, gastric bypass patients may absorb liquid vitamins better than solid or chewable. If bypass patients choose to use tablets, a good rule of thumb is they must be no larger than the eraser of a pencil. If larger, they may be cut or ground (be certain they're not time release). For convenience sake, chewables may be better than tablets. Chewing breaks them down, making absorption easier. Saliva has some digestive enzymes that also help you absorb the supplement.

Adjustable band patients should use chewable or liquid supplements. Depending on your band restriction, it can be very easy for a tablet to get stuck. Very unpleasant!

Select a multivitamin that contains the listed amounts of the vitamins and minerals in Table 3-1. If you are a male or postmenopausal female, your surgeon may recommend a supplement without iron unless you are at risk of anemia. Please remember that these are general requirements. Your surgeon will tell you if you have additional needs.

TABLE 3-1   **Recommended Contents for a Daily Multivitamin**

Vitamin or Mineral	Men	Women
Iron	8 mg/day	18 mg/day
Thiamine	1.2 mg/day	1.1 mg/day
Vitamin B12	2.4 mcg/day	2.4 mcg/day
Folic acid	400 mcg/day	400 mcg/day
Zinc	11 mg/day	8 mg/day
Biotin	30 mcg/day	30 mcg/day
Vitamin K	120 mcg/day	90 mcg/day

REMEMBER

If you had gastric bypass, take two multivitamin supplements per day. For band patients, take one.

Liquid supplements need to be stored in the refrigerator after opening.

Calcium supplements

After surgery you need to take a calcium supplement with 200 to 300 milligrams (mg) vitamin D per pill. Yes, multivitamins have calcium and vitamin D, but it isn't enough.

REMEMBER

As with the multivitamin, your calcium supplement needs to be liquid or chewable for the first month after surgery. Actually, because calcium pills tend to be large, you're better off taking chewable, liquid, powder, or lozenge supplements after the first month as well. (Liquid may be better absorbed by gastric bypass patients.) You sure don't want to get that pill stuck!

TIP

Look for calcium citrate. Your new pouch produces little acid, and while other forms of calcium require stomach acid for absorption, calcium citrate does not.

After weight loss surgery, men and premenopausal women need 1,200 milligrams of calcium a day. Postmenopausal women need 1,500 milligrams each day. However, you can't take it all at once. Your body can only absorb about 600 milligrams at once, so calcium supplements usually come in 500 to 600 milligram doses. As such, you need to divide your doses — one in the morning and one at night. (And if you need more calcium, another one in the afternoon.) To maximize absorption, take your calcium supplements a couple of hours before or after your multivitamin supplement.

Your supplement regimen may look something like this:

>> 8 a.m. calcium supplement

>> 10 a.m. multivitamin supplement

>> 8 p.m. calcium supplement

>> 10 p.m. multivitamin supplement (if you have had bypass surgery)

Other supplements

Your surgeon will tell you what other vitamin and mineral supplements you require and when to take them. The following list gives you an overview of the three most commonly needed supplements:

>> **Vitamin B12:** You absorb vitamin B12 when stomach acid releases it from protein foods. Because after surgery you don't have as much acid production and you're eating less protein, you may be at risk of a vitamin B12 deficiency. B12 supplements come in a sublingual (under the tongue) form, which is better absorbed than a pill. Alternatively, your surgeon may give you injections of B12.

>> **Iron:** Dietary iron comes in two forms:

- *Heme iron* is found in animal protein and is easily absorbed.

- *Nonheme iron* is found in many vegetables, fruits, whole grains, and nuts as well as in meat, but it's not as well absorbed as heme.

Iron deficiency can result in fatigue and lethargy. No one wants that, right? It is fairly common in menstruating women and adolescents. Avoid drinking a lot of tea, because the tannins in tea decrease the absorbability of iron. To increase your natural absorption of nonheme iron, have some form of vitamin C (citrus fruits, tomato, peppers) at each meal. Iron supplements come in tablet or capsule form and should be taken two hours before or after your calcium supplement.

>> **B complex vitamins:** B complex vitamins, also called B50 complex, include many B vitamins that are found in a variety of foods including whole grains, fruits and vegetables, meats, and dairy. They're important in helping your

body use carbohydrates, and they play a role in appetite control. Deficiencies of some of the B vitamins, like thiamine, can result in neurological symptoms, some of which may be irreversible. The B vitamins are water-soluble, meaning they are not retained for long lengths of time in your body, and must be replaced frequently.

Remember, these supplements are used to supplement (not take the place of) healthy food. They need to be taken as directed for the rest of your life. It's a requirement, not a recommendation.

Meeting your protein goal with supplements

You may have difficulty getting in your 60 to 80 grams of protein a day. Remember, when you first start eating after surgery, you can only consume about 2 ounces of food. Even if you choose high-protein foods (like eggs at 3.5 grams per ounce), this is a max of 21 grams of protein a day from your meals. A far cry from what your body needs to heal! In the first few months after surgery, meeting your protein needs from food alone is almost impossible. This is where protein supplements come in. Like multivitamin supplements, these are meant to be used in addition to the healthy proteins you eat.

If you don't receive adequate protein over time, you'll experience muscle wasting and weakness, which will sabotage your weight loss efforts. Muscle helps you burn more calories, and if you're too weak to exercise, you won't build muscle. (Oh, and did we mention that lack of protein also causes hair loss?)

Taking a look at your options

A plethora of protein supplements are available. The challenge is finding one that tastes good, has a palatable texture, is affordable, and is the right kind of protein. Some types provide everything you need to maintain lean body mass, but others don't, so reading labels is very important.

REMEMBER

The highest quality protein comes in the form of whey protein. Whey, a liquid byproduct of cheese production, is rapidly digested and absorbed. It doesn't sit in the stomach very long, so it tends to be well tolerated. Some supplements have whey concentrates or whey isolates. Whey concentrates have a small amount of lactose. If you have a severe lactose intolerance, you may want to look for whey isolates, which are lactose free. Avoid supplements containing collagen, because it's not a high-quality protein.

Protein supplements come in a variety of forms. You can find shakes, drinks, puddings, bars, teas, and soups. You can also purchase unflavored, odorless protein supplements that you can mix into your food. Because protein supplements can be somewhat expensive, your support group is a great place to find out what other people like without having to incur the expense of trial and error. Some companies send samples to surgery centers so you can try before you purchase.

Getting enough protein daily

Focus on eating high-quality protein at breakfast, lunch, and dinner when possible. By using a protein supplement once or twice a day in the place of snacks, you can be sure to get enough protein in your diet. Track the grams of protein you consume daily so you're certain to get the recommended amount of protein based on your specific needs (generally 60 to 80 grams each day).

Like with all types of supplements, protein supplements should not be your whole source of protein. You may be tempted by the seemingly simple solution of meal-replacement supplements and bars. They're blends of several kinds of protein including whey, casein, and soy, and may have added vitamins and minerals, carbohydrates, fiber, and fat. However, they're meant to be used as an occasional meal replacement, not on a regular basis as a meal replacement. Real foods provide many more nutrients than a meal replacement bar ever can.

Your dietitian should be able to provide you with a list of appropriate supplements available in local stores. Other protein supplements are manufactured by the same companies who sell specialized supplements and must be ordered. However, more and more surgeons are selling some supplements out of their offices.

Chapter **4**

Planning to Succeed: The Art of Meal Planning

Ever feel like you're spinning your wheels where meal planning is concerned? If you're like many people, you spend a lot of time wandering around the grocery store but end up

» Without the components of a complete meal

» Throwing a lot of uneaten food away

» With outrageous grocery bills

» With a bunch of food in the cart that wasn't planned for

By spending a little time upfront and then just a few minutes each week in planning, you can have healthy home-cooked meals every day.

You may think you don't have time to cook, but surely you can make 20 to 25 minutes available. It's not too much to ask after you have invested in weight loss surgery. Why not give yourself every opportunity to be successful? You don't have to entirely give up eating out, but if you take the time to prepare even a few meals each week, you may find the food is better and more satisfying (not to mention easier on the pocket book). A majority of the recipes in this book take 25 minutes or less to prepare. Actual time before serving may take longer because of marinating, baking, or chilling, but the time you have to actively be doing something will be 25 minutes or less.

In this chapter we show you how to plan and organize your meals in order to ensure you're meeting your nutritional needs and become a smart and efficient grocery shopper. The system we present in this chapter works really well if you give it a chance. Commit to using it for a few weeks. It won't take long before you're able to see real time and money savings. Like anything else, it becomes a habit. You are, after all, forming lots of new routines to continue down the path of a healthier, more fulfilling life.

Discovering Why to Plan Ahead

"If you fail to plan, you plan to fail." You've probably heard this quote before. In no case is it more appropriate than when you're planning your meals. If you don't adequately plan for healthy, quick, and convenient meals, achieving your weight loss goal is going to be very difficult.

No one said this weight loss journey was going to be easy. You didn't get to the point in your life where surgery was an option by really thinking about what and when you were going to eat a week in advance. Mealtime was probably a "whatever is handy, quick, and cheap" proposition. Planning meals ahead of time may be a foreign concept for many of us who lead busy lives (and who doesn't these days?).

Not to worry! We're going to give you the tools to be able to plan meals. It will take a little work at first, but trust us, you will come to love being able to go to the grocery only once a week. Fast food will come to have a whole new meaning! You'll enjoy having fresh, healthy foods at your fingertips. Eating nutrient-rich foods on a daily basis will give you more energy and time and just make you feel better in general.

You save time

How much time do you spend each day thinking about what you're feeding yourself and/or your family? It may be more time than you think. You can make the process much more efficient and take all the guesswork out of each meal by taking a little time one day a week and planning your meals for the week. You no longer spend time wandering the aisles at the grocery store trying to figure out what you want to prepare. There are no more dashes to the store for a forgotten ingredient, and there's no need to thaw something last-minute for a meal. With planning, it's already done.

Most families prepare the same seven or so meals over and over. The first thing to do is to write down everything you and your family eat in a typical week. Then examine the list and identify places where you can substitute healthier ingredients, prepare something in a different way, or add more nutritious components for a more balanced diet. Of course, we don't expect you to completely change everything you eat, but making a number of small changes can add up to big improvements.

TIP

Commit to trying new recipes as well (like the ones in this book). You could make Sunday night "new recipe night" at your house and try at least one new recipe each week. Then add to your "library" of menus as you find recipes you and your family like.

Because food companies have listened to consumer input and developed foods that can be prepared quickly, the grocery store has lots of time-saving, convenient foods. However, you have to be very careful to purchase healthy convenience foods. Following are some examples of good choices:

>> Roasted chicken

>> Vegetables in bags that can be popped in the microwave

>> Prepackaged salad greens

>> Prewashed and chopped fruits and vegetables

>> Healthy frozen dinners (lowfat, no added sugar, easy on the refined carbs like pasta)

>> Instant grains

TIP

If you post the weekly menu plan somewhere visible, it's very easy for someone else in your household to take the initiative to begin meal preparation if you get hung up in traffic. Now that is a time saver!

You save money

If you go to the grocery store without a list, you'll be tempted to buy foods that are unhealthy and will go to waste. Having a list in hand at the store and going only once a week or less will definitely save money. You'll be more efficient in your spending and resist impulse buying. Planning meals also allows you to

>> Look at the grocery ads to take advantage of bargains.

>> Utilize leftovers. Sunday night's leftover pot roast becomes Tuesday night's barbeque sandwiches.

>> Make double recipes to stockpile in the freezer for future busy evenings.

>> Purchase frequently used items in bulk.

You can eat hassle-free

Imagine waking up and knowing exactly what you're going to eat for breakfast and having your lunch and snack already packed for the day. You get home after a long day at work and know exactly what you're preparing for dinner. You put dinner in the oven and have time to go for a walk while it's cooking. When you return home you make a few last-minute preparations and — *voilà!* — dinner is ready! The best part is, everything you need for the day was already purchased and you didn't have to stop at the store on the way home, saving you a lot of extra time.

Sounds good, doesn't it? Well, by preplanning your meals, you can easily make this a reality.

Laying the Groundwork for Meal Planning

This chapter includes "The Art of Meal Planning" in the title because smart, advanced preparation and thought really is a little like art. It's all about composition and presentation. The composition of your meals is very important in terms of eating a variety of nutrient-rich foods. You know how important protein is, but just as important are whole grains, fruits and vegetables, lowfat or fat-free dairy, and healthy fats. Each of your meals should be composed of a food from each of these groups.

Have you ever thought of food as beautiful? The next time you go to the grocery store, take a minute in the produce section to look at all of the vibrantly colored fruits and vegetables — reds, oranges, purples, greens, and yellows. Notice the different textures of the skins and leaves. A dinner of grilled chicken breast, mashed potatoes, and cauliflower looks pretty blah, doesn't it? But if the chicken breast is served with a baked sweet potato and broccoli, the varied colors make it much more appealing.

This section shows you how to examine your regular meals to see how they measure up in nutritional composition and find out where you can improve them to make them a real work of art.

Breaking down your favorite foods

To get started with healthy meal planning, write down on separate pieces of paper your favorite foods (entrées, sides, desserts, and snacks) that you eat on a weekly basis. If you have a family, enlist their help. Every meal should have all the food groups represented, so on each page, make a checklist:

>> Protein

>> Whole grains and starches

>> Fruits

>> Vegetables

>> Healthy fats

>> Lowfat or fat-free dairy

Break down each meal into components to see if all food groups are represented, and then look for healthy modifications. For example, say your family's favorite meal is hamburgers and French fries. The hamburger is basically meat and a bun, so this is an easy one. The meat patty satisfies the protein requirement, and you can make it healthier by using lean ground beef, ground turkey breast, or a veggie burger. Make the bun whole grain, and another food group is satisfied. Yes, you may also put on pickle, lettuce, onion, and tomato (what we refer to as PLOT), but consider using Romaine lettuce or spinach instead of low-nutrient iceberg lettuce. And PLOT isn't a complete serving of vegetables, so you'll need to add something else to the meal. You can add some mayo, if it's lowfat or fat free, a little ketchup, and mustard (no change necessary there). Modify French fries by preparing baked fries or baked chips.

Now check in with the checklist. The meal satisfies the requirements for protein, whole grain, healthy fat, and, if you add some carrot sticks or lowfat coleslaw on the side, vegetable. Do you see a fruit or dairy? Perhaps you could add some watermelon or apple slices and put a piece of lowfat cheddar cheese on the burger. Or you can drink a glass of milk 30 minutes after the meal is finished or snack on a container of yogurt later in the day.

Table 4-1 shows what your chart for burgers and fries may look like.

Some foods may fall into more than one group. For example, pizza may fall into grain, protein, and dairy. Then you only have to add extra vegetables (maybe a salad) and some fruit.

TABLE 4-1 **Burger Night**

Food Group	Item	Modification
Protein	Hamburger patty	Lean ground beef patty, ground turkey breast patty, or veggie burger
Whole grains or starches	Bun	Whole-grain bun
	Fries	Baked fries or baked chips
Fruits	*None in original menu*	Add apple or watermelon slices
Vegetables	Lettuce	Consider romaine or spinach instead of iceberg
	Tomato, onion, dill pickle	No modification needed
	Insufficient vegetables in original menu	Add carrots or lowfat coleslaw to complete vegetable serving
Healthy fat	Full-fat mayo	Lowfat mayo or sliced avocado
Lowfat or fat-free dairy	Cheese, if applicable	Lowfat cheese, or add milk or yogurt later in the day

Making a list and checking it twice

Take the information you wrote down in the preceding section (menu and ingredients) and transfer this information to an index card or small notebook. You now have a meal plan at your fingertips.

Your card may look something like this:

Menu:

>> Hamburger

>> Baked fries

>> PLOT

>> Carrots with homemade ranch dip

>> Apple slices

Ingredients:

>> Ground turkey breast

>> Whole-grain buns

>> Mustard

- » Lowfat mayo or avocado

- » Ketchup

- » Lowfat cheese

- » PLOT (pickle, Romaine lettuce, onion, and tomato)

- » Frozen French fries

- » Baby carrots

- » Fat-free sour cream

- » Lemon juice

- » Dried parsley

- » Granulated garlic

- » Salt and pepper

- » Apples

Every week, pick out the meals you're going to have and select the new recipes you're going to try. Consider your schedule. If you know you have evening commitments, plan easy, quick meals for those evenings. Save the more time-consuming menus for weekends or other days when you have more time.

Look at the ingredients, check to see what ingredients you have in your refrigerator or pantry, and make a list of the things you need to purchase for the week.

Begin to develop your own grocery list. You can do this on the computer very easily. Think about the foods your family uses on a regular basis. Weekly, enlist their help in circling the foods you need as you need them. That way if someone eats the last piece of cheese, he's responsible for marking it on the list. Another timesaver for you!

TIP

If you want to take your list a step further to save even more time, pick up a map of your grocery store at the customer service desk, if available. Sort your list according to how the store is laid out so you don't have to backtrack. If you have to go to more than one store weekly, sort into two lists.

Stay flexible! Sometimes you'll want to take advantage of seasonal produce or sale items, or you just won't want green beans, and you absolutely can make modifications to your set meals. Perhaps you'd rather have beets than green beans one night. No problem! Just make the change to your list. Maybe the asparagus at the store looks really good and is on special. You can also modify existing menus with new recipes you find in this book.

Shopping Smart Aisle by Aisle

Smart eating requires smart shopping. This means purchasing foods that are healthy, convenient, and good, which can take a little time and may make you feel totally overwhelmed. You will need to compare items and make notes.

TIP

To make shopping easier, as you prepare the meals you have on your weekly menu, make notes of brands you like. You may find that other people in your family are willing to help out with the weekly shopping if you have a detailed list complete with brand names.

The best buys for your nutritional buck are nutrient-rich foods. These are foods that give you a lot of nutrition for fewer calories. It often has nothing to do with how much a food costs. Even though many fast foods and processed foods are inexpensive, they cost you a lot in terms of health and weight gain. When grocery shopping for nutrient-rich foods, follow these tips:

>> Look for foods that are as close to their original form as possible. The more foods are processed, the more vitamins and minerals have been stripped out of them. They also often lack the fiber of their less-processed counterparts.

>> Look for foods that are in season. Strawberries in December are going to be expensive and probably not very good. Buy frozen or wait until June.

>> Look for locally grown foods. Fruits and vegetables that have been shipped across the country have lost many of their nutrients en route. When was the last time you visited your local farmers market? Not only is it fun, but you can't get better vegetables and locally produced products.

TIP

Visualize your grocery store. What do you see around the outside edge of the store? Generally, it's produce, dairy, meats, and frozen foods. Now visualize what you see in the middle. That's where you find chips, cookies, soda pop, and processed foods. Get the drift? Focus most of your shopping around the edge of the store and shop smart on the inside aisles. In general

>> Buy foods that are the least processed you can find.

>> Shop with a list.

>> Don't shop when you're hungry.

>> If possible, shop alone. Focusing on healthy foods and buying just what you need is easier without the influence of a spouse or child with a sweet tooth.

>> Just because a food claims to be a healthy choice, doesn't always mean it is. The fronts of boxes and packaging are meant to sell items to consumers. You have to read labels!

Produce

When it comes to buying produce, knock yourself out! Just don't get carried away. Purchase only what you need and will eat for the week. Experimenting with fruits and vegetables you haven't tried before may introduce you to a new favorite healthy food. Look for seasonal and locally grown foods. Some produce is good eaten raw, and you can keep an eye out for produce packaged in microwavable bags to let you quickly cook vegetables for a side. Don't forget about frozen fruit and vegetables. These items can be useful later in the week when you may have eaten the fresh produce you purchased.

Try to buy produce in a variety of colors — green, red, yellow, orange, and yellow. The more color you incorporate, the more vitamins, minerals, and fiber you give your body (without many calories!).

TIP

Avocados are a great source of monounsaturated fats, which are heart healthy. They're also loaded with calories, so eat smart. One-eighth of an avocado is 45 calories (the same as a teaspoon of oil).

Meat, poultry, and seafood

Meat, poultry, and seafood are generally along the back wall of the grocery store.

>> Look for the words *round* or *loin* (tenderloin, ground round, sirloin) when purchasing meat. These terms indicate lean cuts of meat.

>> Fish is always a good option unless it's breaded or fried. Fatty fish (salmon and mackerel) are particularly good for you because of the omega-3 fatty acids, which are healthy fats.

>> Go ahead and purchase poultry with the skin. It retains more moisture if cooked with the skin on. Just be sure to pull it off before eating.

>> When purchasing ground turkey, be sure to get ground turkey *breast.* Some ground turkey has the skin and dark meat ground into it.

>> Meat and fish in pouches or cans are a real time saver. They also tend to be lower in sodium than deli meats.

>> Remember that you can also get protein from beans, tofu, and dairy like cottage cheese.

Dairy

The dairy aisle can be confusing. What exactly is lowfat? Is butter better than margarine? Follow these tips:

>> Look for cheese and cream cheese that has less than 75 calories and 6 grams of fat per serving.

>> Look for trans-fat-free margarine to use on a daily basis. You can use butter occasionally, but do it sparingly.

>> Drink 1-percent or fat-free milk. If you're used to whole milk, this may take a little getting used to, but hang in there and it will grow on you.

>> When buying yogurt, look for the fat-free variety with no added sugar. Greek yogurt is a great product, having twice the protein of other yogurts. It can also be used in the place of sour cream in many dishes.

Grains and cereals

Grains and cereals can be very confusing. How can sugary cereals be whole grain? Are all breads labeled *whole wheat* healthy? The truth about whole grain is really pretty simple.

REMEMBER

When purchasing bread, crackers, English muffins, pastas, and cereals, look for products that say *100% whole grain* or *100% whole wheat.* If a loaf of bread just says *whole wheat,* it's white bread with caramel coloring added to it. And sugary cereals labeled *whole grain* may have a little whole grain but the majority is still made of white flour. *100%* is the key that ensures you'll get some good vitamins and minerals as well as fiber. If in doubt, look at the ingredients. If you see the word *enriched,* put it back!

Center aisle staples

Thought you should focus on the perimeter of the store, you have to forge into the center aisles for some foods.

Many of the fats are located in the center aisles. Since oils, salad dressings, and condiments comprise much of the fat in a typical diet, knowing what you're buying is particularly important.

>> Buy regular salad dressings with no more than 100 to 150 calories per 2-tablespoon serving. And remember that you don't have to eat

2 tablespoons; 1 is often sufficient. If you have GBP, you may get dumping syndrome from eating full-fat salad dressings.

>> Reduced-fat dressings should have no more than 100 calories per 2 tablespoons. It's still important to measure.

>> If you must use mayo, look for reduced-fat or fat-free versions. If you only like full fat or the salad dressing kind, measure it carefully and use sparingly.

>> Use olive oil, peanut oil, and canola oil when you can in place of other oils. These oils are healthy, but still loaded with calories, so use sparingly!

>> Remember that trans fats are bad for you. Even though the label may say *trans fat free,* look for the word *hydrogenated* in the ingredients. If you see this word, put it back!

What about canned goods? They can be great timesavers. Contrary to what many people believe, they can also be very healthy. Vegetables for canning are picked at their peak and processed quickly; they aren't sitting on a truck for days at a time. However, canned beans, soups, and vegetables can be high in sodium. When possible, buy reduced-sodium brands. Rinse canned beans and vegetables and add back a little water before heating to serve. Doing so greatly reduces the sodium content. Purchase canned fruits that are canned in their own juice or water (not syrup).

Focus on broth-based soups instead of cream-based soups. They are much lower in calories and fat. Homemade soups are super easy to make yourself and let you control the sodium and calories. You can put all the ingredients in a crockpot before you leave the house in the morning and have soup ready when you come home.

Frozen foods

We love frozen fruits and vegetables! They are a great go-to food for those nights when you get in late and need to put a healthy supper on the table quickly. Like canned vegetables, these frozen alternatives can be very healthy. Avoid any that are breaded or have cream or cheese sauce on them.

A plethora of frozen dinners are on the market. Many of them claim to be healthy, and some actually are. The trouble is that many are often too low in calories and pasta heavy to be satisfying, sometimes having less than 200 calories and leaving you hungry later.

When checking the ingredients in a frozen meal, apply the same principles to frozen dinners that we applied to your menu. Does it have protein, whole grains, vegetables, fruit, a little fat (usually not a problem), and lowfat or fat-free dairy? If you're lucky, a typical frozen meal may have whole grains, a dab of vegetables, and a little protein. You can always pump up the calories and nutrition by adding a salad or another vegetable, a piece of fruit, and 30 minutes after the meal, a glass of milk. Look for meals that have 200 to 300 calories, less than 5 grams of saturated fat, less than 600 milligrams of sodium, and more than 15 grams of protein.

Don't forget to watch the sugar! Manufacturers sneak it into everything — ketchup, spaghetti sauce, bread, salad dressings, peanut butter, and the list goes on and on. You have to look at the ingredients and look for words that indicate sugar, like dextrose, cane syrup, high fructose corn syrup, honey, and so on. If one of these words appears in the first three ingredients, avoid that food.

Understanding Nutrition Labels

We talk a lot about reading labels. They can be very confusing. Manufacturers often design packaging so that you think you are getting a nutritious food, when in fact, it's full of sugar or sodium or the portion size is ridiculous.

As with the weekly meal planning, getting the information you need from labels takes a little time at first. You already know some buzzwords to look for that determine whether or not a food is something you want to eat (to name a few, remember hydrogenated fat, enriched flour, and high fructose corn syrup?). In this section we go over some other basics to take the mystery out of nutrition and ingredient labels.

Finding out what all those numbers mean

Information about a food product gives you what you need to make good decisions about what you eat. Think it is a little too much information? The good news is that the numbers on the food label, by law, have to conform to a standard format. So once you get used to the label, it will be easy to compare similar products to make good choices. Figure 4-1 shows a label for granola cereal.

1. **Serving Size.** This bag has six servings (not one!). Each serving is ½ cup. Measure, measure, measure! All the rest of the nutrition information pertains to a single serving.

2. **Calories per serving.** Each serving has 280 calories. If you eat half the bag, you have to triple the calories. If you eat the whole bag, you have eaten 1,680 calories!

3. **Fats.** In particular, pay close attention to the unhealthy fat (saturated and trans). Keep saturated fats as low as possible, and avoid trans fats all together.

4. **Cholesterol.** The American Heart Association recommends limiting cholesterol to less than 300 milligrams a day. Cholesterol is found only in animal foods.

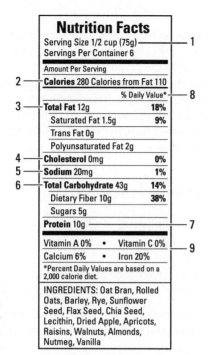

FIGURE 4-1:
Nutrition label for
a box of granola
cereal.

© John Wiley & Sons, Inc.

5. **Sodium.** Limit sodium to less than 2,300 milligrams a day. Remember, the more processed a food is, the higher it is likely to be in sodium.

6. **Carbohydrate.** Fiber and sugars fall under carbohydrates. Aim for 25 grams of fiber a day if you're a female and 30 if you're a male. Sugars may include naturally occurring sugar like the lactose in milk and fructose in fruit. You need to read the ingredients to look for sources of added sugar.

7. **Protein.** Aim for 60 to 80 grams (or the number of grams that have been specifically recommended for you) of protein a day.

8. **% Daily Values.** These numbers are based on a 2,000 calorie diet and are a rough guideline to tell if a food is high or low in a particular nutrient. For example, this label means if you are following a 2,000 calorie diet, the fat in this food provides 18 percent of the recommended fat allowance for the day.

    ● If a product has 5 percent or less, it's low in that nutrient. This could be good or bad, depending on the nutrient. If it's sodium, it's a good thing. If it's fiber, maybe not so good.

    ● If a product has more than 20 percent, it's high in that nutrient. Again, this can be good or bad.

9. **% Daily Value of vitamins and minerals.** These numbers for vitamin A, vitamin C, calcium, and iron are a good way to compare levels of nutrients between similar foods.

Reading ingredient labels in addition to nutrition labels lets you know *exactly* what you are eating. Ingredients are listed in descending order according to weight. For example, look at the ingredients for the granola cereal in Figure 3-1. From this list you should be able to tell that the cereal contains no enriched or refined grain, hence it's 100 percent whole grain. It does have some sugar (the fruit), but it appears toward the end of the ingredients so there is relatively little sugar (and no added sugar) per serving. Compared to many other cereals, this one has fewer ingredients, so it may be a good choice.

Making the label work for you

So what's the bottom line when comparing similar items and deciding what to buy?

>> **Know what a portion size is.** It may not be the whole bag, muffin, or so on. This can make a huge difference in how many calories you consume each day.

>> **Check protein.** Eat 15 to 20 grams of protein at each meal. This is about 2 to 3 ounces. Your protein for the day should equal about 30 percent of your daily calories.

>> **Eat enough carbs.** Carbohydrates should equal about 40 to 50 percent of your daily calories. It may take a while, but the goal is to consume a minimum of 100 grams a day.

>> **Make sure you get enough fiber.** Aim for 25 to 30 grams a day. Good sources of fiber are 100 percent whole grains, fruits, and vegetables.

>> **Minimize saturated fat and avoid trans fats.** If you see the word *hydrogenated* in the ingredient list, don't buy it.

>> **Avoid added sugar.** When reading the ingredient list, look for sources such as high fructose corn syrup, dextrose, sucrose, honey, and brown sugar.

Chapter 5

Kitchen and Pantry Makeover

As you begin this new journey of food and cooking after weight loss surgery, nothing can be more important than having a kitchen well stocked with all the correct equipment and staples. Your space may be limited, but with careful planning you can make the most of the area you have.

Whether you're a cooking pro or a beginner, this chapter guides you through the details of necessary knives, utensils, cookware, and small appliances. Each serves a function and makes being in the kitchen more time efficient. In addition, we provide a list of dry, refrigerated, and frozen staples to make sure the next time you start a recipe you're not dashing out the door for a forgotten ingredient.

Preparing Your Kitchen: Purging and Organizing

You're ready to start cooking, but you have no idea where anything is. You have kitchen gadgets, trinkets, and gag gifts that everyone knew you had to have to make your kitchen more exciting. But now's the time to figure out what you do and don't need to make your cooking successful. Clean out the junk and get your kitchen organized!

TIP

Start with three boxes. The first box is for things to keep, the second box is for donations, and the third box is for trash. Divide your kitchen into sections, sorting into the three boxes. Trying to tackle the whole kitchen all at once can be overwhelming and you may waver over gidgets and gadgets. Get boxes two and three out of the kitchen before you change your mind and clutter up the kitchen again.

After going through all your cupboards, organize your kitchen so that it makes the most out of your space. Professional kitchens are set up in a manner where the person hired to do a specific job doesn't waste time walking from one end of the kitchen to the next. For example, the baker has all baking items and pans needed to do the job close to where production is happening. Even the ovens are within a short distance. The salad chef, on the other hand, is closer to the sinks, strainers, and refrigerators. You can optimize your time in the kitchen if yours is set up the same way. Have your knives close to the cutting boards; cooking utensils, pots, and pans closer to the stove and oven; and spices and herbs close to the food preparation areas. Put dishes, silverware, cups, and glasses close to the dish washing area.

The maxim, "Out with the old and in with the new" is never more appropriate than when cleaning out your kitchen. Having ineffective equipment slows prep time and can be downright dangerous. Equipment should be sturdy when placed on an even surface. Cords should be securely attached. If cords have internal wires showing or not attached properly, they can be a fire hazard or give you an electrical shock.

Examining Essential Tools

Cooking can only become easy with the proper utensils. Having an understanding of the essentials makes kitchen time easier and more enjoyable. Which cookware and utensils should you buy? You want to get the best that your budget allows. Even though competing products may look the same on the outside, there are different levels of quality.

Cookware

Cookware is essential in your kitchen, and price does determine quality. More-expensive cookware has a heavier bottom to help conduct heat more evenly and aid in keeping food from burning to the bottom. In addition, different cookware is infused with different metals, and nonstick coatings are added to the finish to help prevent sticking once food is in the pan. Inexpensive cookware is lighter, so doesn't conduct heat evenly. This can cause cold spots that make your food cook unevenly. The nonstick coating is lighter as well and scratches more easily. In general, cheaper cookware typically lasts one to two years. More-expensive cookware sometimes comes with a lifetime warranty.

Different sizes of cookware serve different functions, and the size of the pan is just as important as what's being cooked in it. If the pan is too large, the empty surface area around the food being cooked is being heated. This gets the pan hotter than intended and causes your food to dry out and, in some cases, burn. When full, your pot or pan should have at least an inch of room from the top to keep the food from splattering out. On the other end of the spectrum, the food should fill at least a third of the pot. If you're sautéing, the bottom of the pan should be at least half covered.

The quality of the pan is important, but which is better: coated or noncoated pans? When shopping for pots and pans, you may notice the higher-end cookware doesn't have nonstick coatings. They don't require coating because the metals are infused in such a way that keeps the food from sticking while cooking. Less-expensive (lower-quality) pans need a coating, or food sticks. But every rule has exceptions, and in this case, it's the omelet pan. This is an 8-inch sauté pan in which eggs and only eggs are cooked. Both high-end and lower quality omelet pans should have a nonstick coating. Use this pan only for eggs, and store it with a small hand towel folded in the middle to keep the surface protected.

REMEMBER

To keep your cookware cooking at its best, take good care of it. Don't put it in the dishwasher, because most dishwasher detergents are too harsh and can harm the finish over time. Hand-wash the pots and pans and dry them thoroughly before storing. If you stack or nest the cookware, put small towels or paper towels in between to protect from nicks and scratches.

Microwaving is a quick and easy way of cooking, but be sure the dishes you use are microwave safe. The microwave heats food differently than standard stove tops, and the dishes are made in such a way to aid cooking food specifically in the microwave. The glass needs to be tempered to keep from shattering when the temperature adjusts, and the surfaces can't have metal pieces. In addition, microwave dishes are normally smaller in size, and they have vents in the lids to allow steam to escape while keeping the food from splattering all over the microwave.

Vegetable steamers are a healthy way of cooking and inexpensive to purchase. Two versions are available. The first is a conventional steamer that comes in three pieces. Water is boiled in a larger pot, and a smaller pot perforated with holes holds the food and fits nestled inside the larger one. Steam seeps through the holes to heat the food, and a fitted lid helps hold the steam in. The second version is an electric steamer. It works the same way, but it's self-contained and sits on your countertop.

Gadgets

Kitchen gadgets make life easier, and the following list makes choosing the right gadget a breeze:

>> **Metal or plastic spatula:** Also known as pancake turners, spatulas come in many different sizes. Metal spatulas are more durable but can scratch your pans. Plastic spatulas are a better choice to keep from scratching the inside of the pan, but make sure your plastic spatula is heat resistant so it won't melt.

>> **Wire whisk:** Use this tool to incorporate air into batters or liquids to make them lighter. You can find plastic whisks, but they don't work as well as metal. Whisks come in different sizes, and you'll find it ideal to have a small, medium, and large in your kitchen.

>> **Mixing spoons:** You need a lot of these because they're such a handy tool, but you won't mind since they're inexpensive. We recommend you have ten. Wooden spoons are perfect for mixing jobs and won't scratch your nonstick cookware. To keep them in good condition, hand-wash these to clean 'em up.

>> **Dry and liquid measuring cups:** Dry measuring cups are used for measuring dry or solid ingredients like flour, mayonnaise, fruits, and vegetables. They typically come in sets ranging in volume from ¼ cup to 1 cup. Liquid measuring cups measure differently than dry ones, so both types are needed. Liquid measuring cups have a small spout for pouring liquids and usually come in sizes ranging from 1 cup to 4 cups.

>> **Measuring spoons:** These come in metal or plastic. Measuring spoons are needed for measuring out small amounts of ingredients. Unlike measuring cups, measuring spoons are used for both dry and liquid measure.

>> **Food scale:** Weighing ingredients to get the right amount is important in some recipes. Scales also help in determining serving sizes. They come in a wide range of prices and features. Small scales, under $10, can give you a weight of a food up to 16 ounces. Some digital scales have computer chips in them that provide you with nutrition information for the food you are eating. You can put your grapes on the scale platform, program the code for the grapes, and the scale gives you a reading for calories, fat, protein, and carbohydrates. Some of these scales have a memory built in so you can tally your intake for the day.

>> **Meat thermometer:** A meat thermometer measures the degree of doneness of meats, poultry, fish, and seafood. Most meat thermometers are not oven-safe, but if you spend a little extra money you can get one that can stay in your protein while it cooks.

>> **Quick-read thermometer:** This simple thermometer is used to measure the internal temperature of any food, cold or hot. They're not oven-proof.

>> **Oven thermometer:** These thermometers are used to make sure the oven is calibrated to correct temperature. Older ovens can be 20 degrees under or over their setting and cause your dish to over- or undercook. If your oven temperature is way off, you can call an appliance repair man to come and adjust it.

>> **Mixing bowls:** When you're preparing multiple dishes or complicated recipes, the more mixing bowls you have, the better. We recommend having three small, three medium, three large, and one really big.

>> **Colander:** Also known as a strainer, this tool is used to let liquid drain out while keeping solids in the colander. They come in plastic or metal.

>> **Garlic press:** You use a press to crush garlic without using a knife. Garlic presses come in plastic or metal, and the metal ones work best by far.

>> **Cheese box grater:** These large graters have four sides. Two are different grating sizes, one is a zester, and one side is a slicer for vegetables and fruits such as zucchini, carrots, and bananas.

>> **Meat pounder:** A pounder, or tenderizer, is used to pound protein or other foods to a thinner size. This is typically done for cuts of meat that aren't as tender as you want or to make the meat a uniform thickness so it cooks evenly.

Knives

In this section we talk about the one of the most neglected but most essential tools in the kitchen. Knives are important, but you can have too much of a good thing. Do you have a knife drawer and/or knife block packed with knives? How many of them are sharp? How many of them are in good condition? How many of them do you actually use? Most of the time you probably find yourself looking for a particular one while pushing the other knives out of the way because you like the feel of the knife or it's sharper.

Gather all your knives and lay them out on the counter for a knife inspection. Check each one for the following points:

>> Is the handle firmly attached?

>> Is the blade straight and free of nicks and gashes?

>> Have you use the knife in the past 60 days?

>> If the knife is dull, can it be sharpened?

If you answer no to any of these questions, throw or give it away.

You don't need knives that can cut through metal blocks and aluminum cans. Those gimmicky sets normally come with 20 knives or more, and you'd be wasting money on knives you'll never use. You only need four basic knives:

>> **Chef's knife:** This essential knife is used for cutting large pieces of food and for dicing and chopping. It comes in 6-, 8-, and 10-inch blades. Most women prefer the 6-inch knife because it suits smaller hands better, and men typically like the feel of an 8-inch blade.

>> **Paring knife:** This knife has a much smaller blade and is used for cutting smaller foods.

>> **Serrated knife:** Also known as a bread knife, the serrated knife is about 8 to 10 inches long and is great for cutting through bread and thick rinds of fruits such as watermelon and pineapple.

>> **Utility knife:** Smaller than a chef's knife and slightly bigger than a paring knife, this one is used for all the foods in between. For example, a utility knife is great for cutting grapefruit and eggplant.

Any of the previously mentioned knives are great for cutting and trimming meat, poultry, seafood, and fish as well.

The quality of the knife is just as important as what type it is, so buy what you can afford. Cheaper knives normally have plastic handles and the blades are thin and not able to be sharpened. More-expensive ones have thicker blades made from high-carbon stainless steel and can be sharpened when they become dull. The part of the blade that runs through the handle is called the tang. Pick knives that let you see the tang run through the entire length of the handle, because knives with a full tang last longer. Knives range from $7 to over $150 each. Protect your investment by washing in soapy water and drying thoroughly before storing. Don't put your knives in the dishwasher, especially if they have wooden handles.

REMEMBER

Keeping your knives sharp is important. Dull knives cause more cuts than sharp ones because when a knife isn't sharp, most people apply more pressure to cut through the food. This excessive pressure can cause more damage if you cut yourself. Food prep also is much quicker with sharpened blades because sharp knives do all the work. Most areas of the country have sharpening services, and the cost is generally around $3 per knife. You can also learn to sharpen them yourself. Most need to be sharpened at least every six months.

Although it's not a knife, a pair of kitchen shears, or scissors, deserves a place in your knife block. You may want to have one pair designated just for food when snipping the stems from herbs, and another pair for opening packages.

Cutting boards

The job of a cutting board is to protect your countertops and to provide a slight cushion for your knife to keep the blade from dulling. Although it may look nice, don't use a glass cutting board. This is the worst on your knives, and when the blade meets the surface of the glass, it slips. Wood and polyurethane boards are the best options. There is some controversy over which cutting board holds bacteria, and the answer is neither, as long as they are cleaned and sterilized well. The advantage to the polyurethane board is that it's dishwasher safe. A wood cutting board needs to be hand-washed and air dried. You may want to have one or more of each on hand. If you're worried about food safety with raw meats, use a polyurethane board that you can be placed in the dishwasher.

Small appliances

The following items make your life in the kitchen much easier:

>> **Blender:** A blender is used for mixing, puréeing, and whipping drinks and small pieces of food. A blender's blades are shaped like an *X* and point down so the liquids and foods are pulled downwards toward the blade. Liquid is needed to help with the blending.

>> **Food processor:** This appliance is used for chopping, dicing, puréeing, and shredding. The blades are *S* shaped and stacked on top of each other. A food processor doesn't require liquid to work. If you are in Stage 3 of the diet progression, smooth foods, use a food processor to make your food smooth but not soupy.

   Note: A food processor and blender are not the same piece of equipment. Take caution when reading recipes, and if the recipe states a food processor, a blender generally won't work.

>> **Mini chopper:** A smaller version of a food processor, a mini chopper typically comes with a 1-cup capacity. It's great for small jobs such as chopping an onion quickly, and it's faster to clean (which saves you time) and takes up less space than a full-sized food processor.

>> **Mixer:** Two types of mixers are used to whip, stir, and blend ingredients together. A hand mixer, great for small jobs, normally has two metal beaters and a wire whisk for whipping. Countertop mixers have an attached bowl, wire whisk, paddle, and dough hook. The countertop mixer costs more money but has a bigger motor to mix larger batches at a time.

>> **Toaster oven:** This miniature oven placed on your countertop has broiling, toasting, and baking functions. It's great for smaller items. Instead of heating up your large oven, you can save electricity with the tinier toaster.

>> **Slow cooker:** You can make lean cuts of meat tender and moist by cooking with low heat over a long period of time in a slow cooker. When quickly cooking lean cuts of protein, the muscle fiber shrinks up, causing the meat to become tough and chewy. However, when slow cooked, the muscle fiber begins to break down after about four to five hours and by the eighth hour the protein is tender and delicious. Slow and low works great for all lean cuts of meat.

A slow cooker can also save you time. How great is it to walk in the door and smell your delicious dinner cooking? Just fix it in the morning and forget it; no rushing around in the evening to feed the hungry troops. If you're rushed for time in the morning, you can assemble the recipe ingredients the night before and put the pot in the refrigerator until morning.

Although electronic countertop "grilling" appliances can reduce the fat and calorie content of some foods, we do not recommend them for people who had weight loss surgery. They don't actually grill (a dry cooking method with indirect heat from below). Instead, they use two heated metal plates with raised metal lines. However, they don't stay hot long enough to sear the food, so the device turns into a steamer. Steam opens the pores of the food and causes the moisture to flow out, leaving you with tough food. Why does this matter to a weight loss surgery patient? To avoid getting food stuck in your pouch, you need your food to be moist and tender, not tough and chewy. So stick to a real grill.

Stocking Your Pantry, Refrigerator, and Freezer with Good Ingredients

Nothing can be more frustrating than going into the kitchen to make a recipe only to find out that you're missing one or two ingredients. Maintaining a running list of staples for your pantry, fridge, and freezer keeps you prepared for almost anything you want to concoct in the kitchen.

Herbs, spices, and more

If you keep the following spices, herbs, oils, and extracts in your pantry, you'll be ready to add a ton of flavor to your dishes.

Herbs and spices:

- Apple pie spice
- Basil, dried
- Bay leaves
- Black pepper
- Caraway seeds
- Cayenne pepper
- Celery seed
- Chili powder
- Cinnamon
- Cloves, ground
- Coriander, ground
- Cumin, ground
- Curry powder
- Dill, dried
- Garlic powder
- Italian seasoning
- Lemon pepper
- Marjoram, dried
- Mustard, dry
- Nutmeg, ground
- Old Bay seasoning
- Onion powder
- Oregano, dried
- Paprika
- Parsley flakes
- Peppercorns
- Poppy seeds
- Pumpkin pie spice
- Red pepper flakes
- Rosemary, crushed
- Sage, dried
- Salt
- Taco seasoning mix
- Tarragon, dried
- Thyme, ground
- Turmeric

Oils:

- Canola oil
- Olive oil
- Peanut oil
- Sesame oil
- Nonstick cooking spray

Extracts:

- Almond extract
- Lemon extract
- Vanilla extract

WHAT'S THE DIFFERENCE BETWEEN HERBS AND SPICES?

Herbs are from the leaf of a plant, and the flavor is found in the natural oil that the leaves exude when the membrane is ruptured. Dried herbs, fresh herbs that have been dried, vary in price from as low as $0.99 to over $5.00 for the same amount. The difference is the cheaper one has more stems added when being processed. The stems are bitter, but this way manufactures can save on cost. When buying dried herbs you get what you pay for, with stems or without.

Spices come from seeds, bark, or berries from a plant and are dried and then ground. For example, cinnamon is the bark from a tree, nutmeg is a seed, and mace is the shell from which the nutmeg is removed. Some spices are sold whole and then ground at home. The most common whole spice is peppercorns, which are placed in a pepper mill and ground when needed.

Storing herbs and spices correctly is essential to maintaining their freshness. Remove fresh herbs from the package they were purchased in. Cut about ½ inch from the bottom of the stems so they can absorb water and stay fresh longer. Then place the freshly cut herbs into 2 inches of water and store them in the refrigerator with a damp paper towel over the top. Some herbs come in small soil-filled pots. Keep the herbs where they can get sunlight and keep them watered. Dried spices and herbs have a one-year shelf life. Write the date on the dried herb or spice container when you unpack it from your grocery bag so you know how long you have had it.

Canned ingredients

Canned items are great to have on hand because they work in all kinds of dishes and are a good option when fresh or frozen ingredients aren't readily available. Plus, because their shelf life is long, you can stock up on these items when they're on sale:

Beans:

- >> Black beans, no salt added
- >> Garbanzo beans, no salt added
- >> Kidney beans, no salt added
- >> Navy beans
- >> Pinto beans
- >> White beans

Fruits:

- >> Applesauce, unsweetened
- >> Apricots in juice
- >> Mandarin oranges in juice
- >> Peaches in juice
- >> Pears in juice
- >> Pineapple in juice

Meats:

- >> Albacore tuna, canned in water or pouch
- >> Chicken, canned or pouch
- >> Crab meat, canned or pouch
- >> Salmon, canned
- >> Shrimp, canned or pouch

Vegetables:

- >> Carrots
- >> Green beans
- >> Mexican-style corn
- >> Mixed vegetables
- >> Mushrooms
- >> Peas
- >> Potatoes
- >> Pumpkin purée
- >> Sweet potatoes
- >> Tomatoes, diced/whole/ stewed, no salt added
- >> Tomato paste, no salt added
- >> Tomato sauce, no salt added

Dry pantry items

Finding yourself without any of the following ingredients is a real bummer. Stock up on these items when you can!

Flour:

- >> All-purpose flour
- >> Quick-mixing flour
- >> Whole-wheat flour

Vinegar:

- >> Balsamic vinegar
- >> Cider vinegar
- >> Red wine vinegar
- >> White vinegar
- >> White wine vinegar

Beans and legumes:

- >> Black beans
- >> Great northern beans
- >> Kidney beans
- >> Lentils
- >> Lima beans
- >> Navy beans
- >> Pinto beans
- >> Split peas

Other:

- >> Baking powder
- >> Baking soda
- >> Cornmeal
- >> Cornstarch
- >> Honey
- >> Pancake syrup, sugar free
- >> Sugar substitute

Refrigerated foods

These refrigerated items are sure to come in handy. Make sure you have the following:

- >> Chili sauce
- >> Chutney
- >> Brown mustard
- >> Dijon mustard
- >> Yellow mustard
- >> Horseradish
- >> Hot pepper sauce
- >> Ketchup
- >> Liquid smoke
- >> Seafood cocktail sauce
- >> Worcestershire sauce
- >> Steak sauce
- >> 100 percent fruit spread
- >> Eggs
- >> Egg substitute
- >> Cheddar cheese, lowfat
- >> Half-and-half, fat free
- >> Milk, nonfat
- >> Butter
- >> Margarine

Frozen fruits and veggies

Always keep frozen fruits and vegetables on hand to add to any recipe or to finish the meal. Following are some ideas:

Fruits:

- Berries, mixed
- Cherries, unsweetened
- Peaches
- Raspberries
- Strawberries, unsweetened

Vegetables:

- Asparagus
- Broccoli flowerets
- Brussels sprouts
- Butternut/winter squash
- Cauliflower
- Corn, whole kernel
- Edamame
- Green beans
- Lima beans
- Peas
- Spinach, chopped or leaf
- Stir-fry mix
- Sweet potatoes
- Vegetables, mixed

Chapter **6**

Top Tips for Food Preparation and Cooking

You may not consider yourself to be a chef, but good cooking can be easier than you think. The great thing about cooking is that you can make it as easy or as challenging as you want it to be. Can't make anything but a bowl of cereal? Look at it as putting food together instead of cooking, and get comfortable with some simple recipes. Are you a foodie with a passion for the kitchen? You can satisfy that interest after surgery, too. Just think of all those "to die for" recipes that can be modified to fit your new lifestyle.

Things do need to change after surgery. After all, for a lot of you, your love of food or lack of time and skill to prepare healthy food is what brought you to the surgeon's office. And after surgery your pouch just can't handle some of the old foods that you ate. Some foods get stuck or just don't "set well" in the pouch.

This book provides you with amazing recipes, but we know you're not going to cook our recipes for the rest of your life. This chapter tells you how to cook after weight loss surgery to suit your tastes, ability, and new lifestyle. Who better to help you than a chef who had gastric bypass himself?

Brushing Up on Food Safety

Food safety is not an option but a necessity. No matter how great your food tastes, if your food, cooking utensils, and cutting boards are not handled properly you meal can be ruined by foodborne illness. In this section you find out how to keep your kitchen and food as clean and safe as possible.

Taking care of fresh and raw foods

Fresh fruits and vegetables and raw meats are always better than processed, but "safety first" is the rule to keep from getting sick. With a few tips and tricks you can ensure all your meals are safe and sound.

After vegetables are picked from the fields they go through a rinse cycle before being packed and shipped to stores for sale. However, a lot of food is cleaned at a time and it doesn't get the tender love and care you personally can give your vegetables and fruits before eating.

TIP

Following are some tips for safely handling and prepping produce:

>> Choose fresh fruits and vegetables carefully. When shopping, look for produce that's not damaged or bruised, and make sure that precut produce is refrigerated.

>> Clean all surfaces and utensils with soap and hot water, including cutting boards, peelers, countertops, and knives that will touch fresh produce. Wash hands with soap and warm water for at least 20 seconds before and after handling fresh fruits and vegetables.

>> Rinse fresh fruits and vegetables, including those with skins and rinds that are not eaten, under clean running water, and avoid using detergents or bleach.

- Remove the outer leaves of leafy vegetables such as lettuce and cabbage before washing.

- Produce with firm skin, such as potatoes, may require rubbing with a vegetable brush while rinsing under clean running water to remove all soil.

- Don't rinse until just before eating, to avoid premature spoilage.

>> Dry fruits and vegetables with a clean towel.

>> Packaged produce labeled *ready to eat, prewashed,* or *triple washed* can be used without further washing.

>> Keep produce separate from all raw meats in your shopping cart, grocery bags, refrigerator, and when prepping food.

- Throw away any produce that will not be cooked if it has touched raw meat or eggs.

- After preparing raw meats, clean your cutting board and knives with hot water and soap before and after preparing fresh fruits and vegetables.

- Store raw meat below ready-to-eat produce and other foods in the refrigerator so it can't leak onto them.

>> Refrigerate all cut, peeled, or cooked produce within two hours. Harmful bacteria may grow on produce and increase the risk of foodborne illness.

Cooking foods to the proper temperature

Raw meats and eggs need to be handled with extreme care to reduce the risk of foodborne illness. Thorough cooking kills harmful bacteria. If you eat meat, poultry, fish, seafood, or eggs that are raw or only partially cooked, you may be exposing yourself to bacteria that can make you ill. This is particularly important for children, pregnant women, the elderly, and those whose immune systems are compromised. Check out the following sections for specific info on safely cooking meats.

WARNING

Salmonella, a bacteria that causes food poisoning, can grow inside fresh, unbroken eggs and raw poultry. Be sure to cook eggs until the yolk and white are firm, not runny. Scramble eggs to a firm texture. Avoid recipes in which eggs remain raw or only partially cooked (for example, mousse, egg drinks, Caesar dressing, and more). Pasteurized eggs or egg substitute can be used instead.

TIP

Use a meat thermometer to ensure that meat, poultry, and fish are cooked to the appropriate temperature. Insert the sterile metal tip into the center and/or the thickest part off the food.

Red meat

Table 6-1 shows the correct cooking temps for red meat, depending on the desired doneness.

TABLE 6-1 ## Red Meat Cooking Temperatures

Doneness	Internal Temperature	Appearance
Rare	120 to 125 degrees	Center is bright red; pinkish toward the exterior portion
Medium rare	130 to 135 degrees	Center is very pink; slightly brown toward the exterior portion
Medium	140 to 145 degrees	Center is light pink; outer portion is brown
Medium well	150 to 155 degrees	Not pink
Well done	160 degrees and above	Uniformly brown throughout
Ground meat	160 to 165 degrees	Uniformly gray throughout

Poultry

Poultry doesn't have levels of doneness. It's either done or it isn't. You know it's done if the juices run clear (instead of cloudy and pink) when you cut into it and a meat thermometer reads approximately 165 degrees for white meat and 185 degrees for dark meat.

Pork

If not cooked to the correct temperature, pork can cause trichinosis, which is a foodborne illness. Table 6-2 tells you how to safely cook pork.

TABLE 6-2 ## Pork Cooking Temperatures

Meat	Doneness	Internal Temperature	Appearance
Roasts, steaks, and chops	Medium	140 to 145 degrees	Pale pink center
	Well done	160 degrees and above	Uniformly brown throughout
Pork ribs and pork shoulders	Medium to well done	160 degrees and above	Thin pink line in the middle
Sausage (raw)	Cooked through	160 degrees	No longer pink
Ham (raw)	Cooked through	160 degrees	Pink if smoked, gray if not smoked
Ham (precooked)	Safely reheated	140 degrees	Pink if smoked, gray if not smoked

Fish and seafood

Fish and seafood need to be handled with care. All fish and seafood have parasites, and proper cooking methods are needed to destroy foodborne pathogens. However, overcooked fish becomes dry and loses its flavor, so monitor it carefully. Check out Table 6-3 for safe cooking instructions. Most seafood is too small to take an internal temperature, so cooking times are used.

TABLE 6-3   Fish and Seafood Cooking Temperatures and Times

Fish or Seafood	Cooking Technique	Internal Temperature or Cooking Duration	Appearance
Tuna, swordfish, and marlin	Any	125 degrees	Flesh is opaque and flakes easily
Other fish (steaks, filleted, or whole)	Any	140 degrees	Flesh is opaque and flakes easily
Medium-size shrimp	Any	3 to 4 minutes	Pink
Large-size shrimp	Any	5 to 7 minutes	Pink
Jumbo-size shrimp	Any	7 to 8 minutes	Pink
Whole lobster	Boil	12 to 15 minutes	Meat turns red and opaque in center
	Broil	3 to 4 minutes	Meat turns red and opaque in center
	Steam	15 to 20 minutes	Meat turns red and opaque in center
Lobster tail	Bake	15 minutes	Meat turns red and opaque in center
	Broil	9 to 10 minutes	Meat turns red and opaque in center
Scallops	Bake	12 to 15 minutes	Milky white or opaque, and firm
	Broil	6 to 10 minutes	Milky white or opaque, and firm
Clams, mussels, and oysters	Any	About 5 minutes	Done when shells open (throw away any that don't open)

WHAT ABOUT SUSHI?

Sushi-grade fish is served raw, but it's handled much differently than fish that's going to be cooked. The fish goes through a rigorous inspection before being graded for sushi, and it's then kept below 40 degrees at all times. However, you are still taking a risk by consuming sushi-like raw meats.

Keeping leftovers safe

Whether frozen or refrigerated, leftovers need to be handled safely. Don't let leftover food that you've cooked and want to save sit out for more than two hours.

When freezing, place the food in an airtight container and freeze within 24 hours. The shelf life varies once frozen, but the food usually keeps close to 100-percent quality for 60 to 90 days. Any longer and the food starts to break down and the quality is significantly compromised.

Refrigerating leftovers is a great way to have a meal all ready to go. Refrigerated food is good for between 72 to 96 hours (three to four days). Soon thereafter the food begins to break down quickly and spoilage sets in. Again, store food in an airtight container.

Reviewing Cooking Methods 101

Different cooking methods produce different results, and having an understanding of what they are will carry over into successful meals every time. You may see the terms *sauté, broil, stew,* and *braise,* but do you know how that applies to food? No matter how great a recipe is, if you cook the food the way you think it should be done instead of the way the recipe intended, or try a cooking shortcut, you have no one to blame but yourself if the meal turns out badly.

REMEMBER

Pot and pan sizes matter, and recipes will turn out differently if the appropriate pan size isn't used. If the pan or pot is too big, the food will likely dry out while cooking. If too small, the food may take longer to cook and become chewy and/or overcooked.

TIP

Some cooking methods are dry, and others are moist. One easy-to-remember rule to follow in choosing between the two is if the animal walks on land, dry cooking methods are recommended, and if it lives in water, moist cooking has better results.

No matter which cooking process you use, improving your understanding of the various methods saves you time and enhances your dishes every time you cook.

Dry cooking methods

Dry cooking methods are recommended when cooking meat from land animals. This includes sautéing, rotisserie cooking, grilling, broiling, roasting, and baking. Sautéing and rotisserie roasting make food especially moist and tender, so are recommended for cooking both meats and fish in the first three months after your surgery when you may experience the most difficulty tolerating foods and preventing sticking.

» **Sautéing:** Cooking food in a preheated pan or griddle with minimum amount of fat

This method of cooking is an easy and preferred procedure because cooking time is short (normally under seven minutes) and because only a few guidelines need to be followed.

- Make certain the pieces of meat are no more than ½ inch thick, or the outside may burn while the inside remains uncooked.

- Preheat the pan before adding meat to ensure that it cooks quickly and retains its moisture.

- *Never* walk away while cooking is in progress. The sauté method requires only two to seven minutes, and overcooking reduces moisture, making food difficult to swallow and digest.

» **Rotisserie cooking:** Cooking food in dry heat while rotating

Rotisserie cooking helps meat retain moisture, so it's a preferred method to improve your protein intake during the first few months after your surgery. Home rotisserie cooking devices are available and generally require little effort, other than time, for food preparation. Most grocery stores and many restaurants sell rotisserie-cooked meats, making moist and tender meats readily available.

Rotisserie-cooked poultry typically cooks with the skin on, but you should discard it to avoid adding unnecessary fat and calories to your meal.

» **Grilling:** Cooking food from heat below

When grilling, a gas flame or a hot charcoal briquette is 3 to 4 inches below a metal or cast-iron grate. The food is slow cooked to the right temperature. The hot dry heat sears in the juices, which keeps the food moist and, depending on the cut, tender. The charcoal or flame adds a distinct flavor and look that cannot be duplicated. Electrically heated indoor grilling gadgets actually steam your food instead of grilling, and in most cases, they cause the meat to become tough and flavorless. (They do add a few pretty grill line marks on the food, though.)

» **Roasting:** Cooking food in dry heat with the aid of fat

To roast food correctly, use a roasting rack and a roasting pan with sides no higher than 2½ to 3 inches. The rack lifts the meat out of the pan and allows the food to be exposed to heat all the way around. Fill the pan ¼ inch with a liquid, such as canned chicken stock, which collects the drippings to start a gravy (and also keeps the drippings from burning when they hit the bottom of the pan). While roasting, baste the food with the stock and drippings from the pan. Never wrap or cover the meat when roasting, because it either breaks the sear (causes the meat to leak juices) or keeps the protein from forming a tight sear, and your protein will be chewy and dry.

>> **Broiling:** Cooking food from heat above

You may already use your oven broiler to brown the tops of casseroles and melt cheese, but that's also a quick way to quickly cook thin cuts of meats, fish, seafood, and vegetables. Preheat the broiler on high before putting food in the oven. Space the food out on the top of a broiler pan (all ovens come standard with them). Add seasoning and, if needed, a little oil. Place the broiler pan in the oven so the food is 6 inches beneath the broiler, and leave the oven door open a crack. At this point you don't want to walk away, because food begins to brown quickly. When desired browning has occurred, flip the food over and broil until desired doneness on the other side.

Moist cooking methods

Moist cooking methods include deep frying, pan frying, stewing, braising, poaching, and boiling. Moist cooking techniques can be used to cook meats, such as poultry, beef, lamb, or pork. Boiling and poaching can cause most meats to be tough unless cooked low and slow to break down the muscle. On the other hand, moist cooking methods, particularly poaching and steaming, are very effective in maintaining the tenderness of fish and seafood.

>> **Deep frying:** Cooking food totally immersed in preheated fat or oil

Deep frying is typically done at 350 degrees so the submerged food is seared on the outside (keeping excess fat from seeping in) and keeps its moisture in. If done correctly, fried food is lower in fat on the inside but higher in fat and calories on the outside. (If the food on the inside is greasy, the food was fried at a temperature below 350 degrees or the oil is old.) That fatty outside, often battered, is where you'll find the most fat. When eating deep-fried food, peel off the fried skin or batter and eat only the moist, tender food on the inside.

>> **Pan frying:** Cooking food partially immersed in preheated fat or oil

Pan frying is the same as deep frying except that the food is only submersed halfway in the heated oil and then turned to finish cooking the other side. Again, discard the fatty outside before eating pan-fried foods.

>> **Stewing:** Cooking small pieces of food submerged in liquid below simmering temperature

Stewing is the key to ready prepared meals. Your recipe can be started in the morning and during the day your food will cook and be ready just in time for dinner. Stews are cooked at a low temperature with the lid on, so most of the liquid is retained in the pot. With most cooking methods, the water in meats and vegetables turns to steam and evaporates, but with stewing, the steam collects on the lid and drips down again, basting the food.

>> **Braising:** Cooking in a closed container with liquid in the oven or on the stove

Braising is very similar to stewing, but the food sits in a small amount of liquid instead of being submerged in it. The food is cooked low and slow.

>> **Poaching:** Cooking food in liquid at a temperature below boiling

Poaching is done on the stove and the liquid is just below a light simmer. This technique works well with fish, seafood, and eggs. Cooking times vary depending on thickness, but on average 5 to 10 minutes is all it takes.

Poaching is usually done around 160 degrees.

>> **Boiling:** Cooking in a liquid at 212 degrees

Boiling is done on the stove. Root vegetables, eggs, pasta, stews, and soups are mostly boiled. Boiling is used to bring soup and stews to a safe temperature when heated, and it cooks root vegetables and pasta quickly.

Cooking and Consuming Meat after Weight Loss Surgery

Foods containing the highest quality protein are beef, chicken, turkey, lamb, eggs, cheese, pork, seafood, fish, shellfish, veal, and liver. Every ounce of these high-quality protein foods has 6 to 8 grams. A 3-ounce piece of chicken breast, for example, contains 21 grams of protein. Processed meats, however, such as hot dogs, bologna, salami, liverwurst, deviled ham, and others, are not high-quality protein foods. A 2-ounce hot dog, for instance, contains only 5 to 7 grams of protein. In addition, processed meats contain large amounts of fillers such as sugar and starches that may possibly cause dumping syndrome. They're also high in fat and sodium. Some of these foods have a rubbery texture that increases the chances of sticking. You can eat deli meat, but only sparingly because of the high sodium content, and choose meats that are highest in protein, such as turkey breast, ham, and top round roast beef.

Other foods high in protein include dairy products, such as cheese and milk. One 8-ounce glass of milk, for instance, may have as much as 13 grams of protein.

Eggs are also high in protein, with 6.5 grams. Eggs can be fried, hard-boiled, poached, scrambled, or prepared as omelets or egg salad, but you may find that certain preparation methods work better than others for you. Everyone is different, so while a hard-boiled egg may work for you, it may not work for your friend.

The following sections provide additional guidance and tips for enjoying various kinds of meat safely while getting the most protein bang for your buck.

Beef

For easier consumption, beef should be cooked medium to rare. Medium is a warm, pink center, and rare is a cool, red center. Refer to Table 6-1 for more specific cooking instructions. When overcooked, beef loses its moisture and becomes tough, chewy, and nearly impossible for the gastric bypass patient to swallow. Ground beef also becomes difficult to digest if overcooked. As a rule, ground beef should be cooked until it turns gray, not brown. Dry heat cooking methods are recommended for all cuts of beef (see "Dry cooking methods" earlier for more info). If moist cooking methods are used, such as stewing or braising, expensive cuts of meat are necessary and should be cooked at low temperatures for prolonged periods of time, up to eight hours, to ensure tenderness.

Poultry

After surgery, you may find that when eating poultry, you prefer dark meat (legs and thighs) to white pieces (breast and wings) because the darker pieces contain more moisture and are easier to chew and swallow. However, this doesn't mean that white poultry can't be eaten, only that it has to be prepared and cooked differently to maintain moisture. When preparing white poultry, thinner cuts are better, preferably only about a quarter of an inch thick. The thickness of the meat can be adjusted by using a meat cleaver to tenderize the piece. You can also ask the butcher to slice the raw breast meat into ¼-inch slices.

Dry heat cooking methods are recommended for poultry. (Check out "Dry cooking methods" earlier to find out more.) For thinner cuts (¼-inch thick), sautéing is best. To sauté poultry, meat should be cooked for a minute and a half on each side in a preheated large skillet over medium-high heat. If the poultry isn't cooked through in 3 minutes, the pan wasn't hot enough or the meat was too thick. The number one reason why white-meat poultry is often too dry to eat is because it's overcooked.

For thicker pieces of poultry, such as a whole bird or large cuts, rotisserie cooking, roasting, grilling, and baking are appropriate dry heat cooking methods. Cook white-meat poultry until it reaches an internal temperature of 165 degrees, and dark meat to 185 degrees. Cooking to a higher temperature than necessary dries out the poultry, and lower temperatures may leave the poultry partially uncooked. Leaving the skin on the poultry while cooking helps with flavor and moisture, but we don't recommend eating it. Skin is fat, and if consumed, you won't have enough room left in your pouch to eat the proper amount of protein. Marinating poultry in acidic marinades helps tenderize the chicken while adding flavor. And remember that leftover poultry can be used for cold salads.

Pork, lamb, and liver

Pork, lamb, and liver are excellent protein sources and most tender when cooked in dry heat (see "Dry cooking methods" earlier for more info). Pork and lamb are good meats to marinate and can be cut up and used in stir-fries or placed on skewers and grilled over medium-low heat. Both American lamb and New Zealand lamb can be found in most supermarkets and some restaurants. American sheep are fed grains, whereas New Zealand sheep eat grass. For this reason, New Zealand lamb sometimes tastes gamy and is not as sweet or tender as American lamb. Beef and chicken liver are very soft and can be made into fresh liver pâté or sautéed and seasoned. However, liver is very high in cholesterol, so consume in moderation. Lamb, liver, and pork can be used in any recipe where beef or poultry is recommended.

Fish and seafood

Fish (from fresh water or the sea) and shellfish such as shrimp, lobster, scallops, oysters, clams, and crab are excellent sources of protein that you will probably find easy to consume after weight loss surgery.

REMEMBER

Fish and seafood is best eaten fresh. Fish that has been frozen has less moisture and flavor. However, beware of fresh fish that smells fishy. Good fresh fish and seafood has almost no smell at all. Don't purchase or consume smelly or slimy fish.

Fish and shellfish may be cooked using moist or dry cooking methods, but moist methods tend to keep the fish and seafood moist while cooking. A popular cooking method for fish is poaching, which is submerging it into a flavored liquid, such as white wine infused with dill, and cooking just below the simmering point (approximately 185 degrees). Poaching is a quick and healthy way to infuse flavor into the fish and shellfish. Other popular cooking methods include grilling, sautéing, and broiling. Most cooked fish and shellfish can be used the next day for cold salad preparations.

Measuring Up: A Guide to Measuring Common Ingredients

Maybe you remember watching Mom or Grandma making a great meal without measuring a thing. You may have old recipes that call for a "handful" or a "chunk" of a food instead of today's recipes that have more precise measurements. Well, Mom and Grandma may not have measured, but after a lot of years of cooking they just knew how much a cup or 4 ounces were by eyeballing the amount.

We still recommend using the proper utensils to get the amounts in a recipe correct. If you're baking, a little more or less of an ingredient can really make the difference between success and failure of the end product. In cooking, the dish may still turn out okay, but the taste may be changed.

TIP

Use your measuring spoons to measure out small amounts of liquids, such as oils, and dry foods, like seasonings. Too much or too little will really make a difference in the finished food. Don't measure over the bowl or the pot, because if you accidentally over-pour, you're stuck. You usually can't get it out after you've put it in! Measurements are level on the top, not heaping. Heaping measures can be double the amount you want, and more is not always better.

The recipes in this book use United States customary units for measurements.

Measuring weight versus volume

One thing that gets folks confused with measuring is weight and volume. All ounces are not equal. Fluid ounces measure liquids like broth, water, milk, or oil. Other ounces measure the weight of solid foods like chicken, flour, or cheese. This may seem puzzling, so check out the following examples:

>> ¼ cup of vegetable oil measures 2 fluid ounces (liquid) but weighs 1½ ounces.

>> ½ cup of shredded cheese also weighs 2 ounces (dry), not four ounces as you may think because of the previous example.

>> ½ cup of puffed rice cereal measures the same volume as ½ cup of peanut butter, but they don't weigh the same!

TIP

When you're reading a recipe:

>> If the ingredient is a solid food, like pasta or meat, and the amount is in ounces, it is weight. Time to break out the food scale.

» If the ingredient is a solid food, like pasta or meat, and the amount is in cups, it is a volume measurement. Use measuring cups.

» If the ingredient is a liquid and the amount is in ounces, it is fluid ounces, not weight. Use the liquid measuring cup.

Measuring liquids

Measure liquids (anything that pours) using the liquid measuring cup. It has a little spout to make pouring easier and leaves some room at the top so you won't spill the contents. Set the measuring cup on the counter and pour in the liquid. You can't get an accurate reading from looking down into the cup, so get down to eye level to check the amount. The liquid level should be right on the marking lines.

Here are some handy measurements for wet ingredients:

» 8 fluid ounces (fl. oz.) = 1 cup (c.)

» 16 fl. oz. = 2 c. = 1 pint (pt.)

» 32 fl. oz. = 4 c. = 2 pt. = 1 quart (qt.)

» 64 fl. oz. = 8 c. = 4 pt. = 2 qt. = ½ gallon (gal.)

» 128 fl. oz. = 4 qt. =1 gal.

TIP

Have several liquid measuring cups of varying size. Getting a reading for ¼ cup in a 1-cup measuring cup is easier than in a 4-cup measuring cup.

Measuring solids

Following are some common measurements for dry ingredients:

» 3 teaspoons (tsp.) = 1 tablespoon (Tbsp.)

» 4 Tbsp. = ¼ cup (c.)

» 5⅓ Tbsp. = ⅓ c.

» 8 Tbsp. = ½ c.

» 12 Tbsp. = ¾ c.

» 16 Tbsp. = 1 c.

» 16 (dry) ounces (oz.) = 1 pound (lb.)

Measuring cups come in graduated sizes, usually starting at ¼ cup and going up to 1 cup. You can also find sets that give you a ⅔ cup and a ¾ cup measure. Having more than one set is a good idea. Stopping to wash and dry measuring cups can be a real hassle when you're cooking.

Following are some tips for measuring common foods:

>> If the recipe calls for a raw protein food to be cooked, the weight in the ingredient list refers to the weight before cooking; for instance, 8 ounces boneless, skinless chicken breast.

>> If the recipe calls for cooked meat, like in a salad, the weight given refers to after cooking; for example, 8 ounces cooked chicken breast.

>> Check the form of the food. The smaller the pieces, the more that fits into the cup. For example, ¼ cup of walnut halves is fewer nuts than ¼ cup chopped walnuts.

>> Recipes call for level measurements, so when you fill the cup with a fine ingredient (such as sugar or flour), take a table knife and run it across the top of the cup to make the food level with the top of the cup.

>> Flour gets packed down in the bag, so it needs to be stirred up in the bag or sifted before measuring. Measure flour by spooning it from the bag into the measuring cup.

>> Brown sugar is measured either unpacked or packed. *Unpacked* means you can just scoop it out with the spoon or cup and level if off. *Packed* means you need to put it into the cup or spoon and pushed down to pack it tightly.

>> Anything semi-liquid, like peanut butter, sour cream, or cottage cheese, is measured in measuring cups unless the recipe specifies weight.

Choosing and using a food scale

If you have a food scale stuck in the back of your cupboard, dig it out, blow off the dust, and put it to good use. You may think weighing out food is a hassle, but it's a skill worth developing. People are not born knowing what 3 ounces of chicken looks like, and the way to learn is by weighing chicken a bunch of times. The more you use the food scale, the better you become at eyeballing portions.

You have a wide choice of food scales available at department stores and home specialty or kitchen stores. Smaller scales can measure up to 16 ounces and are used mostly for determining portion sizes. Home kitchen scales can weigh foods up to 10 pounds or more and are great for cooking measurements. Make sure your scale has a function to set the scale to zero weight, or tare. Some scales give you a reading with a moving pointer and others have a digital screen. Digital scales weigh out in fractions and the display may be easier to read than scales with a pointer.

Some digital scales have food codes programmed in so you can get nutrition information as well as weight. You just enter the code and weigh out your food, and there you have it: calories, carbohydrates, fat, protein, and maybe some other nutrients depending on the specific programming. This feature is especially great for figuring out how many calories you're eating in foods that don't have nutrition labels, like fruit. How many grapes are in ½ cup depends on the size of the grapes. Is that a small, medium, or large apple? Most of us underestimate the sizes. The scale tells you how much you are eating and you don't have to guess at the size. Some also include a memory function so as you weigh your food throughout the day, it keeps a running total of your calories and grams of protein, carbs, and fat.

TIP

If you're trying to figure how many grams of protein you're eating in your fish, chicken, beef, or pork, weigh the food after cooking. Some of the water in these foods cooks out, so the cooked food weighs less than the raw food. The excess water weight can throw off your nutrition calculations.

Figuring out pasta measurements can be confusing. Say a recipe calls for 2 cups of cooked pasta and you don't want to make extra. How much dry pasta do you need to start with? Part of the answer depends on the shape of the pasta. The size and shape dictates how much will fit in a measuring cup so weight is always the best option for measuring pasta. Generally, 8 ounces of dry pasta equals 4 cups of cooked pasta. So in this case you weigh out 4 ounces on your food scale and cook it up. No leftovers! The exception to the rule is egg noodles. Eight ounces of egg noodles cook up to 2½ cups.

Using Alcohol in Cooking

The main reason alcoholic beverages are used in recipes is to add flavor. After all, the most premium of extracts with the most concentrated flavors are alcohol-based, particularly vanilla.

In many recipes the alcohol is an important component to achieve a desired chemical reaction in a dish. Alcohol causes many foods to release flavors that cannot be experienced without the interaction of alcohol. Beer contains yeast which leavens breads and batters. Alcoholic beverages also helps break down tough fibers in marinades. In addition, some dishes use alcoholic content to provide entertainment, such as flambé and flaming dishes. As for fondue, wine and kirsch are added because they lower the boiling point of the cheese, which helps prevent curdling.

Alcohol evaporates even without heat, and the majority burns off during the cooking process. How much remains in the dish depends on the cooking method and amount of cooking time. Those alcohol-soaked fruitcakes turn into solid bricks before the alcohol evaporates. A bottle of beer in a long-simmered stew doesn't leave a significantly measurable alcohol residue, but does add a rich, robust flavor. A quick flambé may not burn off all the alcohol, whereas a wine reduction sauce leaves little if any alcohol content. Heat and time are the keys. Obviously, uncooked foods with alcohol retain the most alcohol.

REMEMBER

In most cases you have to use your own judgment on substituting alcohol in recipes. Sweet recipes require different substitutions than savory. Amounts also make a difference. For example, you don't want to use a quarter cup of almond extract to replace the same amount of amaretto liqueur. And remember, even with reasonable replacements, the final product won't be what the original recipe intended.

Making Healthy Substitutions

When it comes to providing a healthier alternative for you or your family's meal plan, substituting ingredients is a great way to decrease calories while increasing flavor and nutrition. However, it's important to understand that not all substitutions are created equal, and while something may save you calories from fat, it may possibly increase calories in other areas such as from sugar.

REMEMBER

Product labels are designed to sell. So understanding how to read the back of the labels where the nutritional information is located helps to go beyond appealing descriptions and keep your pantry free of unhealthy substitutions. The front product label is usually colorful and highlights words such as *natural, 10% more, now with more fiber, made with less sugar,* and *fat free*. Although these claims are true, what they're not telling you is in most cases they have increased other areas of the formulation to bring back flavor that was lost during the making of the product. Generally sugar and/or sodium content is increased, especially in fat-free and lowfat products.

The healthy-substitution market is filled with new products on a monthly basis, and some are worth mentioning:

>> **Salad dressing:** Always use vinaigrette dressing instead of cream based. A great product is vinegar-based spray salad dressing. It adds a ton of flavor with the added benefit of no calories or fat.

>> **Butter:** "I Can't Believe It's Not Butter" spray is a good product that adds almost no calories or fat but covers your food and adds butter flavor.

» **Eggs:** Eggs are nutritious, but do contain saturated fat, so you can make them healthier by just using the egg whites or egg substitutes. Egg substitutes are made from real egg whites with the benefits of added vitamins and minerals. The yellow color comes from the added beta carotene.

» **Cheese:** We don't recommend fat-free cheese, because it lacks flavor and doesn't melt, but lowfat cheese is a good substitution idea. If a recipe calls for 1 cup of cheddar cheese, substitute with lowfat cheddar, or use just a half cup of a sharper cheese with stronger flavor.

» **Sour cream and cream cheese:** These foods are generally used as garnishes or in small amounts, so fat-free versions work fine.

TIP

If you're changing a recipe that has been a family favorite, change one ingredient at a time. Making too many changes at once could change the final product so much that it ends up inedible!

Saving calories and cutting the fat

One of the easiest ways to make your food healthier and reduce calories is by reducing or substituting high-fat ingredients. A little bit of fat carries a bunch of calories. Remember that:

» 1 gram protein = 4 calories

» 1 gram carbohydrate = 4 calories

» 1 gram fat = 9 calories

You can substitute many high-fat regular ingredients with lower-fat versions or similar products. Use the following list as your guide.

Sour cream substitutes:

» Plain nonfat Greek yogurt

» Fat-free sour cream

Cheese substitutes:

» Lowfat, skim-milk cheese

» Cheese with less than 5 grams of fat per ounce

Ricotta cheese substitutes:

>> Lowfat or nonfat cottage cheese

>> Part-skim or nonfat ricotta cheese

Milk/cream substitutes:

>> 1 percent or nonfat milk

>> Fat-free half-and-half

Ground beef substitutes:

>> Extra-lean ground beef

>> Lean ground turkey or chicken

Sausage substitutes:

>> Lean ground turkey sausage

>> 95 percent fat-free sausage

>> Soy-based sausage products

Mayonnaise and salad dressing substitutes:

>> Lowfat mayonnaise

>> Lowfat or fat-free dressings

Butter substitutes:

>> Lowfat margarine

>> Spray margarine

Checking out other ways to save calories

Another way to reduce your calorie intake is by using less of the ingredient. Many times a recipe calls for sautéing something in 2 tablespoons of oil. Usually you can cut this amount in half. Reducing the amount of cheese in a recipe is an easy change. You can also put in less pasta and/or rice so the dish is easier for you to tolerate as well as lower-calorie. Another easy place to cut back is in a recipe that includes nuts. Nuts are typically included just for flavor, not to dominate the food. Don't decrease the amount of vegetables, though!

You can leave many ingredients out entirely. Sometimes an ingredient is added for appearance sake or as a garnish. You don't have to top a taco with sour cream *and* guacamole. If the ingredient isn't critical to the recipe, just don't put it in.

You can change some ingredients. If a cooking recipe (not for a baked item) calls for sugar, you may consider a sugar substitute. In addition, herbs and spices can add a lot of flavor without calories. They're interchangeable and can be substituted to suit your tastes.

You can change the cooking method. We provide you plenty of excellent options at the beginning of this chapter to help you pick the right cooking method for your food, so find a healthier selection for the dish you want to make.

Relying on Convenience Foods

We're all looking for timesavers. You get home at dinnertime and the last thing you want to do is spend an hour standing in the kitchen and fixing dinner. Using convenience foods can really save you time and money. Money? Yup, your time is worth money, and convenience foods can result in less food waste.

Note that we're talking convenience foods here, not highly processed food. If you have a recipe that calls for shredded carrots and you buy preshredded carrots from the produce department, that's a convenience food, not a highly processed food. We mean convenience foods that are pretty much in their natural state, no additives, no long list of ingredients, just the food itself put into a different form to save you time.

The produce department is a great place to save time. You can buy all kinds of vegetables already cleaned, cut, and ready to go. Some of these come in plastic steamer bags. No more excuses that you don't know how or don't have the time to prepare fresh veggies. You can buy fresh fruit already cleaned and cut. Probably the biggest sellers are the prepackaged lettuce varieties and salads. If you buy a packaged salad mix with all the toppings, pick one that that has a light dressing.

Frozen vegetables are also a quick-dinner solution, but watch out for packages that come with unhealthy sauce included. Try cooking plain frozen vegetables and then adding a little spray butter and a sprinkle of your favorite herbs.

If a recipe calls for cooked chicken, a rotisserie chicken from the deli is a great timesaver. You could also use a rotisserie turkey breast and then you have only white meat. It's cooked and ready to go; you just need to remove the skin from the meat and the meat from the bones.

2

Now You're Cooking! Healthy and Delicious Dishes

IN THIS PART . . .

Rise and shine for a good, balanced breakfast.

Prepare food fast (that isn't fast food) for lunches that aren't to be taken lightly and healthy dinners you'll love.

Get fabulous recipes for main dish entrées featuring poultry, beef, pork, lamb, fish, seafood, and vegetarian options.

Get plenty of variety with recipes that are weight-loss-surgery friendly.

IN THIS CHAPTER

» **Starting the day on track**

» **Waking up with easy fruit and yogurt dishes**

» **Scrambling more than an egg**

» **Loving whole grains in the morning**

» **Taking more time for leisurely weekend breakfasts**

Chapter **7**

Balanced Breakfasts

In the old days, before surgery, you may have been a breakfast skipper. Now that you have your pouch and follow the rule of eating three regular meals a day (right?), you're a breakfast eater. You may not feel hungry when you get up, but your pouch needs to be fed. Eating breakfast jump starts your metabolism. Hello to another day of losing weight! You also need to keep your body's blood-sugar level stable to feel your best. Skipping breakfast, or any meal, is likely to make you feel lightheaded and unfocused and may give you a headache.

You should eat breakfast within 90 minutes of getting up, so this may take some planning on your part. If you're always in a rush, turn to one of the on-the-go meals included in this chapter. We also tell you which recipes can be made the night before for a quick start to your day.

Starting Your Day the Pouch-Friendly Way

Starting the day with a pouch-friendly meal can help set you up for on-track eating the rest of the day. Making healthy food choices gives you a positive attitude toward eating to carry you right through dinner. It may be harder for you to get some foods down in the morning, so choose breakfast foods that won't get stuck. Getting food stuck your first meal of the day can make for an unpleasant start and limit your food choices for the rest of the day.

TIP

Sometimes after surgery, when you wake up in the morning your stomach pouch may feel unsettled, or if you had AGB, your band may feel "tight." This is due to bodily fluids that collect in your pouch overnight. Sipping a warm beverage, such as decaffeinated tea or warm water, can help calm your pouch and make it easier for you to eat breakfast.

WARNING

Coffee, both regular and decaffeinated, may not be tolerated in the early months after surgery because coffee beans themselves can be irritants. Caffeine is also a diuretic, so decaffeinated tea may be your best choice after surgery.

Take 20 to 30 minutes to eat your breakfast, and if you're in a big hurry to get out the door in the morning, make a breakfast that you can take with you. Pick a recipe that you can make in five minutes or less. Or if you want to have a more leisurely family breakfast on the weekend, choose a recipe that takes longer. We include recipes that taste yummy, so your entire family can enjoy.

REMEMBER

Note that the portion sizes in these recipes are intended for people who are at least a few months out from surgery. If you're still eating smaller meals, split the recipe into more portions and eat only the amount you need.

Waking Up Your Pouch Gently with Yogurt and Fruit Recipes

Getting your pouch ready to take on the day is not easy for some. So begin with a few sips of warm liquid such as decaf coffee, herbal tea, or warm water to allow the pouch to relax and get ready to start taking in breakfast. Fruit is about 80 percent water, so it's easy to eat. In addition, it's loaded with vitamins and minerals. Fruit doesn't provide protein, though, which is where yogurt comes in.

TIP

Yogurt is a good choice for breakfast because it's fast and easy to punch up with added flavors. Even most people with lactose intolerance can eat yogurt without discomfort. Be sure to look at the labels and buy nonfat yogurt or light yogurt. Light yogurt is usually fat free and has less sugar because artificial sweetener is added. Of course, nonfat yogurt is also fat free, but it has added sugar. The nutrition facts tell you how many grams of sugar are in a serving. Lactose, or milk sugar, is naturally occurring and doesn't cause problems with dumping syndrome; the added sugars are the ones that create problems. To see if the yogurt has added sugar, check if sugar or fructose appears in the list of ingredients.

Spicy Pumpkin Yogurt

STAGE: SMOOTH FOODS	PREP TIME: 5 MIN	YIELD: 2 SERVINGS

INGREDIENTS

1 cup light vanilla yogurt

½ cup canned pumpkin

¼ teaspoon cinnamon

⅛ teaspoon allspice

⅛ teaspoon ground ginger

⅛ teaspoon nutmeg

Sugar substitute to taste

1 teaspoon vanilla extract

½ teaspoon liquid butter extract

DIRECTIONS

Combine all ingredients. Chill until ready to serve.

PER SERVING: *Calories 90 (From Fat 0); Fat 0g (Saturated 0g); Cholesterol 0mg; Sodium 70mg; Carbohydrate 16g (Dietary Fiber 3g); Protein 5g; Sugar 10g.*

VARY IT! You can substitute the light yogurt with plain nonfat yogurt or nonfat Greek yogurt.

TIP: You can mix this up the night before and stick it in the refrigerator for a grab-and-go breakfast.

Triple Berry Yogurt Parfait

STAGE: SOFT FOODS	PREP TIME: 5 MIN	YIELD: 1 SERVING

INGREDIENTS

4 medium strawberries, tops removed, chopped

2 tablespoons blueberries

2 tablespoons raspberries

1 or 2 packets sugar substitute, or to taste

¼ teaspoon vanilla extract

½ cup light vanilla yogurt

DIRECTIONS

1 In a small bowl mix the berries, sugar substitute, and vanilla.

2 Place half the yogurt in the bottom of an 8-ounce glass. Add half the berry mixture over the yogurt. Layer the remaining yogurt and berries.

PER SERVING: *Calories 110 (From Fat 0); Fat 0g (Saturated 0g); Cholesterol 0mg; Sodium 65mg; Carbohydrate 22g (Dietary Fiber 3g); Protein 4g; Sugar 14g.*

VARY IT! Substitute the light yogurt with plain nonfat yogurt or nonfat Greek yogurt.

NOTE: Although this recipe may seem high in sugar, the sugar naturally occurs from the fruit and yogurt, not from added sugars. Berries and natural sugars are usually well tolerated after surgery, so you can enjoy this appealing recipe with strawberries, blueberries, and raspberries layered with creamy yogurt.

TIP: If you make the berry mixture a day in advance, it becomes more syrupy.

Exploring Easy Egg Dishes

Did you know that an egg is one of nature's most nutritious foods? Eggs are a high-quality protein food, are low in sodium, and contain vitamins and minerals. They're also inexpensive and easy to prepare.

REMEMBER

Cook eggs with medium to low temperature and careful timing. When eggs are cooked at too high a temperature or for too long at a low temperature, the whites shrink and become tough and rubbery and the yolks become tough and may turn gray-green.

TIP

After surgery some people have difficulty tolerating eggs. This has a lot to do with the texture: If a cooked egg is too rubbery, like a hardboiled egg, you may have trouble getting it down and keeping it down. Try a fluffy scrambled egg instead.

Havarti Scramble with Salmon

STAGE: SOFT FOODS | PREP TIME: 5 MIN | COOK TIME: 5 MIN | YIELD: 4 SERVINGS

INGREDIENTS

6 large eggs

¼ cup nonfat milk

2 ounces havarti cheese

Salt and pepper to taste

1 teaspoon minced chives

1 teaspoon butter

½ cup canned salmon, no skin or bones

DIRECTIONS

1 Crack eggs into a small mixing bowl, add milk, and whisk together for 1 minute.

2 Cut havarti into small pieces and add to the egg mixture along with salt, pepper, and chives.

3 Melt butter in a 10-inch sauté pan over medium heat. Place egg mixture in pan and cook for 2 minutes, stirring often, scraping up the egg from the bottom and gently folding over. Add the salmon and cook for an additional 2 minutes or until well cooked and fluffy.

PER SERVING: *Calories 220 (From Fat 120); Fat 13g (Saturated 6g); Cholesterol 305mg; Sodium 310mg; Carbohydrate 3g (Dietary Fiber 0g); Protein 20g; Sugar 3g.*

TIP: To reduce cholesterol and fat, use ¼ cup fresh or frozen egg substitute to replace each whole egg.

VARY IT! You can substitute salmon with bay shrimp. Keep the cooking time the same.

THE MANY USES OF EGGS

Eggs are known as breakfast entrées, but they're also used in a variety of ways. Some ways you may have used eggs and didn't even know it are as follows:

- **Binding** ingredients, in meatloaf or croquettes
- **Leavening** ingredients, rising baked foods like soufflés and sponge cakes
- **Thickening** ingredients, in custards and sauces
- **Emulsifying,** or blending, ingredients, in mayonnaise, salad dressings, and hollandaise sauce

Canadian Bacon and Spinach Frittata

STAGE: REGULAR FOODS	PREP TIME: 6 MIN	COOK TIME: 25 MIN	YIELD: 8 SERVINGS

INGREDIENTS

12 large eggs

8 ounces Canadian bacon, cut into ¼-inch cubes and cooked

½ cup chopped green onions

½ teaspoon paprika

¼ teaspoon garlic powder

¼ teaspoon dried mustard

¼ teaspoon salt

¼ teaspoon black pepper

2 cups fresh baby spinach

1 cup shredded lowfat sharp cheddar cheese

DIRECTIONS

1 Preheat the oven to 350 degrees. Spray a 9-x-9-inch baking dish with nonstick spray.

2 In a large mixing bowl whisk eggs for 2 minutes. Add the Canadian bacon, green onions, and spices and mix well. Pour the mixture into the baking dish and top with baby spinach and cheddar cheese.

3 Bake for 25 minutes, or until the center of frittata is firm. Let cool for 5 minutes before cutting.

PER SERVING: *Calories 175 (From Fat 91); Fat 10g (Saturated 4g); Cholesterol 332mg; Sodium 541mg; Carbohydrate 3g (Dietary Fiber 1g); Protein 18g; Sugar 1g.*

Having Healthy Whole-Grain Mornings

A wide variety of whole grains provide valuable vitamins and minerals. Whole grains are high in fiber and help you feel full longer. Some whole grains, like oatmeal, are good sources of soluble fiber, which helps lower bad cholesterol. Many whole grains are convenient, quick to make, and taste good, making them perfect foods for busy mornings.

Choose products that list whole-grain foods as the first ingredient in the ingredient list. Look for the key words *whole* or *whole grain* before the grain ingredient's name.

REMEMBER

Labels and packaging are designed to get you to purchase their product. Beware of foods labeled with the words *multigrain, stone-ground, 100% wheat, cracked wheat, seven-grain,* or *bran* because they are usually *not* 100 percent whole-grain products. In addition, brown color is not an indication of a whole grain; it can come from molasses or other added ingredients. Read the ingredient list to see if something is truly a whole grain.

WARNING

Whole grains use warm, moist environments to expand, and your pouch is the perfect place. After whole grains are eaten, they expand in your pouch and may cause you discomfort and/or vomiting. To help prevent too much expansion, add more liquid while the whole grain is cooking. This requires a longer cook time, but better it absorbs liquid in the pot than in your pouch. As a general rule of thumb, increase the liquid by one fourth. For example, rice is usually cooked at a ratio of 1 cup rice to 2 cups liquid, but instead use 2½ cups liquid to 1 cup rice. *Note:* We have already adjusted the liquid for the recipes in this book.

Quinoa Pilaf with Dried Cherries and Pecans

STAGE: REGULAR FOODS	PREP TIME: 5 MIN	COOK TIME: 30 MIN	YIELD: 8 SERVINGS

INGREDIENTS

1½ cups quinoa

2 teaspoons butter

3¼ cups nonfat milk

⅓ cup dried cherries

½ teaspoon vanilla extract

¼ cup chopped pecans

¼ cup sugar substitute

DIRECTIONS

1 Place quinoa in a colander and rinse under warm running water for 3 minutes to rinse off its natural bitter coating. Drain well.

2 In a large skillet, heat butter over medium heat. Stir in quinoa and cook 2 to 3 minutes or until lightly toasted. Add milk, cherries, vanilla, and pecans.

3 Bring to a simmer, cover, and cook 20 to 25 minutes, or until quinoa is tender. Stir in sugar substitute.

PER SERVING: Calories 200 (From Fat 50); Fat 5g (Saturated 1g); Cholesterol 5mg; Sodium 50mg; Carbohydrate 30g (Dietary Fiber 4g); Protein 8g; Sugar 7g.

NOTE: Quinoa (pronounced *keen*-wah) is a gluten-free nutty whole grain that when cooked has an amazing flavor and texture. This may be a new grain to you, but after you make this dish you'll want to include it as a regular part of your diet. Quinoa has more protein than other grains and is a great source of fiber. It's an excellent choice for vegetarians because it contains all the essential amino acids, making it a complete protein.

Banana Bran Muffins

STAGE: REGULAR FOODS	PREP TIME: 10 MIN	COOK TIME: 20 MIN	YIELD: 24 SERVINGS

INGREDIENTS

6 cups Grape-Nuts Flakes

5 cups whole-wheat flour

5 teaspoons baking soda

3 cups Splenda

4 large eggs

1 quart lowfat buttermilk

1 teaspoon vanilla extract

1 cup unsweetened applesauce

6 large bananas, mashed

DIRECTIONS

1 Preheat the oven to 400 degrees. Add all ingredients to a large bowl and mix well.

2 Fill muffin cups ⅔ full and bake for 20 minutes.

PER SERVING: *Calories 266 (From Fat 21); Fat 2g (Saturated 1g); Cholesterol 37mg; Sodium 494mg; Carbohydrate 56g (Dietary Fiber 7g); Protein 9g; Sugar 13g.*

TIP: To bake two muffins at a time, fill two center muffin cups with batter and the empty cups with water and bake for about 15 minutes.

NOTE: Commercially prepared muffins are high in fat and sugar, both of which can cause problems after GBP surgery, but these healthy banana muffins use unsweetened applesauce to replace the oil, and bananas and Splenda add sweetness.

TIP: The batter keeps in the refrigerator for up to a week, so you can mix it up and then take out just enough to bake a few muffins each time you want some.

Honey, Almonds, and Oats Breakfast Bar

STAGE: REGULAR FOODS	PREP TIME: 5 MIN	COOK TIME: 3 MIN	YIELD: 8 SERVINGS

INGREDIENTS

1⅓ cups Wheat Chex or Shreddies cereal, broken into smaller pieces

⅔ cup crispy brown rice cereal

⅔ cup sliced almonds

⅓ cup instant whole oats

⅓ cup honey

½ cup all-natural creamy peanut butter

¼ teaspoon liquid butter extract

DIRECTIONS

1 In a large bowl, toss together the cereals, almonds, and oats. Grease an 8-x-8-inch dish with nonstick cooking spray. Set both aside.

2 In a medium saucepan over medium heat, stir together the honey and peanut butter. Cook mixture until it's heated through but not simmering, about 1½ minutes, stirring constantly to keep it from burning to the bottom of the pan.

3 Remove from heat and quickly stir in butter extract. Pour the mixture into the bowl with the cereals and mix well.

4 Press into the prepared pan. Let cool until set. Cut into bars and serve.

PER SERVING: *Calories 241 (From Fat 112); Fat 13g (Saturated 1g); Cholesterol 0mg; Sodium 131mg; Carbohydrate 25g (Dietary Fiber 3g); Protein 6g; Sugar 13g.*

TIP: The bars can be prepared ahead of time and stored in an airtight container for a week. If you're out running errands or traveling, they're a good food to wrap up and take with you because they don't need refrigeration.

Swiss Oatmeal

STAGE: REGULAR FOODS	PREP TIME: 10 MIN	CHILL TIME: 8 HR OR OVERNIGHT	YIELD: 3 SERVINGS

INGREDIENTS

½ cup old-fashioned rolled oats or thick-cut rolled oats

½ cup nonfat milk, 1% milk, or plain soy milk

½ teaspoon cinnamon

1 cup blueberries

1 medium banana, sliced

¾ cup plain nonfat Greek yogurt

1 teaspoon vanilla extract

1 tablespoon chopped pecans, walnuts, or almonds

1 tablespoon ground flax meal

Sugar substitute to taste

DIRECTIONS

1 Mix oatmeal, milk, and cinnamon in a tightly covered container. Store in the refrigerator overnight or for at least 8 hours.

2 Before eating, stir in the remaining ingredients.

PER SERVING: *Calories 187 (From Fat 30); Fat 3g (Saturated 0g); Cholesterol 0mg; Sodium 40mg; Carbohydrate 31g (Dietary Fiber 5g); Protein 11g; Sugar 5g.*

VARY IT! Substitute your favorite berries, apples, or peaches for the blueberries and banana.

TIP: The oatmeal keeps in the refrigerator for a couple of days, but don't add the other ingredients until you're ready to eat.

GOOD OLD OATS

One of the most popular whole grains is oats, which are used in a wide variety of foods from breakfast cereals to meatloaf to desserts. Different kinds of oatmeal have different cooking times and uses.

- **Steel-cut oats** are hulled and cracked oats that are chopped into little pieces. They require a longer cooking time and are chewier than other types. You can usually find them at your natural food store or in the health food section of your grocery store.

- **Old-fashioned oats** are also from hulled and cracked oats, but they're steamed and rolled to flatten them. This is usually the least expensive type of oats.

- **Quick oats** are old-fashioned oats that have been rolled thinner to make them cook up faster. They're softer than the thicker oats.

- **Instant oatmeal** comes is packets and usually has flavoring and sugar added. Buy the unflavored ones and add your own sweeteners and flavors to make it the way you like it and cut down on the added sugars.

Steel-Cut Oats with Almonds and Cherries

STAGE: SOFT FOODS	PREP TIME: 5 MIN	COOK TIME: UP TO 30 MIN	YIELD: 2 SERVINGS

INGREDIENTS

½ cup steel-cut oats

½ cup water or cold chai-spiced tea

1 cup nonfat milk

2 tablespoons almond butter

Vanilla, to taste

Pinch of salt

1 cup halved fresh cherries

DIRECTIONS

1 In a medium saucepan, combine oats, water or tea, and milk and bring to a boil over medium heat.

2 Reduce the heat to low heat and stir every few minutes until the oats are thickened, about 20 to 25 minutes.

3 Remove from the heat and stir in the almond butter, the salt, and the vanilla.

4 Add the fruit and serve.

PER SERVING: *Calories 270 (From Fat 100); Fat 11g (Saturated 1g); Cholesterol 2mg; Sodium 719mg; Carbohydrate 35g (Dietary Fiber 4g); Protein 10g; Sugar 17g.*

VARY IT! You can substitute blueberries for cherries if you prefer.

Steel-Cut Oats with Egg and Spinach

STAGE: SOFT FOODS	PREP TIME: 5 MIN	COOK TIME: UP TO 30 MIN	YIELD: 1 SERVING

INGREDIENTS

¼ cup steel-cut oats

1¼ cup water

½ cup liquid egg white

1 teaspoon butter

1 egg

1 cup raw spinach

Salt and pepper, to taste

Smoked paprika, to taste

Italian seasoning, to taste

DIRECTIONS

1 In a small saucepan, combine the oats with the water and bring to a boil.

2 Reduce the heat and simmer until thickened, about 20 minutes.

3 Whisk in the liquid egg white and stir for 1 minute.

4 While the oats are cooking, warm the butter in a small skillet until melted.

5 Add the whole egg to the butter and lower the heat to medium low; cook until the yolk is set. Remove the egg from the pan and set aside.

6 Add the spinach and stir until wilted.

7 Add the egg and spinach to the oatmeal in a bowl. Top with salt and pepper, smoked paprika, and Italian seasoning to taste.

PER SERVING: *Calories 191 (From Fat 50); Fat 6g (Saturated 3g); Cholesterol 10mg; Sodium 463mg; Carbohydrate 16g (Dietary Fiber 3g); Protein 20g; Sugar 1g.*

Berrycotta Pancakes

STAGE: SOFT FOODS | PREP TIME: 10 MIN | COOK TIME: 10 MIN | YIELD: 6 SERVINGS

INGREDIENTS

¾ cup whole-wheat flour

¾ cups all-purpose flour

1 teaspoon baking powder

¼ teaspoon baking soda

¼ teaspoon salt

1 ½ teaspoons sugar

2 tablespoons melted butter

¾ cup part-skim ricotta cheese

1 large egg

½ cup orange juice

⅓ cup nonfat milk

½ teaspoon vanilla extract

1 cup blueberries, fresh or frozen

DIRECTIONS

1 In a bowl, combine both flours with baking powder, baking soda, salt, and sugar. In another bowl, whisk together the butter, ricotta cheese, egg, orange juice, milk, and vanilla.

2 Combine and stir the wet and dry ingredients until just blended. Gently stir in the blueberries.

3 Spray a skillet or griddle with nonstick cooking spray and heat over medium heat. Spoon a small amount of batter onto the hot skillet and cook for about 2 minutes or until browned on the underside, then flip the pancake. Cook until golden brown.

PER SERVING: Calories 229 (From Fat 69); Fat 8g (Saturated 4g); Cholesterol 56mg; Sodium 272mg; Carbohydrate 32g (Dietary Fiber 3g); Protein 9g; Sugar 8g.

VARY IT! Substitute the blueberries with diced apples or peaches.

TIP: If you have any extra, these pancakes freeze well and can be reheated in the microwave for a quick breakfast on another day.

NOTE: Regular syrup has loads of sugar, so serve these pancakes with sugar-free syrup or a dollop of 100 percent fruit preserves.

IN THIS CHAPTER

» Preparing an altogether meal:
   One-dish wonders

» Exploring the possibilities of eggs

» Enjoying a sandwich or a wrap

» Making salads work for you

Chapter **8**

Bunches of Lunches and Brunches

The word lunch may bring thoughts of "What do I eat? What can I pack?" while brunch brings thoughts of relaxation and social time. But whether you're hurried or leisurely and whether it's lunch or brunch, you can make a meal that fits your time schedule and your health needs. By planning ahead, you can make some of your lunch or brunch the night before so you aren't rushing around in the morning to get your food together.

Lunches and brunches are easy when you always have staples on hand. Keep your pantry stocked with canned low-sodium beans, prepacked fish, whole-grain pasta, and plenty of spices. In your refrigerator, make sure you have eggs, several types of shredded cheeses, fat-free sour cream, hot sauce, lowfat salad dressings, lowfat mayo, and reduced-sodium deli meats. Also, don't forget nature's easy foods: fruits and veggies. With these few items you have plenty of options to makes quick, painless, and nutritious meals.

REMEMBER Eat three meals a day. If you're planning to have brunch hours after you wake up, you still need to eat a small breakfast like a protein shake or smoothie to get started. If you wait too long to eat, you may not feel well by the time brunch rolls around.

When you can't have a meal at home, packing your lunch can make your eating easier and save you money. And besides, getting in your car, waiting in drive-through, and driving back to work is not fast food. Following are some tips for improving your homemade to-go lunch:

>> Pack condiments or vegetables separately so they don't make your sandwich soggy.

>> Try new flavors of condiments, such as the many flavors of mustards, or add some herbs to your light mayo.

>> Use a thermos for hot or cold food.

>> Find a lunch buddy or buddies at work. You can take turns bringing in lunch so you get a day off.

>> Don't forget your lunch! When you pack your lunch bag, drop your keys in it so you can't leave home without it.

>> Wash out your lunch box regularly. Bacteria can grow anywhere.

Note that the portion sizes in the following recipes are intended for people who are months out from their weight loss surgery. If you are still eating very small meals, adjust the portion sizes as necessary to meet your needs.

Putting Together One-Dish Meals

Three cheers for one-dish meals! Cleanup is easy and the food combinations are endless. And we're not just talking your traditional casseroles mixed with canned soup. You can make your altogether meal hot or cold, fresh on the spot or made ahead.

TIP One-pot meals often feature pasta or rice, and by following a couple of tips you can lower the risk of problems that those foods often cause for weight loss surgery patients. Mixing flour and water leads to paste that can lump up like dough and won't set well in your pouch. Use whole-wheat pasta instead of regular, because it doesn't get as gummy. Cook rice with more liquid so that it swells up more before you eat it, not when it's in your pouch. And be sure to eat very small portions of rice and pasta.

KEEPING COOL

If you're making your lunch or brunch ahead of time, make sure to get it into the fridge and keep it cold until it's time to cook it or pack it. Nobody wants to get sick from improperly handled food. To keep bacteria from multiplying, refrigerated food must be kept below 40 degrees.

When you leave the house, insulated, soft-sided lunch bags or boxers are best for keeping foods cold. Remember to put in a frozen gel pack to keep food cold until you're ready to eat. You can also freeze an uncarbonated beverage in a plastic bottle (just don't fill it all the way to the top) and use that in your lunch bag to keep your food cold.

Cheesy Chicken Enchiladas

STAGE: REGULAR FOODS	PREP TIME: 10 MIN	COOK TIME: 12 MIN	YIELD: 6 SERVINGS

INGREDIENTS

8 ounces cooked and shredded boneless, skinless chicken breast

½ cup shredded lowfat cheddar cheese

1 ½ cups shredded pepper jack cheese, divided

Six 6-inch whole-wheat flour tortillas

1 ½ cups Enchilada Sauce (see the following recipe)

DIRECTIONS

1 Preheat the oven to 350 degrees. Using nonstick cooking spray, grease a 9-x-13 baking dish.

2 In a small bowl, combine chicken, lowfat cheddar cheese, and ½ cup pepper jack cheese; toss until mixed well.

3 Place ⅓ cup of cheese and chicken mixture into the center of one whole-wheat tortilla, tightly roll, and place seam down into the baking dish. Repeat with the remaining five tortillas.

4 Place ¼ cup of enchilada sauce over each stuffed enchilada and top with the remaining pepper jack cheese. Bake for 12 minutes, or until cheese is melted and bubbly.

Enchilada Sauce

¼ cup vegetable oil

2 tablespoons all-purpose flour

¼ cup chili powder

One 8-ounce can low-sodium tomato sauce

1 ½ cups water

¼ teaspoon ground cumin

¼ teaspoon garlic powder

¼ teaspoon onion powder

1 In a small pot, heat oil over medium-high heat.

2 When the oil is hot, add the flour and chili powder.

3 Reduce heat to medium and cook until light brown, stirring constantly to prevent the flour from burning.

4 Add the tomato sauce, water, cumin, garlic powder, and onion powder to the pot and stir until smooth. Continue cooking for 10 minutes, or until thickened slightly.

PER SERVING: *Calories 370 (From Fat 135); Fat 15g (Saturated 7g); Cholesterol 60mg; Sodium 540mg; Carbohydrate 31g (Dietary Fiber 4g); Protein 25g; Sugar 4g.*

Vegetable Lasagna

STAGE: SOFT FOODS | PREP TIME: 15 MIN | COOK TIME: 45 MIN | YIELD: 8 SERVINGS

INGREDIENTS

2 cups part-skim ricotta cheese

1 large egg

1 teaspoon dried Italian seasoning

2 large, fresh yellow summer squash, sliced into ¼-inch rounds

2 large, fresh zucchini, sliced into ½-inch rounds

4 cups fresh baby spinach, stems removed

3 cups Cheese Sauce (see the following recipe)

DIRECTIONS

1 Preheat the oven to 350 degrees. Using nonstick cooking spray, grease a 9-x-13 baking dish.

2 In a small mixing bowl, combine ricotta cheese, egg, and Italian seasoning and mix well.

3 Place half of the summer squash on the bottom of the pan to form a single even layer. Spread half the ricotta cheese mixture over the summer squash. Top the cheese with an even layer of half the spinach. Layer half the zucchini on top of the spinach. Repeat the layers of yellow squash, cheese, spinach, and zucchini with the remaining quantities of each. Pour cheese sauce over the top of the lasagna.

4 Place in the preheated oven and bake uncovered for 45 minutes.

Cheese Sauce

¼ cup butter

2 cloves garlic, minced

½ cup all-purpose flour

1 teaspoon salt

½ teaspoon black pepper

3 cups nonfat milk

1 cup shredded lowfat sharp cheddar cheese

1 Melt butter in a medium pot over medium-high heat. When it's fully melted, add the garlic and sauté for 30 seconds. Add the flour to the pot and whisk until it forms a paste. Add salt and pepper; stir for 1 minute.

2 Very slowly add about 1 cup of the milk, whisking constantly. When the flour mixture is smooth, add the remaining 2 cups of milk and bring to a simmer. This may take up to 5 minutes, but continue stirring constantly to keep the milk from burning to the bottom of the pan.

3 When the mixture comes to a simmer, turn the heat down to medium low and stir in the cheddar cheese. When the cheese melts, remove the pot from heat.

PER SERVING: *Calories 260 (From Fat 110); Fat 12g (Saturated 7g); Cholesterol 60mg; Sodium 570mg; Carbohydrate 21g (Dietary Fiber 3g); Protein 17g; Sugar 9g.*

Stuffed Avocados with Chicken-Corn Salsa

STAGE: REGULAR FOODS	PREP TIME: 10 MIN	CHILL TIME: 2 HR	YIELD: 4 SERVINGS

INGREDIENTS

1 cup ½-inch pieces of cooked chicken

½ cup frozen corn, defrosted under cold water

½ cup low-sodium canned black beans

¼ cup chopped fresh cilantro

1 clove garlic, minced

½ teaspoon chili powder

½ teaspoon cumin

¼ cup fresh lemon juice

¼ cup diced red onion

1 tablespoon olive oil

2 avocados

DIRECTIONS

1 In a large mixing bowl, combine chicken, corn, black beans, cilantro, garlic, chili powder, cumin, lemon juice, onion, and olive oil and mix well.

2 Refrigerate mixture for 2 hours.

3 Peel the avocados, then cut in half and seed. Place avocado halves flat side up and fill each with ½ cup of the chicken-corn salsa.

PER SERVING: *Calories 290 (From Fat 180); Fat 20g (Saturated 3g); Cholesterol 30mg; Sodium 100mg; Carbohydrate 19g (Dietary Fiber 9g); Protein 15g; Sugar 2g.*

TIP: When choosing avocados, they should be firm to the touch yet soft when you apply pressure. Hass avocados are the most common, and they should be dark in appearance. If they're green, they're not ripe yet.

TIP: If you don't have time to cook your own chicken, you can pick up a rotisserie chicken from the deli and cut the meat into ½-inch pieces.

Piña Colada Fruit 'n Cheese

STAGE: SOFT FOODS	PREP TIME: 5 MIN	YIELD: 1 SERVING

INGREDIENTS

¼ cup thawed and chopped frozen strawberries

½ medium banana, sliced

½ teaspoon sugar substitute

½ teaspoon vanilla extract

⅛ teaspoon coconut extract

⅛ teaspoon rum extract

½ cup lowfat cottage cheese

DIRECTIONS

Combine strawberries, banana, sugar substitute, vanilla, coconut extract, and rum extract in a medium bowl and mix well. Pour fruit mixture over cottage cheese.

PER SERVING: *Calories 170 (From Fat 30); Fat 3g (Saturated 1g); Cholesterol 10mg; Sodium 370mg; Carbohydrate 21g (Dietary Fiber 2g); Protein 14g; Sugar 13g.*

VARY IT! Fresh strawberries can be used instead of frozen ones.

Preparing Egg Dishes with Style

Because eggs are high in protein and can be kept soft, they are an ideal food for someone who's undergone weight loss surgery. Eggs have many different applications, from scrambled eggs to light and airy soufflés. No other food is as versatile or can be so diverse in so many recipes.

Egg substitutes are often used to help lower the fat and cholesterol contents of a dish. These products are made mostly of egg whites, which contain a good amount of protein. They're excellent to use in dishes that contain high-fat ingredients, like cheese, to help keep the calories and fat content lower.

TIP

If you're making scrambled eggs, you can substitute the whites of two eggs for each whole egg. So if you're scrambling four eggs for breakfast, make it healthier by using two whole eggs and four more egg whites. If you want to reduce the cholesterol even more, use one whole egg and six egg whites.

Crustless Seafood Quiche

STAGE: REGULAR FOODS	PREP TIME: 15 MIN	COOK TIME: 30 MIN	YIELD: 6 SERVINGS

INGREDIENTS

4 large eggs, whisked

1 cup fat-free sour cream

1 cup part-skim ricotta cheese

¼ cup grated Parmesan cheese

1 teaspoon onion powder

1 teaspoon nutmeg

1 cup shredded pepper jack cheese

4 ounces crabmeat, canned or fresh

4 ounces cooked bay shrimp

6 large mushrooms, thinly sliced

1 tablespoon chopped green onion

1 teaspoon lemon juice

DIRECTIONS

1 Preheat the oven to 350 degrees. Spray an 8-x-8 baking dish with nonstick cooking spray.

2 In a medium mixing bowl, combine eggs, sour cream, ricotta, Parmesan, onion powder, and nutmeg and whisk for 2 minutes or until smooth.

3 In a small mixing bowl, combine jack cheese, crab, shrimp, mushrooms, green onions, and lemon juice and mix well.

4 Spread seafood mixture evenly into the baking dish. Pour the egg mixture over the seafood mixture.

5 Place the dish in the oven and bake for 30 minutes, or until a knife inserted in center comes out clean. Let stand 5 minutes before serving.

PER SERVING: *Calories 273 (From Fat 128); Fat 14g (Saturated 8g); Cholesterol 234mg; Sodium 418mg; Carbohydrate 9g (Dietary Fiber 0g); Protein 25g; Sugar 4g.*

VARY IT! Shredded cooked chicken can be substituted for seafood.

NOTE: Though egg substitute can be used in many recipes, it's not a good option here because egg yolks are needed to bind the quiche.

WHITE EGGS OR BROWN? IT DOESN'T MATTER!

Eggshell color has nothing to do with the nutritional value, flavor, or cooking of the egg. The color of the shell comes from the breed of chicken laying the egg. White-feathered chickens with white ear lobes lay white-shelled eggs, and hens with red feathers and red ear lobes lay brown eggs.

Berry Delicious Egg Custard

STAGE: SOFT FOODS | **PREP TIME: 5 MIN** | **COOK TIME: 35 MIN** | **YIELD: 4 SERVINGS**

INGREDIENTS

1 cup water

2 large eggs

4 teaspoons sugar substitute

1 teaspoon vanilla extract

¼ teaspoon salt

2 cups nonfat evaporated milk

1 cup raspberries

1 cup blueberries

¼ teaspoon nutmeg

DIRECTIONS

1 Preheat the oven to 350 degrees. Pour 1 cup of water into a 9-x-13-inch baking pan and place it to the side. Using non-stick cooking spray, grease an 8-x-8 baking dish.

2 In a small bowl, beat together the eggs, sugar substitute, vanilla, and salt until well blended. Then pour the nonfat evaporated milk into the egg mixture and stir until blended.

3 Mix together the raspberries and blueberries and spread on the bottom of the 8-x-8 pan. Pour the egg custard mixture over the top.

4 Place the 8-x-8 dish into the 9-x-13 pan that's filled with water. (This creates a double boiler and prevents the custard from curdling.)

5 Bake for 35 minutes, or until a knife inserted in the center of the custard comes out clean. After removing the finished custard from the oven, sprinkle the nutmeg on top.

PER SERVING: *Calories 178 (From Fat 28); Fat 3g (Saturated 1g); Cholesterol 111mg; Sodium 326mg; Carbohydrate 24g (Dietary Fiber 3g); Protein 13g; Sugar 21g.*

WARNING: Be sure not to use sweetened condensed milk, made by adding a whole bunch of sugar to whole milk and then removing 50 percent of the water. The high added-sugar content can cause dumping syndrome if you have had GBP.

Satisfying Hunger with a Sandwich or Wrap

Sandwiches are classic lunchtime food, whether warm or cold. A hot toasted sandwich is always a satisfying treat on a leisurely weekend day. Wraps, which are often like sandwiches but with a tortilla instead of bread, are perfect for toting with you for workday lunches. In this section we give you both kinds of recipes to help get you through the day.

Pimento Cheese and Tomato Wrap

STAGE: REGULAR FOODS	PREP TIME: 5 MIN	YIELD: 2 SERVINGS

INGREDIENTS

1 cup shredded lowfat cheddar cheese

2 tablespoons light mayonnaise

1 teaspoon chopped pimento (normally found near the olives in the grocery store)

¼ teaspoon onion powder

4 slices ripe tomato

Two 6-inch whole-wheat tortillas

DIRECTIONS

1 Place cheese, mayonnaise, pimento, and onion powder in a food processor and blend for 15 seconds. Scrape down the sides of the bowl with a rubber spatula and remix for another 15 seconds.

2 Place ½ cup pimento cheese mixture into the center of a tortilla and top with 2 slices of tomato. Roll the tortilla, cheese, and tomatoes up into a tightly wrapped tube. Repeat with the remaining ingredients.

PER SERVING: *Calories 231 (From Fat 86); Fat 10g (Saturated 4g); Cholesterol 17mg; Sodium 641mg; Carbohydrate 17g (Dietary Fiber 2g); Protein 17g; Sugar 1g.*

VARY IT! Monterey jack, provolone, and pepper jack cheeses work great in place of cheddar cheese. You can also use whole-grain crackers instead of tortillas.

TIP: The cheese mixture lasts up to five days if kept in an airtight container in the fridge.

Making Unbeatable Salads

One of the questions frequently asked is, "When can I eat salad again?" Because salads typically have raw vegetables in them, it may be a month or more before you can comfortably tolerate them. Some vegetables, like celery, need to be cut into smaller pieces so they don't stick. Also, be sure to peel any fruit to minimize the chances that it will get stuck and cause discomfort.

REMEMBER

Chew, chew, chew. Prevention is the best remedy for getting food stuck.

If you use a commercially prepared salad dressing, choose a light or reduced-fat variety. Salad dressings are fat based, and fat carries a lot of calories with the flavor. If you have had GBP, the high-fat salad dressings may cause the highly unpleasant experience of dumping syndrome.

Orzo and Salmon Salad

STAGE: REGULAR FOODS	PREP TIME: 10 MIN	COOK TIME: 20 MIN	YIELD: 6 SERVINGS

INGREDIENTS

½ medium cucumber, peeled, halved, seeds removed, and cut into ½-inch cubes

4 plum tomatoes, cut into ½-inch cubes

¾ teaspoon salt, divided

¾ cup dry orzo

3 tablespoons plus 2 teaspoons olive oil

2 tablespoons fresh lemon juice

⅓ cup chopped fresh dill

½ cup sliced mushrooms

½ cup diced red bell pepper

½ teaspoon black pepper, divided

1 pound salmon fillet, about 1 inch thick, cut into 6 pieces

DIRECTIONS

1 In a strainer, toss the cucumber, tomatoes, and ½ teaspoon of the salt and let drain for 15 minutes.

2 In a large pot of boiling, salted water, cook the orzo until just done, following the package directions. Drain the pasta and rinse with cold water until the orzo is cool to the touch.

3 Toss the orzo with 3 tablespoons of the olive oil, lemon juice, dill, mushrooms, red bell pepper, ¼ teaspoon of the black pepper, and the drained tomatoes and cucumbers.

4 Preheat the oven broiler. Coat the salmon with 2 teaspoons oil, the remaining ¼ teaspoon salt, and the remaining ¼ teaspoon pepper.

5 Place the salmon on a baking sheet and broil on the top oven rack for 4 minutes. Turn salmon over and broil an additional 4 minutes. The fish is done when it's golden brown outside and still translucent in the center and the meat flakes easily with a fork.

6 Plate orzo salad with the salmon pieces on top.

PER SERVING: *Calories 254 (From Fat 104); Fat 12g (Saturated 2g); Cholesterol 43mg; Sodium 352 mg; Carbohydrates 18g (Dietary Fiber 2g); Protein 20g; Sugar 3g.*

Quick Seafood Salad

| STAGE: REGULAR FOODS | PREP TIME: 10 MIN | CHILL TIME: 2–4 HR | YIELD: 2 SERVINGS |

INGREDIENTS

½ cup cooked baby shrimp

½ cup cooked scallops

½ cup cooked crabmeat

¼ cup minced celery

1 clove garlic, minced

2 tablespoons lemon juice

2 tablespoons cocktail sauce

1 teaspoon fat-free sour cream

1 teaspoon light mayonnaise

DIRECTIONS

In a large mixing bowl, combine all ingredients and mix well. Refrigerate for 2 to 4 hours before serving.

PER SERVING: *Calories 161 (From Fat 20); Fat 2g (Saturated 0g); Cholesterol 131mg; Sodium 561mg; Carbohydrate 7g (Dietary Fiber 1g); Protein 26g; Sugar 3g.*

TIP: When shopping for shrimp, try to find smaller shrimp rather than larger prawns. The larger the shrimp, the more fibrous it is, and the more difficult it is to chew thoroughly.

NOTE: We like to use the foil-packed seafood that's located near the canned fish at grocery stores. In addition, most markets have precooked seafood at the fish counter.

Grilled Chicken and Pecan Salad

STAGE: REGULAR FOODS	PREP TIME: 5 MIN	COOK TIME: 8 MIN	CHILL TIME: 4–6 HR	YIELD: 4 SERVINGS

INGREDIENTS

½ teaspoon paprika

½ teaspoon garlic powder

½ teaspoon onion powder

¼ teaspoon black pepper

¼ teaspoon salt

1 pound boneless skinless chicken breast

1 teaspoon olive oil

¼ cup minced celery

1 teaspoon lemon juice

¼ cup chopped green onions

¼ cup pecans, chopped

¼ cup light mayonnaise

DIRECTIONS

1 Prepare a medium-hot fire in a charcoal or gas grill.

2 In a medium mixing bowl, combine paprika, garlic, onion powder, black pepper, and salt. Brush the chicken with oil and then toss with the spice mixture.

3 Place the chicken on the hot grill and cook for 4 minutes. Turn the chicken over and grill an additional 4 minutes. Test doneness by inserting an instant-read thermometer into the thickest part of the chicken and checking that it registers 165 degrees.

4 Let chicken cool until you can handle it; then cut into ½-inch cubes. In a medium mixing bowl, combine chicken, celery, lemon juice, green onions, pecans, and mayonnaise and mix well.

5 Refrigerate for 4 to 6 hours before serving.

PER SERVING: *Calories 240 (From Fat 120); Fat 13g (Saturated 1g); Cholesterol 70mg; Sodium 350mg; Carbohydrate 4g (Dietary Fiber 1g); Protein 27g; Sugar 1g.*

Poached Herb Chicken Salad with Tangy Dressing

STAGE: REGULAR FOODS	PREP TIME: 15 MIN	CHILL TIME: 15 MIN	YIELD: 4 SERVINGS

INGREDIENTS

Four 4-ounce skinless chicken breasts

¼ cup chopped scallions (including the green)

1 cup fresh herbs (basil, thyme, parsley, cilantro, or other favorite), chopped

½ teaspoon salt

½ teaspoon pepper

2 cloves garlic, sliced

Zest of ½ orange or lemon

Tangy Dressing (see the following recipe)

DIRECTIONS

1 In a large saucepan, place the chicken, scallions, herbs, salt, pepper, garlic and citrus peels and cover with water.

2 Bring to a boil and then reduce to simmer for 15 minutes. Remove from the heat.

3 Cool for 15 minutes and remove the chicken from the other ingredients.

4 Shred and add the Tangy Dressing to the chicken. Stir until incorporated.

Tangy Dressing

¼ cup mango vinegar or mango rice wine

2 tablespoons flavored oil (for example, orange or lime)

¼ cup canola oil

¼ cup water

2 tablespoons Hoisin sauce

1 tablespoon Dijon mustard

In a small bowl, combine all the ingredients and whisk until blended.

PER SERVING: *Calories 339 (From Fat 219); Fat 24g (Saturated 3g); Cholesterol 73mg; Sodium 596mg; Carbohydrate 4g (Dietary Fiber 0g); Protein 25g; Sugar 2g.*

Curried Apple and Tuna Salad

STAGE: REGULAR FOOD	PREP TIME: 10 MIN	CHILL TIME: 2–4 HR	YIELD: 2 SERVINGS

INGREDIENTS

1 small Granny Smith apple, peeled, cored, and chopped

1 tablespoon lemon juice

¼ cup minced celery

¼ cup chopped green onions

½ cup peeled, seeded, and diced cucumber

4 ounces canned tuna in water, drained and flaked

¼ cup plain nonfat yogurt

2 teaspoons light mayonnaise

½ teaspoon curry powder

2 teaspoons sugar substitute

¼ teaspoon garlic powder

Salt to taste

DIRECTIONS

1 Combine apple, lemon juice, celery, green onions, cucumber, and tuna in a bowl, toss lightly, and set aside.

2 In a separate small bowl, add yogurt, mayonnaise, curry, sugar substitute, garlic powder, and salt and mix well. Pour dressing over the apple-tuna mixture and mix well. Refrigerate for 2 to 4 hours before serving.

PER SERVING: *Calories 133 (From Fat 30); Fat 3g (Saturated 1g); Cholesterol 20mg; Sodium 524mg; Carbohydrate 15g (Dietary Fiber 2g); Protein 12g; Sugar 9g.*

Eggless Egg Salad

STAGE: REGULAR FOODS | PREP TIME: 10–15 MIN | YIELD: 2 SERVINGS

INGREDIENTS

6 ounces extra-firm tofu, drained

¼ cup plain, nonfat Greek yogurt

1 tablespoon light mayonnaise

1 teaspoon yellow or Dijon mustard

⅛ teaspoon salt

⅛ teaspoon pepper

⅛ teaspoon ground turmeric

2 tablespoons pickle relish

DIRECTIONS

1 In a medium bowl, mash the tofu with a fork until it looks like cooked, mashed egg whites.

2 Add the remaining ingredients and stir with a small spatula until blended evenly.

3 Enjoy with sliced seedless cucumbers or stuffed in a whole-grain pita with lettuce.

PER SERVING: *Calories 148 (From Fat 68); Fat 8g (Saturated 1g); Cholesterol 5mg; Sodium 301mg; Carbohydrate 9g (Dietary Fiber 1g); Protein 13g; Sugar 5g.*

Chapter **9**

Umm . . . Tastes Like Chicken: Poultry Dishes

P oultry is one of the most versatile protein sources. You can eat it hot or cold, baked, grilled, broiled, or sautéed, by itself or mixed with an endless number of complementing ingredients. In this chapter we provide chicken and turkey dishes that are cooked with a variety of methods. When you're comfortable with these preparations, you'll have endless options for experimenting and creating your own recipes.

Whether you're cooking chicken, turkey, or small Cornish hens, the internal temperature needs to reach 165 degrees for white meat and 180 degrees for dark meat before you stop cooking. The meat continues to cook after you remove it from the heat source, so it will reach the food-safety-recommended temperatures of 170 and 185 degrees, respectively, on its own. The actual cook time will vary based on the size of the cuts.

Popular Poultry Cooking Methods

Cooking methods are especially important when preparing poultry because it's an easy food to overcook. Dry, overcooked poultry is difficult to eat because it's likely to get stuck when passing through the pouch or gastric band. The following two methods for properly cooking various types of poultry will provide you with moist, tender, and flavorful meals — increasing your enthusiasm to cook high-quality meats and improve your protein intake.

Sautéing

When you sauté food, you cook it in a preheated pan or griddle with a small amount of added fat such as oil or butter. Because you start with a hot pan and fat, the cooking time is short (usually under 7 minutes), which makes sautéing a popular method. Keeping an eye on the cooking food when you sauté is easy to do, and it's actually an important guideline because unmonitored sautéed food can quickly overcook. Because food cooks so rapidly, pieces of meat need to be small and uniform so that the inside isn't still undercooked when the outside is burning.

CONSIDERING FREE-RANGE AND ORGANIC CHICKEN

When shopping for chicken, you may notice some labels indicating that the product is free range or organic. *Free range* means the birds have access to the outside, as opposed to living their whole lives in small cages. The demand for free-range chicken has grown because people believe the birds are treated more humanely. However, no standard is in place for how much space or time birds need outside the coop. You may think of the chickens happily pecking around the grass, but their "free range" may be a small plot of dirt or gravel.

Organic chicken requires stricter standards. The birds must have access to the outdoors, and their indoor space is larger than nonorganic birds. They're fed certified organic feed and treated with antibiotics only when needed, not routinely, and probiotics are often used to replace growth-promoting drugs. Providing better living conditions and higher standards for animal welfare contributes to the higher cost for organic chicken.

Roasting

Roasting, if done correctly, can be a great way to cook large cuts of poultry. If done with a roasting rack, it sears the juices in from all sides, whereas baking only sears the top. To roast, place in a shallow pan with a baking rack to lift the poultry just above the pan so it can cook from 360 degrees. The follow instructions provide general guidelines for roasting:

1. **Preheat your oven to 500 degrees.**

2. **Using a roasting pan with 3-inch-high sides, add water or broth to fill the pan with 1 inch of liquid.**

   If you plan to use the liquid as gravy, chicken broth adds more flavor than water. The liquid in the pan keeps the drippings from the poultry from burning or evaporating from the pan.

3. **Place your roasting rack over the liquid and put the cut of poultry on the rack.**

   The roasting rack lifts the poultry just above the pan so the heat from the oven can cook the bird all the way around.

4. **Place your prepared poultry into the preheated oven and roast for 5 minutes.**

   The high heat sears the outside of the bird and locks in the moisture.

5. **Turn down the heat to 325 degrees and continue to roast until your poultry is cooked to your desired doneness.**

   To use a meat thermometer, insert it into the thickest part of the poultry and stay clear of cartilage and bone. The thermometer takes about 20 seconds to register the internal temperature.

   Some meat thermometers are oven safe, meaning they can be left in the meat while it cooks in the oven, but unless yours specifically states "oven safe," assume it isn't. Remove it from the oven as soon as you get a temperature reading.

Roasting bags are available in stores, but they don't really roast your food. They *braise* the food (cook it in liquid), causing poultry to be moist but chewy.

REMEMBER

Poultry skin, which is fat, naturally bastes (moistens) the poultry as it cooks. When you're grilling, baking, or roasting, you can leave the skin on, but remove the skin before eating to avoid adding extra fat to your meal. If you choose not to use the skin when cooking, baste the chicken with a healthy substitute such as canola or olive oil to help keep it moist.

Roasted, Sautéed, and Baked Poultry

This section has recipes that will keep your house wafting with the aroma of delicious poultry. These easy-to-make dishes will keep your family coming back for more.

REMEMBER

A typical chicken breast is more than one serving. A serving of cooked chicken is 3 ounces by weight, and most chicken breasts are 6 or more ounces. To ensure that you divide each dish into the correct number of appropriately sized servings, check the weight on the label to make sure you start with the right amount of meat, and take note of each recipe's yield.

Chicken with Peppers and Olives

STAGE: REGULAR FOODS	PREP TIME: 10 MIN	COOK TIME: 30 MIN	YIELD: 6 SERVINGS

INGREDIENTS

2 tablespoons olive oil, divided

1½ pounds boneless, skinless chicken breast, cut into six 4-ounce pieces

2 cloves garlic, crushed

1 large red onion, sliced

3 medium bell peppers (red, green, and yellow), cut into strips

½ cup pitted green olives

2 tablespoons capers

One 8-ounce can no-salt-added tomato sauce

1 cup low-sodium chicken broth

2 teaspoons chopped fresh marjoram

½ teaspoon black pepper

DIRECTIONS

1 Heat 1 tablespoon of oil in a large sauté pan over medium-high heat. Brown the chicken pieces on all sides. Remove the chicken from the pan and set aside.

2 Add the remaining 1 tablespoon of oil to the pan and sauté the garlic and onion until softened, about 2 minutes. Stir in the bell peppers, olives, capers, and tomato sauce.

3 Return the chicken to the sauté pan and add the broth, marjoram, and pepper. Cover and simmer for 20 minutes, or until the chicken reaches 165 degrees internally.

PER SERVING: *Calories 240 (From Fat 80); Fat 9g (Saturated 2g); Cholesterol 65mg; Sodium 400mg; Carbohydrate 11g (Dietary Fiber 3g); Protein 29g; Sugar 5g.*

VARY IT! You can substitute fresh oregano for marjoram if you prefer.

NOTE: Capers, which are unripened flower buds, have a distinctive flavor and texture, so don't leave them out of this recipe. They come packed in a brine that contains salt, and you can rinse them if you like, but it won't change the sodium content very much.

Turkey Cutlets with Thyme–Tomato Sauce

STAGE: REGULAR FOODS	PREP TIME: 5 MIN	COOK TIME: 12 MIN	YIELD: 8 SERVINGS

INGREDIENTS

8 teaspoons olive oil, divided

2 pounds turkey cutlets

1 teaspoon salt, divided

1 teaspoon black pepper, divided

1 tablespoon chopped fresh thyme

1 teaspoon minced garlic

3 cups chopped tomato

2 tablespoons white wine vinegar

DIRECTIONS

1 Heat 4 teaspoons of the oil in a large skillet over medium-high heat.

2 Sprinkle turkey on both sides with ½ teaspoon salt and ½ teaspoon pepper. Add turkey to the pan and cook for 2 to 5 minutes on each side, or until done. Remove from the pan and keep warm.

3 Add the remaining 4 teaspoons of oil, thyme, and garlic to pan. Sauté for 1 minute.

4 Add the tomatoes and cook for 1 minute, stirring frequently. Stir in the remaining ½ teaspoon salt, ½ teaspoon pepper, and vinegar. Serve over turkey.

PER SERVING: Calories 180 (From Fat 45); Fat 5g (Saturated 1g); Cholesterol 45mg; Sodium 390mg; Carbohydrate 3g (Dietary Fiber 1g); Protein 29g; Sugar 2g.

TIP: If tomatoes aren't in season, you can use a drained 28-ounce can of diced tomatoes. However, this will increase the sodium content of the dish.

TIP: Turkey cutlets are thin slices of turkey breast. The cutlets cook quickly, so keep an eye on the clock.

Mojo Chicken

STAGE: REGULAR FOODS	PREP TIME: 15 MIN	MARINATE TIME: 8–24 HR	COOK TIME: 45 MIN	YIELD: 8 SERVINGS

INGREDIENTS

1 pound boneless, skinless chicken breasts cut into 4-ounce portions

1 pound skinless chicken thighs cut into 4-ounce portions

¼ cup fresh lime juice

¼ cup fresh lemon juice

3 cloves garlic, minced (see Figure 9-1)

1 tablespoon chopped fresh oregano

1 tablespoon olive oil

DIRECTIONS

1 Place the chicken in a large resealable bag and pour the remaining ingredients over the top. Let it marinate in the refrigerator for at least 8 hours or up to 24 hours.

2 Preheat the oven to 350 degrees.

3 Place the chicken in a roasting pan and pour marinade over chicken. Roast for 45 minutes or until internal temperature is 165 degrees.

PER SERVING: Calories 150 (From Fat 35); Fat 4g (Saturated 1g); Cholesterol 80mg; Sodium 85mg; Carbohydrate 2g (Dietary Fiber 0g); Protein 24g; Sugar 0g.

HOW TO EXTRACT, PEEL AND MINCE GARLIC

BREAK OFF ONE SECTION OR CLOVE. PRESS HARD AND PUSH SIDEWAYS.

LAY THE CLOVE ON A HARD, FLAT SURFACE. PRESS DOWN ON IT WITH YOUR THUMB TO CRACK THE PAPERY CASING. PEEL OFF ALL THE LAYERS.

PLACE THE CLOVE IN A GARLIC MINCER. CRANK THE HANDLE TO PRESS THE GARLIC THROUGH. SCRAPE OFF WITH A KNIFE.

OR

USE A SHARP KNIFE TO CUT AND MINCE AS FINELY AS POSSIBLE. PRESS DOWN ON GARLIC WITH THE FLAT SIDE OF THE KNIFE TO RELEASE THE JUICES.

FIGURE 9-1: How to peel and chop garlic.

Illustration by Elizabeth Kurtzman

Poached Chicken with Lowfat Cream Sauce

STAGE: SOFT FOODS	PREP TIME: 5 MIN	COOK TIME: 15 MIN	CHILL TIME: 15 MIN	YIELD: 4 SERVINGS

INGREDIENTS

1 pound skinless chicken breasts, sliced into 4-ounce pieces

1 tablespoon dried herbs, such as thyme, basil, oregano, or Herbs de Provence

1 clove garlic, sliced

½ teaspoon salt

½ teaspoon pepper

Lowfat Cream Sauce (see the following recipe)

¼ cup freshly grated Parmesan cheese (optional)

DIRECTIONS

1 In a medium saucepan, combine all the ingredients.

2 Cover with cold water and bring to a boil.

3 Reduce the heat to medium-low and simmer for 10 minutes.

4 Remove from the heat and cool for 15 minutes. Remove the chicken from the stock. (You can use the stock for a soup if you like.)

5 Pour the Lowfat Cream Sauce over the chicken. Top with Parmesan, if desired.

Lowfat Cream Sauce

½ cup powdered nonfat dry milk

2 tablespoons cornstarch

1 cup cold chicken or vegetable stock

¾ cup teaspoon dried seasoning blend (basil, thyme, pepper)

½ teaspoon salt

1 While the chicken is poaching, in a small saucepan, mix all the ingredients.

2 Whisk together and stir over medium heat until thickened. Do not stop stirring.

3 Once thickened remove from the heat.

PER SERVING: Calories 219 (From Fat 34); Fat 4g (Saturated 1g); Cholesterol 77mg; Sodium 879mg; Carbohydrate 13g (Dietary Fiber 0g); Protein 31g; Sugar 9g.

Chicken with Tomato-Mushroom Sauce

STAGE: REGULAR FOODS	PREP TIME: 15 MIN	COOK TIME: 20 MIN	YIELD: 8 SERVINGS

INGREDIENTS

¼ cup olive oil

2 pounds boneless, skinless chicken breasts, cut in half

½ teaspoon salt

½ teaspoon pepper

3 tablespoons all-purpose flour

½ cup white wine

2 medium tomatoes, peeled and chopped

½ cup fresh sliced mushrooms

½ cup chopped green onions

1 clove fresh garlic, chopped

½ cup chicken broth

DIRECTIONS

1 Heat the olive oil in a large sauté pan over medium–high heat.

2 Salt and pepper the chicken breasts. Lightly coat with flour. Add them to the pan and sauté until chicken is golden brown, approximately 3½ minutes on each side.

3 When the chicken is browned on both sides, add white wine and scrape the bottom of the pan with a spatula to deglaze the pan.

4 Add the tomatoes, mushrooms, green onions, garlic, and chicken broth to pan. Simmer for 10 minutes or until the chicken is cooked through. The sauce will thicken while cooking.

TIP: Fresh chicken breasts are thicker on one end than the other end. To make sure the chicken cooks evenly, pound the chicken breast with a meat mallet until it's even thickness.

NOTE: The recipe gets a lot of flavor from a technique called *deglazing*: a room-temperature liquid is added to a hot pan and the pan is scraped to lift the caramelized goodness off the bottom and mix it into the sauce.

VARY IT! If you don't want to use wine in the sauce, you can use extra chicken broth instead. Turkey cutlets can also be substituted for the chicken.

PER SERVING: *Calories 220 (From Fat 70); Fat 9g (Saturated 2g); Cholesterol 65mg; Sodium 260mg; Carbohydrate 5g (Dietary Fiber 1g); Protein 27g; Sugar 2g.*

Poached Chicken in Herbs with Tangy Dressing

STAGE: SOFT FOODS	PREP TIME: 5 MIN	CHILL TIME: 8 HR OR OVERNIGHT	COOK TIME: 15 MIN	YIELD: 4 SERVINGS

INGREDIENTS

1 pound skinless chicken breasts, sliced into 4-ounce pieces

1 tablespoon dried herbs, such as thyme, basil, oregano, or Herbs de Provence

1 clove garlic, sliced

½ teaspoon salt

½ teaspoon pepper

Tangy Dressing (see the following recipe)

DIRECTIONS

1 In a medium saucepan, combine the chicken, dried herbs, garlic, salt, and pepper. Cover with cold water and bring to a boil.

2 Reduce the heat to medium–low and simmer for 10 minutes.

3 Remove from the heat and cool for 15 minutes. Remove the chicken from the stock. (You can use the stock for a soup if you like.)

4 Shred the chicken and add the Tangy Dressing. Chill overnight.

Tangy Dressing

¼ cup mango vinegar or mango rice wine

2 tablespoons flavored oil (for example, orange or lime)

¼ cup canola oil

¼ cup water

2 tablespoons Hoison sauce

1 tablespoon Dijon mustard

In a small bowl, combine all the ingredients and whisk until blended.

PER SERVING: Calories 339 (From Fat 219); Fat 24g (Saturated 3g); Cholesterol 73mg; Sodium 596mg; Carbohydrate 4g (Dietary Fiber 0g); Protein 25g; Sugar 2g.

Herb-Roasted Cornish Game Hens

STAGE: REGULAR FOODS	PREP TIME: 10 MIN	COOK TIME: 45 MIN	YIELD: 4 SERVINGS

INGREDIENTS

2 Cornish hens

½ teaspoon salt

1 teaspoon black pepper

2 sliced garlic cloves

2 teaspoons minced fresh rosemary

2 teaspoons minced fresh thyme

1 bay leaf

2 shallots, roughly chopped

1½ carrots, roughly chopped into 1-inch pieces

1½ stalks celery, roughly chopped into 1-inch pieces

1 lemon

DIRECTIONS

1 Preheat the oven to 375 degrees.

2 Rinse the Cornish hens with cold water, remove giblets (if included), and pat dry. Season with salt and pepper inside and out. Stuff the inside of the hens with garlic, rosemary, thyme, and ½ bay leaf each.

3 Place the shallots, carrots, and celery on the bottom of a roasting pan and place the hens on top of the vegetables. Squeeze juice from the lemon all over the hens.

4 Roast in the oven until the hens are golden brown and crisp and the juices run clear when the thigh is pierced with a sharp knife, about 45 minutes. Transfer the hens to a serving platter and let rest for about 5 minutes, and then remove the bay leaf before serving.

PER SERVING (INCLUDING VEGETABLES): *Calories 160 (From Fat 35); Fat 4g (Saturated 1g); Cholesterol 110mg; Sodium 410mg; Carbohydrate 6g (Dietary Fiber 1g); Protein 25g; Sugar 2g.*

TIP: The vegetables in this recipe are at the bottom of the pan to add flavor to the chicken. If you want to eat them with the hen, be sure to cut up the celery and carrots into small pieces so they don't get stuck.

NOTE: Although Cornish game hen may sound gourmet, it's simply a young male or female chicken, not a game bird. In the United States they were first used in the early 1950s and have been a hit ever since. Because of their small size, each bird makes two perfect servings.

Chicken in Mushroom Wine Sauce with Pasta

STAGE: REGULAR FOODS	PREP TIME: 15 MIN	COOK TIME: 25 MIN	YIELD: 4 SERVINGS

INGREDIENTS

1 teaspoon butter

¼ pound mushrooms, quartered

½ cup dry red wine, divided

2 tablespoons all-purpose flour

½ teaspoon salt

¼ teaspoon black pepper

1 pound boneless, skinless chicken breast, cut into 4-ounce pieces

2 tablespoons olive oil

½ cup diced onion

1 cup thinly sliced fennel bulb (discard bottom inch of bulb)

1 clove garlic, minced

2 teaspoons balsamic vinegar

¼ pound whole-wheat angel hair pasta

DIRECTIONS

1 Melt butter in a medium sauté pan over medium-high heat. Add the mushrooms and sauté, stirring frequently. When the mushrooms soften and give off liquid, reduce heat to medium and cook until liquid evaporates.

2 Stir in ¼ cup of the wine. Increase the heat to high and boil until most of the wine evaporates. Remove mushrooms from the pan and set them aside.

3 Combine the flour, salt, and pepper on a plate. Dredge each piece of chicken in the flour mixture and shake off the excess.

4 Wipe out the sauté pan. Add olive oil to sauté pan and heat over medium-high heat. When oil is hot, turn the heat down to medium and add the chicken. Brown the chicken on both sides, about 3 minutes a side. Remove chicken from the pan and set aside.

5 Add the onion and fennel to the drippings in the pan, cooking over medium heat until the onion softens and fennel begins to brown.

6 Stir in the garlic and cook 2 to 3 minutes more. Increase heat to high and stir in the remaining ¼ cup wine.

7 Add the sautéed mushrooms and return the chicken to the pan. Cover tightly, reduce heat, and bring to a simmer. Cook until chicken is thoroughly cooked, about 5 minutes. Remove from heat and stir in balsamic vinegar.

8 Prepare angel hair pasta according to package directions until it's soft all the way through, not al dente; drain. Serve immediately with chicken and mushroom sauce.

PER SERVING: *Calories 350 (From Fat 90); Fat 10g (Saturated 2g); Cholesterol 70mg; Sodium 390mg; Carbohydrate 28g (Dietary Fiber 4g); Protein 31g; Sugar 3g.*

Turkey, the White Meat Burger

Sometimes you just feel like having a burger. But after weight-loss surgery, many people have difficulty tolerating beef. It just may not "sit well." However, you can still have a burger if you swap the beef for ground turkey.

Ground meat is less likely to get stuck because the stringy meat fibers have been mechanically broken down for you. In the meat case you can find ground turkey and ground turkey breast. Ground turkey is less expensive than ground turkey breast because it's made with both white and dark meat, and usually has some turkey skin added. So although you save some money, ounce for ounce you get less protein and more fat with regular ground turkey.

REMEMBER

Even ground meat can be difficult to swallow and digest if it gets dry, so cook the turkey burgers just until they reach an internal temperature of 165 degrees. This temperature is low enough to keep your turkey burgers moist while ensuring they're thoroughly cooked.

Greek Turkey Burgers with Yogurt Sauce

STAGE: SOFT OR REGULAR FOODS	PREP TIME: 15 MIN	COOK TIME: 20 MIN	YIELD: 4 SERVINGS

INGREDIENTS

1 cup minced mushrooms

1 pound lean ground turkey or chicken (at least 90 percent lean)

¼ cup minced onion

1 cup chopped fresh spinach

¼ cup feta, crumbled

½ cup cooked brown rice

2 eggs

¼ teaspoon salt

1 teaspoon dried oregano

2 teaspoons light olive oil

Yogurt Sauce (see the following recipe)

DIRECTIONS

1 In a medium bowl, mix the mushrooms, ground turkey or chicken, onion, spinach, feta, rice, eggs, salt, and oregano with a fork until incorporated.

2 Heat a skillet over medium heat, and add the oil; swirl the pan.

3 With a quarter-cup measurement, make patties at ½-inch thick to fit four at a time in the pan.

4 Brown on each side 3 to 4 minutes each until browned and no longer pink (they should register 165 degrees on a meat thermometer).

5 Remove from the heat and serve with the Yogurt Sauce.

Yogurt Sauce

½ cup plain, nonfat Greek yogurt

2 tablespoons dried dill

1 small cucumber, diced

¼ cup whole milk feta, crumbled

½ lemon, zest and juice

Combine all ingredients in a small bowl until mixed well.

PER SERVING: Calories 325 (From Fat 146); Fat 16g (Saturated 6g); Cholesterol 103mg; Sodium 485mg; Carbohydrate 15g (Dietary Fiber 2g); Protein 31g; Sugar 5g.

A Casserole Everyone Will Flock To

Casseroles are one-dish meals. They always have some sort of liquid added, so they're moist and easy to eat after you have had weight loss surgery. They're easy to make, too: You can put them in the slow cooker or prepare them ahead of time and refrigerate them until it's time to heat. Leftovers can be packed for lunch or frozen for another time-saving meal. One of our favorite things about casseroles is that they often taste better the next day! Just remember to reheat the food to 160 degrees before eating.

Spicy Picante Turkey Casserole

STAGE: REGULAR FOODS	PREP TIME: 15 MIN	COOK TIME: 30 MIN	YIELD: 6 SERVINGS

INGREDIENTS

2 teaspoons olive oil

9 ounces ground turkey breast

½ cup sliced green onions

2 cups sliced mushrooms

8 ounces canned diced green chilies, drained

1½ cups mild picante sauce

2 cups cooked brown rice

6 tablespoons light sour cream

½ cup shredded sharp cheddar cheese

DIRECTIONS

1 Preheat the oven to 350 degrees. Coat an 8-x-8-inch baking pan with nonstick spray.

2 Heat the oil in a large skillet over medium heat. Brown the ground turkey until it has no pink, and drain excess fat from pan. Add the onions and mushrooms and cook until soft.

3 Stir in the chilies and cook for 2 minutes. Add the picante sauce. Stirring constantly, cook until thickened, about 5 minutes.

4 Combine the rice and sour cream and spread at the bottom of the baking pan. Add the turkey mixture evenly on top. Sprinkle with the shredded cheese. Bake for 15 to 20 minutes, or until hot and cheese is melted.

PER SERVING: *Calories 240 (From Fat 90); Fat 10g (Saturated 4g); Cholesterol 50mg; Sodium 760mg; Carbohydrate 23g (Dietary Fiber 4g); Protein 13g; Sugar 4g.*

TIP: If you want the rice to have more flavor, cook it in low-sodium broth instead of water. To help with tolerance, be sure to "overcook" the rice by letting it cook longer in more liquid than usual.

Chapter **10**

Let's Meat in the Kitchen: Beef and Pork Recipes

"Will I be able to eat red meat again after surgery?" is a question we often hear. Red meat is one of those foods that works for some people and not for others, even if they've had the same surgery. So the response to this question is answered by your pouch. If you had gastric bypass surgery, you may find that red meat does not "set well" in your pouch, meaning it will make your pouch feel uncomfortable. No matter what kind of weight-loss surgery you had, the meat fibers can be difficult to chew thoroughly and can get stuck in the stoma or the band, causing great discomfort.

When you decide to eat red meat, start with ground meat. The fibers are already broken down, so it is easier to tolerate than a piece or chunk of meat. Choosing the right grade and cut of meat and using the best cooking method make all the difference in the world in how well you tolerate it. In this chapter we show you which grades and cuts of beef and pork are best, and we provide lots of delicious and easy recipes in which to use them.

Note that the portion sizes in this chapter may be too large if you're still in the postsurgery diet progression. Be sure to check each recipe's yield and adjust for your needs as necessary.

REMEMBER

Choosing Beef and Pork You Can Eat after Surgery

U.S. Department of Agriculture grades are based on nationally uniform standards, so no matter where in the United States you buy meat, it must meet the same criteria. Grading of meat for quality is voluntary and the meat plant must pay for the service of having their products graded.

USDA beef grades

The USDA (U.S. Department of Agriculture) designates eight beef grades, used to classify the meat according to *marbling*, or the fat running through the muscle, and age of the beef. The three grades commonly available to consumers are

>> **Prime:** Prime meat is heavily marbled which makes for a tender and flavorful steak. Only 2 percent of graded beef is prime. Prime meats are generally served in restaurants and sold in high-end grocery stores.

>> **Choice:** The majority of graded beef is graded choice. It's moderately marbled and is still tender, but the flavor isn't as great as prime.

>> **Select:** Select beef has very little marbling therefore the cooked meat is drier, tougher, and has less flavor than prime and choice cuts.

The grade is the quality of the meat when inspected. It doesn't necessarily affect tolerance when eaten, although tender meat tends to be better for weight loss surgery patients than drier, tougher pieces.

Which cuts makes the cut

Not all steaks are created equal. The tenderness of a steak depends on where the steak is cut from. Beef is a muscle, and the more the muscle is worked, the leaner and less fatty it will be. Steaks that have less fat are not as tender and tend to be tough if overcooked. Top round, bottom round, and blade steaks are examples of leaner steaks. When the muscle is worked less, it gets more marbling, thin lines of fat throughout, making it more tender. Examples of tender steaks are fillet mignon, New York strips, and rib-eye.

Following are some common cuts of meat:

>> **Chuck steaks:** The chuck section, the shoulder area, includes the first five ribs as well as the shoulder-blade bone. In most cases chuck steaks are downright tough, and some cuts contain large amounts of gristle and fat. We only recommend low and slow cooking, such as in a slow cooker, for these cuts.

>> **Rib steaks:** The rib section is located just behind the chuck/shoulder area and contains the next seven ribs. This is where the prime rib roast is found. The steaks from this rib section are of high quality with just the right amount of marbling and great texture and tenderness. We recommend this cut of meat, which is great for grilling.

>> **Short-loin steaks:** The short-loin section is located just behind the rib section, in the upper middle area of the back. Steaks cut from the short loin are of great quality. The tenderloin, which is known for its tenderness and rich flavor, is found here. The T-bone and porterhouse steaks are also from this section. Cuts from the short loin are highly recommended for those just starting to add a solid piece of red meat to their diet after their weight loss surgery because they're moist, tender, and good in any beef dish.

>> **Sirloin steaks:** The sirloin section is behind the loin section and in some areas of the country is referred to as the hip area. Sirloin steaks are fairly large but thin, and the meat isn't as tender as the short-loin cuts, but they have great flavor. Because these cuts require a little more chewing, they're best for those who have been on a regular diet for at least six months and have tolerated short-loin steak. This cut is great for stews and roast.

>> **Flank steak:** The flank steak is located on the underside belly area, directly below the short loin and sirloin. Steaks from this area have a rich, beefy flavor but *must* be sliced thin and against the grain to keep the texture of meat from being chewy.

We do not recommend flank steak, because it's too stringy and chewy to be digested well.

Cooking Phenomenal Ground-Beef Dishes

Who hasn't started with a pound of ground beef and made a meal for six or more people? Few other high-protein foods have the versatility and low price of ground beef. From stews to burgers, ground meats can be the complement to the dish or the center of attention. We use ground beef in the recipes in this section, but you can substitute ground venison, bison, or turkey.

Ground beef comes from different cuts of meat that determine the fat content and price of the beef. Not all types of ground meat work for all recipes. If you're making a ground-meat dish that has other ingredients in it to help keep it moist, you can use a leaner ground beef, one with 5 to 10 percent fat. If you're making burgers, use a ground beef with more fat, 15 to 20 percent, because the fat keeps the meat moist. Grilling extra-lean beef patties gives you a dry, tough burger.

Whether you choose extra-lean or regular ground beef, it all contains about equal amounts of iron, vitamin B12, niacin, and protein. Regular ground beef has more calories than lean ground beef because it has more fat. A 3-ounce serving of broiled 95 percent lean ground beef has 140 calories and 5 grams of fat, versus a 3-ounce broiled serving of 80 percent lean ground beef with 210 calories and 14 grams of fat.

WARNING

Because ground meat is exposed to more bacteria during processing, it doesn't keep as long as a solid piece of meat. You can refrigerate it for up to two days or keep it in the freezer for three months.

TIP

If you have an adjustable gastric band (AGB), ground meats generally work better than a solid piece of meat. Grinding meat breaks down its fibers so it's less likely to get lodged trying to pass through the band. But even with ground meats, be sure to chew, chew, chew.

Salisbury Steak with Sautéed Vegetables

STAGE: SOFT FOODS | PREP TIME: 10 MIN | COOK TIME: 20 MIN | YIELD: 6 SERVINGS

INGREDIENTS

1 pound lean ground beef

¼ cup fresh minced parsley

2 tablespoons chopped green onion

½ teaspoon salt

½ teaspoon black pepper

¼ cup plus 1 teaspoon all-purpose flour

1 tablespoon olive oil

1 cup sliced onion

1 cup sliced green bell pepper

1 cup chopped tomatoes

1 tablespoon minced garlic

1 tablespoon tomato paste

2 cups low-sodium beef broth

¼ cup dry red wine

½ teaspoon dried thyme

DIRECTIONS

1 Combine the ground beef, parsley, green onion, salt, and pepper in a mixing bowl. Divide evenly into 4 equal portions and shape each into a ¾-inch thick patty.

2 Place ¼ cup flour into a shallow dish and dredge each patty in flour.

3 Heat oil in a medium sauté pan over medium-high heat. When oil is hot, add patties and sauté 3 minutes on each side or until browned; remove from pan.

4 Add the onion, green pepper, and tomatoes to pan and sauté for 5 minutes. Stir in garlic and tomato paste and cook for 1 minute.

5 Sprinkle the onion mixture with 1 teaspoon flour and cook for 1 minute. Stir in the broth and wine; then add thyme. Return meat patties to the pan and bring broth to a boil.

6 Reduce heat to medium low, cover, and simmer 10 minutes. *Note:* Sauce will be thin like soup.

PER SERVING: *Calories 230 (From Fat 111); Fat 12g (Saturated 4g); Cholesterol 46mg; Sodium 266mg; Carbohydrate 11g (Dietary Fiber 2g); Protein 18g; Sugar 3g.*

Home-Style Meatloaf with Tomato Gravy

STAGE: REGULAR FOODS	PREP TIME: 15 MIN	COOK TIME: 1½ HR	YIELD: 8 SERVINGS

INGREDIENTS

1 teaspoon olive oil

1 medium onion, diced small

3 cloves garlic, minced

2 teaspoons dried thyme

½ teaspoon black pepper

2 pounds lean ground beef

1 cup wheat bran

4 tablespoons ketchup

1 tablespoon Worcestershire sauce

½ cup finely chopped flat-leaf parsley

2 large egg whites, beaten

Tomato Gravy (see the following recipe)

DIRECTIONS

1 Preheat the oven to 350 degrees. Coat a 9-x-5-x-3-inch loaf pan with nonstick cooking spray.

2 Heat the olive oil in a medium skillet. Sauté the onion and garlic until translucent but not brown, about 5 minutes. Add the thyme and pepper and sauté for 2 minutes. Remove pan from heat and allow to cool.

3 Combine the ground beef, bran, ketchup, Worcestershire sauce, parsley, and egg whites in a bowl and mix well. Stir in the cooled onion mixture.

4 Fill the loaf pan with the beef mixture. Bake the loaf approximately 1 hour 20 minutes, until the internal temperature of the meatloaf reaches 160 degrees. Top with Tomato Gravy.

Tomato Gravy

1 tablespoon canola oil

1 cup chopped onion

¼ teaspoon black pepper

One 16-ounce can no-salt-added tomato purée

1 teaspoon chopped fresh parsley

¼ teaspoon chopped fresh thyme

1 Heat the oil in a large sauté pan over medium-high heat. Add onion and sauté for 2 minutes.

2 Add black pepper, tomato purée, parsley, and fresh thyme. Bring to a light simmer for 5 minutes, stirring occasionally.

PER SERVING: *Calories 290 (From Fat 130); Fat 15g (Saturated 5g); Cholesterol 75mg; Sodium 210mg; Carbohydrate 16g (Dietary Fiber 5g); Protein 26g; Sugar 6g.*

Greek Meatballs with Yogurt Sauce

STAGE: SOFT FOODS | **PREP TIME: 10 MIN** | **COOK TIME: 40 MIN** | **YIELD: 6 SERVINGS**

INGREDIENTS

1 cup bread crumbs

¼ cup nonfat milk

¼ cup crumbled reduced-fat feta cheese

¼ cup fresh minced mint

2 tablespoons chopped green onion

2 teaspoons dried oregano leaves

1 egg, lightly beaten

1 pound lean ground beef

1 tablespoon olive oil

1 tablespoon minced garlic

Two 14.5-ounce cans low-sodium diced tomatoes

Yogurt Sauce (see the following recipe)

DIRECTIONS

1 Combine bread crumbs, milk, feta, mint, green onion, oregano, and egg in a mixing bowl. Stir in ground beef and mix lightly but well. Shape the mixture into 12 meatballs, each about 1 inch in diameter.

2 Heat oil in a large sauté pan over medium–high heat. When oil is hot, add the meatballs and brown on all sides, about 5 minutes. Remove them from the pan and cover with foil to keep them warm.

3 Add garlic to the pan and sauté for 1 minute. Stir in tomatoes and cook for 10 minutes. Return meatballs to the pan and simmer for 5 minutes or until cooked through. Serve with Yogurt Sauce.

Yogurt Sauce

¼ cup crumbled reduced-fat feta cheese

¼ cup nonfat Greek yogurt

2 tablespoons lemon juice

¼ teaspoon black pepper

Combine all ingredients in a bowl and stir well. Cover and chill until ready to use.

PER SERVING: *Calories 310 (From Fat 120); Fat 13g (Saturated 5g); Cholesterol 85mg; Sodium 430mg; Carbohydrate 23g (Dietary Fiber 3g); Protein 23g; Sugar 7g.*

Making Meaty Meals on a Stick

Meals on a stick, often called kebabs, are a great way to keep portion sizes in line because you can portion out the protein, fruits, and vegetables on each skewer. Kebabs are quick cooking in the oven or on the grill and fun to eat!

Spicy Pork Kebabs with Pineapple

STAGE: REGULAR FOODS	PREP TIME: 10 MIN	MARINATE TIME: 30 MIN	COOK TIME: 40 MIN	YIELD: 8 SERVINGS

INGREDIENTS

1 cup low-sodium soy sauce

1 teaspoon red pepper flakes

2 cloves garlic, minced

One 16-ounce can of pineapple chunks, drained, with pineapple juice reserved

2 pounds pork tenderloin

Sixteen 6-inch wooden skewers soaked in water for 20 minutes

DIRECTIONS

1 Combine soy sauce, red pepper flakes, garlic, and reserved pineapple juice in a large mixing bowl.

2 Slice tenderloin into 1-inch cubes. Add pork to marinade and marinate 30 minutes.

3 Preheat the oven to 325 degrees.

4 Fill skewers with alternating pieces of pineapple and pork, saving the marinade. Spray a baking sheet with nonstick cooking spray and place kebabs on baking sheet. Brush them with the marinade.

5 Bake for 30 to 40 minutes, until the internal temperature of the pork is 160 degrees.

PER SERVING: *Calories 160 (From Fat 25); Fat 3g (Saturated 1g); Cholesterol 75mg; Sodium 330mg; Carbohydrate 10g (Dietary Fiber 1g); Protein 24g; Sugar 8g.*

TIP: Some people have difficulty tolerating pineapple because it's a fibrous fruit that can cause sticking. Using canned pineapple instead of fresh can help with this, but if neither works for you, just substitute another fruit in this recipe.

Oriental Steak Strips with Mushrooms and Cherry Tomatoes

STAGE: REGULAR FOODS	PREP TIME: 10 MIN	MARINATE TIME: 1 HR	COOK TIME: 5 MIN	YIELD: 4 SERVINGS

INGREDIENTS

1 pound beef tenderloin, cut into 16 thin 3-inch strips

½ cup low-sodium teriyaki sauce

½ cup chopped green onion

1 tablespoon garlic powder

1 tablespoon sesame oil

8 small button mushrooms, washed

16 cherry tomatoes, washed

¼ teaspoon olive oil

Eight 6-inch wooden skewers soaked in water for 20 minutes

DIRECTIONS

1 Place the beef, teriyaki sauce, green onion, garlic powder, and sesame oil into a medium mixing bowl, and marinate for 1 hour in the refrigerator.

2 When done marinating, thread a piece of meat onto each skewer by piercing through one end and then the other. Add 2 cherry tomatoes, 1 mushroom, and a second piece of meat onto each skewer.

3 Heat a large skillet on medium–high heat and add olive oil. When olive oil is hot, add skewers and sauté for 1 minute on each side.

PER SERVING: *Calories 170 (From Fat 60); Fat 6g (Saturated 2g); Cholesterol 60mg; Sodium 320mg; Carbohydrate 6g (Dietary Fiber 1g); Protein 23g; Sugar 3g.*

Creating Can't-Go-Wrong Meaty Dinner Salads

Meats aren't just for hot dishes. If you have leftover beef or pork and plan to eat the leftovers, eat the meat cold in a salad. Reheating the meat will overcook it and it will be dry, tough, and difficult to get down (especially if you try to reheat in the microwave). If you want to make a meaty salad but don't have any leftover meats, choose reduced-sodium meats from the deli or rotisserie meats from the hot case.

Taco Salad

| STAGE: REGULAR FOODS | PREP TIME: 20 MIN | COOK TIME: 10 MIN | YIELD: 4 SERVINGS |

INGREDIENTS

1 pound lean ground beef

1 teaspoon garlic powder

1 teaspoon onion powder

1 teaspoon ground cumin

2 teaspoons chili powder

½ teaspoon salt

½ teaspoon black pepper

1 tablespoon corn starch

½ cup water

2 cups chopped lettuce

4 teaspoons shredded lowfat cheddar cheese

4 teaspoons sliced black olives

4 teaspoons chopped tomatoes

4 teaspoons mild salsa

DIRECTIONS

1 In a medium skillet, sauté the ground beef over medium-high heat until no longer pink, approximately 5 minutes. Drain the fat from meat. Return the pan to heat and add garlic powder, onion powder, cumin, chili powder, salt, and pepper to the meat.

2 In a small bowl, mix the cornstarch and water. Add to the pan and sauté for 3 minutes.

3 To plate the salads, place ½ cup of warm taco meat in the center of each dish. Top each with ½ cup lettuce and 1 teaspoon each of cheese, olives, tomatoes, and salsa.

PER SERVING: *Calories 230 (From Fat 110); Fat 12g (Saturated 5g); Cholesterol 75mg; Sodium 440mg; Carbohydrate 5g (Dietary Fiber 1g); Protein 24g; Sugar 1g.*

Chilled Roasted Vegetable Salad with Pork Tenderloin

STAGE: REGULAR FOODS	PREP TIME: 20 MIN	COOK TIME: 1½ HR	CHILL TIME: 2 HR	YIELD: 6 SERVINGS

INGREDIENTS

1 large baking potato

1 small onion, chopped

½ cup sliced carrots, cut into ¼-inch round slices

1 clove garlic, minced

3 tablespoons olive oil

1 teaspoon dried thyme

1 teaspoon chili powder

1 teaspoon dried rosemary

½ teaspoon salt

½ teaspoon black pepper

½ cup sliced yellow squash, cut in half lengthwise and cut into ¼-inch half-circle slices

½ cup sliced zucchini, cut in half lengthwise and cut into ¼-inch half-circle slices

1 pound raw pork tenderloin, cut into ½-inch cubes

DIRECTIONS

1 Cook the potato by baking for 45 minutes or until soft when pricked with a fork. Let the potato cool; then peel, cut in half, and slice into ¼-inch pieces.

2 Preheat the oven to 350 degrees.

3 Combine onion, carrots, garlic, olive oil, thyme, chili powder, rosemary, salt, and pepper in a large bowl and toss well. Place mixture into a 9-x-13-inch baking dish and roast in the oven for 20 minutes, stirring halfway through.

4 Remove the dish from the oven and mix in the potatoes, squash, and zucchini. Cook for another 10 minutes.

5 Remove the dish from the oven and stir in the pork cubes, and then cook for another 10 to 15 minutes until the internal temperature of the pork is 160 degrees. Let the dish chill for 2 hours before serving.

PER SERVING: *Calories 197 (From Fat 86); Fat 10g (Saturated 2g); Cholesterol 42mg; Sodium 239mg; Carbohydrate 11g (Dietary Fiber 2g); Protein 17g; Sugar 2g.*

Preparing Pork and Beef Main Entrées

"What's for dinner?" is the question of the day in the late afternoon. The typical response is a protein food, and protein remains the star of the show in these recipes. After weight loss surgery, you can combine a piece of meat with fruit or veggies to make a total meal. No matter how far out you are from surgery, meeting the protein guidelines from your surgeon will always be important.

Eating the same food prepared the same way can be monotonous. We bet the following recipes are something new for you. They'll be a treat for your family and are good enough for when company's comin'.

Don't be afraid to get all your prep done the morning or the day before. This speeds things up when you get home and gives you a head start on dinner. You can buy some vegetables already cut up from the produce department. They may cost a bit more, but your time is valuable, and there is less waste because you don't have to trim the produce and you may be able to buy a smaller quantity, getting just what you need.

Pork Loin with Greens and Exotic Mushroom Fried Rice

STAGE: REGULAR FOODS	PREP TIME: 10 MIN	COOK TIME: 30 MIN	YIELD: 4 SERVINGS

INGREDIENTS

8 ounces pork loin or pork chop, trimmed of excess fat and chopped

1 tablespoon canola oil

1 tablespoon peanut oil or canola oil

3 cups raw mixed greens, such as kale, Swiss chard, spinach, or turnip greens

1 cup chopped portobello, oyster, shiitake, or button mushrooms

1 egg

2 cups cooked brown rice

1 tablespoon soy sauce (not light)

1 teaspoon dark sesame oil

1 large green onion, minced

DIRECTIONS

1 In a large skillet or wok, sauté the pork in the canola oil until browned, about 10 to 15 minutes.

2 Remove from the heat and add the greens and mushrooms to the same pan, with the additional 1 tablespoon of oil. Stir-fry until wilted.

3 Crack the egg in the pan with the vegetables moved to the side, and stir with a fork or tongs until blended and it starts to scramble. Then mix the egg into the vegetables.

4 Lower the heat to medium low and add the rice, soy sauce, sesame oil, and pork. Stir for a few minutes until all are incorporated. Top with the green onion.

PER SERVING: Calories 277 (From Fat 104); Fat 12g (Saturated 2g); Cholesterol 36mg; Sodium 317mg; Carbohydrate 26g (Dietary Fiber 3g); Protein 17g; Sugar 1g.

Spanish Steak with Black Bean Salsa

STAGE: REGULAR FOODS	PREP TIME: 15 MIN	COOK TIME: 5 MIN	YIELD: 4 SERVINGS

INGREDIENTS

Four 4-ounce thin-sliced, boneless sirloin steaks

1 tablespoon olive oil

3 tablespoons lime juice

2 teaspoons butter

3 cloves garlic, peeled and minced

Salt and freshly ground black pepper to taste

1 fresh lime, cut into wedges

DIRECTIONS

1 Place the steaks between two sheets of plastic wrap and pound with a meat mallet to make them ¼-inch thick.

2 Heat the olive oil in a large sauté pan over high heat. Just before the oil starts to smoke, drop the steaks in, one or two at a time. Be very quick; cook each side no more than 1 minute.

3 When the steaks are cooked, remove them and cover to keep warm. Remove the pan from heat. Immediately deglaze the pan by adding lime juice and scraping up drippings from the bottom of the pan with a rubber spatula.

4 Add butter and garlic to the pan. Return the pan to low heat and cook until the garlic starts to brown. Pour the sauce over the steaks, season with salt and pepper, and serve with fresh lime sections and Black Bean Salsa (see the following recipe).

Black Bean Salsa

1 large tomato, cut into pieces

1 tomatillo, cut into pieces

½ small onion, cut into small pieces

4 cloves garlic, peeled and left whole

3 tablespoons chopped fresh cilantro

½ teaspoon cumin

6 tablespoons fresh lime juice

1 jalapeño pepper, seeded and veins removed

½ teaspoon salt

1 cup canned no-salt-added black beans, rinsed and drained

1 Place all ingredients except black beans into a food processor and pulse for 15 seconds. Using a rubber spatula, wipe down the sides of the bowl and pulse for 15 more seconds.

2 Stir in black beans. Serve ½ cup black bean salsa with each steak.

PER SERVING: *Calories 340 (From Fat 170); Fat 19g (Saturated 7g); Cholesterol 75mg; Sodium 490mg; Carbohydrate 17g (Dietary Fiber 4g); Protein 29g; Sugar 4g.*

Pork Tenderloin Cutlets with Pear and Ginger Sauce

STAGE: REGULAR FOODS	PREP TIME: 15 MIN	COOK TIME: 20 MIN	YIELD: 8 SERVINGS

INGREDIENTS

2 pounds pork tenderloin, cut into eight 4-ounce portions

1 teaspoon salt

1 teaspoon ground pepper, or to taste

2 teaspoons canola oil

3 tablespoons cider vinegar

2 tablespoons sugar

⅔ cup dry white wine

1 cup reduced-sodium chicken broth

1 medium firm, ripe pear, peeled, cored, and cut lengthwise into eighths

¼ cup thin slices fresh ginger root

6 green onions, trimmed and sliced into ½-inch lengths

2 teaspoons cornstarch

2 teaspoons cold water

DIRECTIONS

1 Season pork on both sides with salt and pepper.

2 Heat the oil in a large nonstick skillet over medium–high heat. Add the pork and cook until browned and just cooked through, 2 to 3 minutes per side. Transfer to a plate and cover to keep warm.

3 Pour off any oil from the pan and return to heat. Add the vinegar and sugar and stir to dissolve the sugar. Cook over medium–high heat until the syrup turns dark amber, about 10 to 20 seconds.

4 Pour in the wine (stand back, as the caramelized sugar may sputter) and bring to a simmer while stirring. Add the broth, pear slices, and ginger and bring to a simmer. Cook for 5 minutes, turning the pear slices occasionally.

5 Add green onions and cook until the pear slices are tender, about 2 minutes more. Add the cornstarch to cold water and stir to mix; then add to the skillet and cook, stirring, until slightly thickened. Reduce heat to low.

6 Return the pork and any accumulated juices to the pan; turn pork to coat with the sauce.

PER SERVING: *Calories 190 (From Fat 35); Fat 4g (Saturated 1g); Cholesterol 75mg; Sodium 360mg; Carbohydrate 10g (Dietary Fiber 1g); Protein 25g; Sugar 6g.*

Chapter 11

Let's Not Forget: Lamb and Other Meats

If life after weight loss surgery isn't enough of a new adventure for you, this chapter gives you the chance to further expand your taste buds. The following recipes include some protein foods that may be new to you or at least not a part of your regular diet.

Although they may sound gourmet or exotic to you, they're common meats in other parts of the world and cultures. For example, though Americans eat less than one pound of lamb per person a year, it's a diet staple in India, Greece, the Middle East, and Australia. You can find lamb at most grocery stores in chops, in roasts, or ground.

Liver tends to be a love-it-or-hate-it food. If you haven't tried it since your mom made you, give our recipe a try. No ketchup needed! We use chicken liver rather than calf or beef liver because chicken liver remains tender after cooking.

Back in the Wild West days, many folks lived on bison and venison. These days you don't have to hunt it on the plains; you can do your hunting in the meat case. You may be able to find bison at the fresh meat counter, but if not, look for ground bison in one-pound chubs in the frozen meat section. (Note that bison meat is sometimes called buffalo meat in the United States.)

Trying Out Lamb, Another Red Meat

Lamb is considered a red meat, but American domestic and imported lambs have very different taste and texture. American lamb is grain fed, which tends to give the meat a sweeter taste and smoother texture. Lamb imported to the United States comes mostly from Australia and is grass fed, which tends to make the meat taste a bit grainy and gamy (strong and tangy).

Lamb, like beef, is easiest to digest when cooked to medium doneness. This gives the fat a chance to melt and flavor and moisten the meat without overcooking. If left rare, the fat doesn't have a chance to cook through the muscle and the lamb may be tough. If cooked medium well to well done, most of the fat is cooked out and the lamb will be tough.

The four main cuts of lamb are the shoulder, rack, leg, and loin. Most of the grilling cuts come from the shoulder. The loin, leg, and racks are frequently used for roasting. Additionally, chops and riblets, the best cuts, are commonly found in your local grocer's meat department.

TIP

Buying lamb can be a bit confusing. Here are a few quick tips for buying the best cut for your recipe:

>> If you need a boneless leg of lamb, choose sirloin. It has the least amount of connective tissue, making it the most tender part of the leg.

>> If your recipe calls for rack of lamb, be prepared: It's the most expensive cut of lamb. Rack of lamb is most commonly served rare to medium rare. If overcooked, the lamb can become tough.

>> If you're looking for lamb chops, go for loin chops. They're the leanest and turn out well when grilled or sautéed.

>> If you want a cut of lamb for low and slow cooking, choose a roast or shoulder. They're larger and tougher than other cuts, so plenty of cooking time over low heat makes them tender.

REMEMBER

When making your lamb selection, choose raw meat with a pinkish color, which indicates freshness, not deep red or pale. Also, only buy cuts that have moderate fat marbling. Lamb is high in fat, so although you want enough marbling to keep the meat juicy and flavorful while cooking, you don't want to overdo it. Purchasing lamb from your local butcher typically gives you more choices, and they can trim outer fat for you.

Leg of Lamb with Thyme and Orange

STAGE: REGULAR FOODS	PREP TIME: 15 MIN	COOK TIME: 10 MIN	YIELD: 8 SERVINGS

INGREDIENTS

1 tablespoon chopped fresh thyme

1 tablespoon orange zest

3 cloves garlic, minced

1 teaspoon salt

1 teaspoon black pepper

2 pounds boneless lamb leg (3–3½ pounds bone-in)

1 tablespoon olive oil

DIRECTIONS

1 Preheat the broiler to high.

2 Combine the thyme, orange zest, garlic, salt, and pepper in a small bowl.

3 Place the lamb on a rimmed baking sheet. Using a sharp knife, make half a dozen ½-inch-deep slits on each side of the lamb. Fill each slit with ½ teaspoon of the thyme mixture. Rub any remaining mixture over both sides of lamb.

4 Brush the lamb lightly with olive oil. Broil until brown and crusty on top, about 5 minutes, and then flip over and broil for 5 more minutes. If needed, continue to broil until a meat thermometer inserted into thickest part registers 135 degrees for medium rare.

5 Transfer lamb to platter and let stand for 15 minutes. Slice thin to serve.

PER SERVING: *Calories 230 (From Fat 130); Fat 15g (Saturated 6g); Cholesterol 75mg; Sodium 360mg; Carbohydrate 1g (Dietary Fiber 0g); Protein 22g; Sugar 0g.*

TIP: To zest an orange, first wash and dry the fruit. Using a medium-fine grater, scrape the peel, stopping when you get to the bitter white layer, called the pith. Or you can use a chef's knife to cut off the colored part of the peel and finely dice it.

TIP: Have the butcher debone a cut if you can't find boneless.

Lamb Vindaloo

STAGE: REGULAR FOODS	PREP TIME: 10 MIN	MARINATE TIME: 8 HR	COOK TIME: 50 MIN	YIELD: 8 SERVINGS

INGREDIENTS

2 pounds boneless lamb loin, cut into ¾-inch cubes

3 tablespoons cider vinegar

2 teaspoons tamarind paste

Salt to taste

1 tablespoon plus 2 tablespoons canola oil

1 large white onion, quartered, plus 2 cups thinly slices onions

6 garlic cloves

2 tablespoons peeled and chopped fresh ginger root

1 teaspoon ground cumin

1 teaspoon ground mustard

2 teaspoons turmeric

½ teaspoon cayenne pepper

3 teaspoons paprika

1 teaspoon ground cinnamon

About 2 ¼ cups hot water

DIRECTIONS

1 Place the lamb cubes in a nonmetallic bowl with the vinegar, tamarind, and salt. Cover and marinade in the refrigerator for at least 8 hours.

2 Put 1 tablespoon of oil, the onion quarters, garlic, and ginger in a food processor, purée, and set aside.

3 Heat 2 tablespoons of oil in large skillet over medium-high heat.

4 Add the sliced onions and sauté until they're caramel brown, stirring constantly to avoid burning. Add the lamb (reserving the marinade) and cook until slightly seared on all sides, about 10 minutes total.

5 Add the onion purée to the pan. Reduce the heat to medium and add cumin, mustard, turmeric, cayenne pepper, paprika, and cinnamon.

6 Add enough hot water to the marinade to make 2½ cups of liquid. Pour it into the pan and bring to a boil, then lower the heat and simmer, partially covered, until the meat is very tender (about 30 minutes).

PER SERVING: *Calories 240 (From Fat 120); Fat 13g (Saturated 4g); Cholesterol 75mg; Sodium 90mg; Carbohydrate 6g (Dietary Fiber 1g); Protein 25g; Sugar 2g.*

Roasted Rack of Lamb

STAGE: REGULAR FOODS	PREP TIME: 15 MIN	COOK TIME: 30 MIN	YIELD: 8 SERVINGS

INGREDIENTS

2 teaspoons fresh thyme

1 teaspoon salt

1 teaspoon black pepper

2 pounds rack of lamb chops

1 tablespoon olive oil

DIRECTIONS

1 Preheat the oven to 350 degrees.

2 Combine the thyme, salt, and pepper in a small bowl. Sprinkle the seasoning all over the meat.

3 Add olive oil to a large skillet and heat over high heat. Brown the lamb for 3 minutes on each side.

4 Transfer the lamb to roasting pan and roast, fat side up, in the middle of the oven for 14 to 16 minutes, or until the internal temperature is 130 degrees for medium rare.

5 Transfer the rack of lamb to a warm platter and let it rest for 10 minutes. Cut the rack into individual chops and serve.

PER SERVING: *Calories 210 (From Fat 110); Fat 12g (Saturated 4g); Cholesterol 75mg; Sodium 370mg; Carbohydrate 0g (Dietary Fiber 0g); Protein 23g; Sugar 0g.*

NOTE: Rack of lamb has a lot of flavor by itself, so be careful not to over-season. A little thyme, salt, and pepper is all that is needed when roasting this delicate cut of lamb.

Greek Meatballs with Tzatziki

STAGE: REGULAR FOODS	PREP TIME: 5 MIN	CHILL TIME: 30 MIN–12 HR	COOK TIME: 6 MIN	YIELD: 4 SERVINGS

INGREDIENTS

1 pound lamb loin ground

4 cloves garlic, minced

3 tablespoons grated onion

3 tablespoons chopped fresh flat-leaf parsley

1 teaspoon ground coriander

1 teaspoon ground cumin

½ teaspoon ground allspice

¼ teaspoon cayenne pepper

½ teaspoon black pepper

Eight 6-inch wooden skewers soaked in water for 20 minutes

1 tablespoon olive oil

Tzatziki (see the following recipe)

DIRECTIONS

1 Place lamb and the next 8 ingredients in a large bowl and mix well. Divide the meat mixture into 8 balls.

2 Mold each piece around the pointed end of a skewer, making a 2-inch oval meatball that comes to a point just covering the tip of the skewer. Lay the skewers on a foil-lined pan, cover, and refrigerate for at least 30 minutes and up to 12 hours.

3 Heat a grill to medium heat. Brush the grill grates with olive oil. Place the skewered meatballs on the grill, turning occasionally, until brown all over and just cooked through, about 6 minutes.

4 Slide meatballs off the skewers onto a serving platter and serve with tzatziki.

Tzatziki

½ medium cucumber, grated

½ cup fat-free sour cream

1 clove garlic, minced

1½ teaspoons lemon juice

1½ teaspoons olive oil

½ teaspoon salt

1 After cucumber is grated, squeeze out all the moisture by placing it in a strainer and pressing against it with the back of a large spoon. Discard the liquid.

2 In a medium bowl, mix together the squeezed cucumber, sour cream, minced garlic, lemon juice, oil, and salt. Refrigerate until ready to use.

PER SERVING: *Calories 290 (From Fat 150); Fat 17g (Saturated 8g); Cholesterol 80mg; Sodium 400mg; Carbohydrate 8g (Dietary Fiber 1g); Protein 24g; Sugar 3g.*

Discovering a Lick-Your-Plate Liver Dish

Come into this section with an open mind. Sure, as a kid you dreaded liver, which no amount of ketchup could improve. But when liver is prepared correctly, you don't need the ketchup bottle to get it down.

Calf and chicken liver are both tasty and can be cooked in similar ways. However, calf liver can only be cooked until pink in the center or it becomes tough and chewy, and chicken liver remains tender even when thoroughly cooked. To cook, sautéing is recommended. Make sure the pan is hot before adding the meat to allow it to cook quickly and stay tender.

Protein-rich liver is loaded with B vitamins, vitamins A and D, iron, selenium, and zinc. However, it's also very high in cholesterol. Ounce for ounce, chicken liver is higher in cholesterol and iron than beef liver and slightly lower in calories. Braunschweiger, or liver sausage, is almost double the calories of fresh animal liver because it is very high in fat, and it has less protein, cholesterol, and iron. If you're a liver lover, limit your intake of any kind of liver to no more than once a week because of the high cholesterol and vitamin A content. (Too much vitamin A over a short period of time can cause hypervitaminosis A, which can cause a host of ailments including liver problems and bone loss.)

Curried Chicken Liver

STAGE: SOFT FOODS	PREP TIME: 5 MIN	COOK TIME: 20 MIN	YIELD: 4 SERVINGS

INGREDIENTS

5 teaspoons curry powder

¼ teaspoon ground cloves

1 teaspoon onion powder

1 tablespoon poppy seeds

1 pinch saffron

1 tablespoon canola oil

¼ teaspoon turmeric

½ teaspoon red chili powder

1 teaspoon minced garlic

1 teaspoon minced ginger

1 pound fresh chicken liver, washed, drained, and trimmed

¾ cup low-sodium chicken broth

DIRECTIONS

1 Mix together the curry powder, cloves, onion powder, poppy seeds, and saffron. Set aside.

2 Heat oil in a large skillet over medium-high heat. Add turmeric, chili powder, garlic, and ginger and sauté for 2 minutes. Add liver and the spice mixture and sauté for 3 minutes.

3 Add the chicken broth. Cover and cook over medium heat for 15 minutes, or until sauce thickens.

PER SERVING: *Calories 190 (From Fat 100); Fat 11g (Saturated 3g); Cholesterol 390mg; Sodium 100mg; Carbohydrate 2g (Dietary Fiber 0g); Protein 21g; Sugar 0g.*

TIP: This dish goes perfectly with whole-grain rice.

Staying Lean with Venison and Bison Meals

Home on the range in your own kitchen is where you can cook bison (also called buffalo in the United States). Bison is becoming more popular with consumers because of its sweet taste and lowfat content. Unlike most beef cattle, which are grain-fed, bison are usually grass- or pasture-fed, which means the meat is lower in saturated fat and cholesterol. Grass-fed animals aren't confined or caged but allowed to roam about, and they're generally free of antibiotics, pesticides, and hormones. (Note that bison may be fed grain and forage just prior to processing.) And there's no need to worry about bison becoming extinct. Through careful breeding, bison numbers have returned.

Venison typically refers to meat from the deer family. Most venison eaten at home comes from animals shot in the wild, but venison farms do exist. Restaurants that have venison listed on their menus generally buy farmed meat. If you haven't tried it before, be prepared for its gamy taste, which some people love.

REMEMBER

Bison and venison are very lean, so they can be tough if cooked past medium. Venison is easiest to digest if cooked to medium rare or medium, although to be safe you may want to cook until it reaches an internal temperature of 155 degrees. Bison is leaner than beef, so to maintain its tenderness you need to cook it low and slow to allow the juices to flow as it's cooking.

Venison Chili

STAGE: SOFT FOODS	PREP TIME: 5 MIN	COOK TIME: 20 MIN	YIELD: 8 SERVINGS

INGREDIENTS

1 pound ground venison

2 teaspoons chopped garlic

½ cup chopped onions

14 ounces no-salt-added tomato sauce

14 ounces no-salt-added diced tomatoes, drained

2 teaspoons chili powder

1 teaspoon ground cumin

½ teaspoon black pepper

1 cup canned black beans, drained

1 cup canned pinto beans, drained

DIRECTIONS

Place all ingredients into a medium pot and bring to a simmer. Cook for 20 minutes.

PER SERVING: *Calories 177 (From Fat 41); Fat 5g (Saturated 1g); Cholesterol 46mg; Sodium 378mg; Carbohydrate 16g (Dietary Fiber 5g); Protein 17g; Sugar 2g.*

Bison Stew

STAGE: REGULAR FOODS	PREP TIME: 10 MIN	COOK TIME: 8 HR	YIELD: 8 SERVINGS

INGREDIENTS

1 pound cubed bison stewing meat

8 small red potatoes cut into quarters

½ cup chopped onions

8 ounces baby carrots

2 cups sliced fresh shiitake mushrooms

One 14.5-ounce can low-sodium beef broth

½ cup all-purpose flour

1 tablespoon Worcestershire sauce

1 teaspoon salt

1 teaspoon dried marjoram leaves

¼ teaspoon pepper

½ cup red wine

DIRECTIONS

Place all ingredients in a crockpot and stir. Cover and cook on medium setting for 8 hours.

PER SERVING: *Calories 250 (From Fat 50); Fat 6g (Saturated 2g); Cholesterol 30mg; Sodium 380mg; Carbohydrate 29g (Dietary Fiber 4g); Protein 18g; Sugar 4g.*

TIP: If your crockpot only has low and high settings, use high to cook and low to keep the dish warm.

TIP: This dish freezes well and is great served over fresh steamed spaghetti squash.

Bison Sliders

STAGE: REGULAR FOODS	PREP TIME: 10 MIN	COOK TIME: 15 MIN	YIELD: 4 SERVINGS

INGREDIENTS

1 pound ground bison meat

½ cup minced fresh mushrooms

¼ teaspoon salt

¼ teaspoon pepper

¼ teaspoon onion powder

¼ teaspoon garlic powder

2 teaspoons canola oil

8 whole-grain mini rolls

Butter lettuce or spinach leaves

Dijon mustard, to taste

DIRECTIONS

1 In a medium bowl, mix the bison, mushrooms, salt, pepper, onion powder, and garlic powder. Form 8 patties.

2 In a large skillet, heat the oil.

3 Add the patties to the skillet and cook at least 4 to 5 minutes each side until no longer pink and/or a meat thermometer inserted into the center registers 155 degrees.

4 Remove from the heat and place each patty on a bun with lettuce and mustard. Serve two sliders per person.

PER SERVING: *Calories 345 (From Fat 116); Fat 13g (Saturated 4g); Cholesterol 62mg; Sodium 494mg; Carbohydrate 28g (Dietary Fiber 1g); Protein 29g; Sugar 4g.*

Chapter **12**

Catching On to Fish and Seafood

Fish and other seafood work well for people recovering from weight loss surgery. When cooked correctly, it's soft and moist and is one of the first solid foods you can introduce back into your diet. Your pouch can tolerate it well, so you don't experience that "ugh" feeling of food not setting well that you may get with meat.

Buying, Storing, and Cooking Fish and Seafood

Fish and seafood taste great, but in order to get great tasting dishes you need to make sure your fish and seafood are in their best condition. This section gives you great pointers on how to store, buy, and cook your proteins from the water. These tips are practical and easy to follow.

Buying tips

The two most common ways to purchase fish are fresh and frozen. Fresh fish is a great option if you live near the coast or your grocery stocks good-quality seafood, but in some landlocked places, frozen is a better choice because fresh fish can take up to two days to get to the store.

Don't buy fresh fish that's slimy to the touch or has a strong odor. The eyes of a fish can tell you a lot as well: If the eyes are cloudy, the fish is old, so make sure they're clear. You can also test freshness by seeing if the flesh of the fish springs back up when you press down on it. Beware of "fresh frozen," which is just a marketing term used for selling frozen fish.

Frozen fish typically comes IQF, individual quality frozen, which means each piece of fish is frozen separately and bagged together. This allows you to take out what you need and leave the remainder for another meal. You may also find *cryovact* frozen fish, which means that each single serving or piece of fish is sealed inside airtight plastic wrap. All frozen fish has an expiration date, so make sure you check the date before you buy.

TIP

Due to high demand for fish and seafood around the world, many types are over-fished or caught or farmed in destructive ways, which can lead to damaged ecosystems and possible extinction of some species. To find out the best choices when shopping for seafood, check out the Seafood Watch guide put out by the Monterey Bay Aquarium, available at www.seafoodwatch.org.

Storing tips

To properly store fresh fish and seafood, follow these steps:

1. **Remove from store wrapping.**

2. **Wipe its surface with a damp cloth. If the fish is whole, wash and pat dry.**

3. **Wrap food in wax paper and place in a tightly covered container.**

4. **Refrigerate immediately at 34 to 36 degrees.**

For long-term storage, freeze immediately.

Here are some tips for storing frozen fish and seafood:

>> If in a sealed package (not store-packaged), keep products in their original sealed packages and store immediately in the freezer.

>> Keep store-packaged products in their original wrapping and seal inside an airtight freezer bag or container. Store immediately in the freezer.

>> Store at 0 degrees or lower.

>> Use within the following recommended storage periods:

- *Lean fish (cod, Dover sole, haddock, snapper):* 6 months

- *Medium-fat fish (halibut, sea bass, orange roughy):* 4 months

- *Fatty fish (salmon, tuna, mahi-mahi):* 2 months

- *Shrimp:* 4 months

Cooking tips

Many people are afraid to cook fish at home, but it doesn't have to be difficult. Fish is not only healthy but also easy to cook. The average cooking time is typically the same as or less than for poultry.

REMEMBER

Overcooking fish makes the meat tough and destroys flavor. Fish is done when the flesh turns opaque and begins to flake easily when tested with a fork. Cooking times vary with each fish and cut. The following are typical cooking times:

>> 10 minutes per inch of fresh or thawed fish cooked without sauce

>> 5 minutes per inch of fresh or thawed fish cooked in a sauce

>> 20 minutes per inch of fish if cooked from frozen

There's a delicate balance between perfectly cooked fish and overcooked fish. For best results, cook fish until it's almost done; then remove it from heat and let stand for a few minutes to finish cooking with residual heat.

Fish is versatile, and many cooking methods work well. The best method is sautéing, which uses high heat and little fat and cooks the fish quickly. The oven also works great when broiling under high heat or baking at 350 degrees. Grilling also works, but make sure the grill isn't too hot; medium heat is recommended.

Stewing and use of a slow cooker are not recommended. When subjected to long cooking, fish becomes mushy and falls apart.

Grilling, Sautéing, and Baking Fish

When shopping for fish, you have dozens of varieties to choose from, even if you don't live near water. Salmon is the most popular fish in the United States and for good reason; it tastes good and is good for you.

If you don't like a strong tasting fish, whitefish is your best choice because of its delicate flavor. And when it comes to seafood, shrimp is the first choice in the United States. About 90 percent of the shrimp consumed in the United States is imported from overseas and a majority of that is farmed-raised. If the option is available to you, buy wild fish and seafood rather than farm raised. Wild fish and seafood have less fat, more protein, and fewer pollutants than farm raised. You can taste the difference.

Angel Hair and Salmon with Spicy Basil Sauce

STAGE: REGULAR FOODS	PREP TIME: 10 MIN	COOK TIME: 20 MIN	YIELD: 3 SERVINGS

INGREDIENTS

1 tablespoon butter

8 ounces fresh salmon, boned and skinned

1 small onion, minced

1 teaspoon chopped fresh jalapeño pepper, seeds and veins removed

1 medium tomato, chopped

¼ cup bottled clam juice

¼ cup dry white wine

½ cup fat-free half-and-half

3 tablespoons finely chopped basil

1 tablespoon finely chopped fresh parsley

½ teaspoon salt

½ teaspoon pepper

4 ounces dry whole-wheat angel hair pasta

DIRECTIONS

1 Cook pasta until it is soft all the way through (not al dente). Drain and set aside.

2 Melt 1 tablespoon butter in a medium sauté pan over medium heat. When the butter has melted, add the salmon and sauté until opaque, 2 to 3 minutes. Transfer to a plate and cut into ¾–inch cubes.

3 Add the onion, jalapeño, and tomato to the pan and sauté for 2 minutes. Add the clam juice and wine. Turn heat to high and boil until sauce thickens, about 5 minutes.

4 Add the half-and-half and basil to the sauté pan. Lightly simmer until the sauce thickens again, about 5 minutes.

5 Turn the heat to low. Fold in the parsley, salt, and pepper. Add the cooked pasta and salmon to the sauce, toss gently, and serve.

PER SERVING: *Calories 302 (From Fat 66); Fat 7g (Saturated 3g); Cholesterol 54mg; Sodium 528mg; Carbohydrate 34g (Dietary Fiber 5g); Protein 24g; Sugar 5g.*

Salmon with Honey–Garlic–Caramelized Onions

STAGE: SOFT FOODS	PREP TIME: 10 MIN	COOK TIME: 35 MIN	YIELD: 4 SERVINGS

INGREDIENTS

1 tablespoon butter

1 large onion, cut in half lengthwise, sliced, and separated into thin rings

1 tablespoon balsamic vinegar

2 teaspoons honey

1 clove fresh garlic minced

1 pound salmon fillets cut into 4 equal pieces

Salt and pepper to taste

DIRECTIONS

1 Preheat the oven to 400 degrees. Spray a baking sheet with nonstick cooking spray.

2 Melt butter in a large skillet over medium-high heat. Add onion rings to the pan.

3 Reduce heat to low and cook onion for 10 minutes, stirring frequently. Reduce heat to low and cook for 10 more minutes. Then stir in vinegar, honey, and garlic.

4 While onions are cooking, rinse salmon and place on the prepared baking sheet. Sprinkle both sides with a little salt and pepper. Bake for 10 to 15 minutes, depending on thickness. Serve topped with onions.

PER SERVING: *Calories 290 (From Fat 160); Fat 18g (Saturated 5g); Cholesterol 70mg; Sodium 95mg; Carbohydrate 7g (Dietary Fiber 1g); Protein 24g; Sugar 5g.*

Tasty Salmon Cakes

STAGE: SOFT OR REGULAR FOODS	PREP TIME: 10 MIN	COOK TIME: 20 MIN	YIELD: 2 SERVINGS

INGREDIENTS

One 14-ounce can salmon

2 eggs

1 tablespoon deli or Dijon mustard

1 large shallot, minced

½ cup celery or green pepper, minced (or 1 tablespoon celery flakes if the fibers are an issue)

1 tablespoon garlic pepper unsalted seasoning, such as Mrs. Dash or other seasoning blend

½ cup crushed corn flakes or whole-wheat panko crumbs

DIRECTIONS

1 Preheat the oven to 400 degrees.

2 In a medium bowl, blend all the ingredients with a fork and form into four patties.

3 Place on a baking sheet lined with aluminum foil and bake for 6 to 8 minutes each side.

4 Cool and serve.

PER SERVING: *Calories 85 (From Fat 12); Fat 1g (Saturated 0g); Cholesterol 8mg; Sodium 329mg; Carbohydrate 10g (Dietary Fiber 1g); Protein 8g; Sugar 1g.*

Herb-Infused Poached Mahi-Mahi

STAGE: SOFT OR REGULAR FOODS	PREP TIME: 10 MIN	COOK TIME: 15 MIN	YIELD: 4 SERVINGS

INGREDIENTS

2 teaspoons refined sesame oil or canola

Four 4-ounce pieces of fresh mahi-mahi or other firm fish such as grouper or swordfish

¼ teaspoon salt

¼ teaspoon pepper

¼ cup white wine

Zest of 1 small lemon

½ cup homemade chicken, vegetable, or fish broth

¼ cup chopped fresh herbs (basil, thyme, chives, dill) or 2 teaspoons dried

Juice of lemon

Mustard-Dill Vinaigrette (see the following recipe)

DIRECTIONS

1 In a skillet, heat the oil on medium-high heat.

2 Season the fish with the salt and pepper and sear on each side for 2 to 3 minutes until browned.

3 Lower the heat to medium and add the wine and lemon zest. Simmer for 2 minutes.

4 Add the broth and herbs and simmer for 8 to 10 minutes.

5 Remove from the heat and add the lemon juice. Season to taste.

6 Add the mustard dill vinaigrette and serve.

Mustard-Dill Vinaigrette

3 tablespoons Dijon or yellow mustard

2 tablespoons minced fresh dill or 2 teaspoons dried dill

2 teaspoons honey or sugar substitute

2 tablespoons fresh lemon juice

¼ cup canola or light olive oil

Pinch of salt

Pinch of pepper

Combine all the ingredients in a jar and shake.

PER SERVING: Calories 376 (From Fat 248); Fat 28g (Saturated 6g); Cholesterol 57mg; Sodium 485mg; Carbohydrate 8g (Dietary Fiber 1g); Protein 23g; Sugar 4g.

Lemon Garlic Dover Sole

STAGE: SOFT FOODS | **PREP TIME: 5 MIN** | **COOK TIME: 6 MIN** | **YIELD: 4 SERVINGS**

INGREDIENTS

1 tablespoon butter

2 teaspoons minced garlic

1 teaspoon lemon pepper

1 pound Dover sole fillets

1 lemon wedge

DIRECTIONS

1 Melt butter in a large skillet over medium–high heat. Stir in the garlic.

2 Season the fish on both sides with lemon pepper. Place the fish in the pan and cook for 2 to 3 minutes on the first side; then turn fillets and cook for an additional 1 minute, or until fish flakes easily with a fork.

3 Squeeze the lemon wedge over the cooked fish to sprinkle with juice.

PER SERVING: *Calories 140 (From Fat 45); Fat 5g (Saturated 2g); Cholesterol 60mg; Sodium 150mg; Carbohydrate 1g (Dietary Fiber 0g); Protein 21g; Sugar 0g.*

Stove-top Weeknight Fish with Leeks and Scallions

STAGE: REGULAR FOODS	PREP TIME: 10 MIN	COOK TIME: 10–15 MIN	YIELD: 3 SERVINGS

INGREDIENTS

2 tablespoons olive oil, divided

Three 3- to 4-ounce fillets of white fish (tilapia, cod, or catfish), fresh or thawed

¼ teaspoon salt

¼ teaspoon pepper

¼ teaspoon dried Herbs de Provence

2 fresh leeks, sliced and rinsed

2 to 3 scallions, minced

1 clove garlic, minced

1 cup chicken stock or ½ cup water and ½ cup white wine

2 to 3 teaspoons dried herbs

½ lemon, zested and juiced

DIRECTIONS

1 Preheat a large skillet on medium heat and add 1 tablespoon of the olive oil.

2 Season the fish with the salt, pepper, and Herbs de Provence.

3 Cook the fish for 3 to 4 minutes on each side until opaque; remove from the heat.

4 Heat the remaining 1 tablespoon of olive oil and add the leeks, scallions, and garlic; stir for a few minutes until soft.

5 Add the chicken stock, or the water and white wine, and the dried herbs. Heat to simmer. Reduce the heat for 3 to 4 minutes.

6 Add the fish back in and simmer for 1 to 2 minutes.

7 Sprinkle with lemon zest and juice.

PER SERVING: *Calories 261 (From Fat 109); Fat 12g (Saturated 2g); Cholesterol 59mg; Sodium 381mg; Carbohydrate 13g (Dietary Fiber 1g); Protein 26g; Sugar 5g.*

Sea Bass with Herb-Spiced Pecans

STAGE: REGULAR FOODS	PREP TIME: 10 MIN	COOK TIME: 15 MIN	YIELD: 4 SERVINGS

INGREDIENTS

¼ cup dry white wine

2 tablespoons white wine vinegar

2 tablespoons finely chopped onion

2 tablespoons fat-free half-and-half

1 large tomato, chopped

1 tablespoon melted butter

1 pound sea bass, skinned and filleted

¼ teaspoon Spice Mixture (see the following recipe)

Spicy Pecans (see the following recipe)

DIRECTIONS

1 In a small saucepan over high heat, bring wine, vinegar, and onion to a boil. Cook until most of the liquid is gone, about 2 minutes.

2 Add fat-free half-and-half and ¾ of the tomato. Turn heat to low and simmer, approximately 6 minutes. Keep warm while cooking fish.

3 Heat the grill to medium-high heat.

4 Brush butter over the fish fillets. Sprinkle the fish with Spice Mixture. Grill for 2 to 3 minutes per side.

5 Ladle the sauce onto a warmed serving plate. Lay the cooked fish fillet on top of the sauce. Sprinkle with the Spicy Pecans and then top with the remaining chopped tomatoes.

Spice Mixture

1 teaspoon paprika

¼ teaspoon onion powder

¼ teaspoon dried basil

¼ teaspoon white pepper

½ teaspoon garlic powder

¼ teaspoon dried thyme

⅛ teaspoon dry mustard

⅛ teaspoon dried oregano

⅛ teaspoon crushed rosemary

Combine all spices in a bowl and set aside.

Spicy Pecans

¼ cup coarsely chopped pecans

¼ teaspoon dried thyme

¼ teaspoon dried oregano

¼ teaspoon Spice Mixture
(see previous recipe)

⅛ teaspoon allspice

2 teaspoons butter

1 Mix all the ingredients except butter in a small bowl.

2 Melt the butter in a small skillet over medium heat and add the spices and pecans. Sauté for 4 minutes or until pecans are golden brown. Transfer nuts to a small dish once toasted.

PER SERVING: *Calories 230 (From Fat 110); Fat 12g (Saturated 4g); Cholesterol 60mg; Sodium 125mg; Carbohydrate 4g (Dietary Fiber 1g); Protein 22g; Sugar 2g.*

NOTE: Although we recommend grilling the fish, this recipe is also great when baked at 350 degrees for about 7 to 9 minutes.

TIP: The spice mixture makes more than you need for this recipe, so store it in an airtight container and use it to season fish, poultry, or vegetables.

Parmesan Baked Haddock

STAGE: SOFT FOODS | **PREP TIME: 10 MIN** | **COOK TIME: 20 MIN** | **YIELD: 4 SERVINGS**

INGREDIENTS

½ cup all-purpose flour

1 pound haddock fillets cut into 4 equal pieces

1 egg white

4 teaspoons grated Parmesan cheese

¼ teaspoon salt

¼ teaspoon pepper

½ teaspoon paprika

DIRECTIONS

1 Preheat the oven to 375 degrees. Put the flour in a shallow bowl or small plate and coat fish on each side with flour.

2 Beat egg white in a bowl with a fork until foamy. Dip fish on each side in egg white.

3 Spray a baking sheet with nonstick cooking spray. Place fish on the baking sheet and sprinkle evenly with Parmesan cheese, salt, pepper, and paprika.

4 Bake for 15 to 20 minutes, or until fish is browned and flakes easily with a fork.

PER SERVING: Calories 120 (From Fat 20); Fat 2g (Saturated 0g); Cholesterol 65mg; Sodium 260mg; Carbohydrate 2g (Dietary Fiber 0g); Protein 23g; Sugar 0g.

A sampling of smooth foods: Coconut Kiwi smoothie (Chapter 14), Mango Cream (Chapter 19), Spicy Pumpkin Yogurt (Chapter 7), and Sweet Potato Bake (Chapter 17).

Soft foods ideal for breakfast: Triple Berry Yogurt Parfait and Havarti Scramble with Salmon (both in Chapter 7)

Soft foods for lunch or dinner: Italian Halibut (Chapter 12), Vegetable Soup (Chapter 20), and Greek Meatballs with Yogurt Sauce (Chapter 10)

Starting the day off right: Swiss Oatmeal and Canadian Bacon and Spinach Frittata (both in Chapter 7)

A few lunchtime options: Curried Apple and Tuna Salad, Orzo and Salmon Salad

Dinnertime favorites: Fresh Spinach Salad with Roasted Corn (Chapter 13)

More tasty choices for dinner: Sautéed Shrimp with Asparagus Tips (Chapter 12)

Delicious appetizers, snacks, and desserts: Apples with Honey Almond Butter (Chapter 18), Chocolate and Strawberry Layered Pudding (Chapter 19), Thai Chicken Wraps (Chapter 15), and Crab-Stuffed Deviled Eggs (Chapter 15).

Italian Halibut

STAGE: SOFT FOODS | PREP TIME: 5 MIN | COOK TIME: 20 MIN | YIELD: 6 SERVINGS

INGREDIENTS

1½ pounds halibut fillets, cut into 6 equal pieces

½ cup sliced mushrooms

¼ cup sliced black olives

1 cup prepared spaghetti sauce

½ cup shredded part-skim mozzarella cheese

DIRECTIONS

1 Preheat the oven to 400 degrees. Spray a baking pan with nonstick cooking spray. Place fish in the pan.

2 Top with the mushrooms and olives. Pour spaghetti sauce over the top and bake for 10 minutes.

3 Remove from the oven and sprinkle with cheese. Bake 10 more minutes or until the fish flakes easily with a fork.

PER SERVING: *Calories 180 (From Fat 45); Fat 5g (Saturated 2g); Cholesterol 40mg; Sodium 380mg; Carbohydrate 6g (Dietary Fiber 2g); Protein 26g; Sugar 3g.*

Serving Up Super Shrimp Recipes

We're not just fishing around in this chapter; there are other treasures in the sea. Shrimp is the most popular seafood. You can find it fresh or frozen, raw or cooked, tail on or tail off.

There are also different sizes of shrimp ranging from colossal to extra small. The larger the shrimp, the more fibrous it is and more chewing it requires. Picking smaller shrimp makes it less likely that the shrimp will cause sticking problems.

No matter the size, they're not shrimpy in the nutrition department. Shrimp are low calorie, lowfat, and high in protein. They are high in cholesterol but have half the amount of cholesterol of eggs for the same weight.

Sautéed Shrimp with Asparagus Tips

STAGE: REGULAR FOODS	PREP TIME: 5 MIN	COOK TIME: 7 MIN	YIELD: 4 SERVINGS

INGREDIENTS

1 tablespoon olive oil

1 cup raw asparagus tips (the top two inches of each spear)

1 pound raw medium shrimp, peeled and deveined (see Figure 12-1)

2 tablespoons garlic, minced

1 teaspoon red pepper flakes

1 tablespoon lemon juice

2 tablespoons white wine

¼ teaspoon salt

1 teaspoon butter

1 tablespoon chopped fresh parsley

DIRECTIONS

1 Heat the oil in a skillet over medium heat. When oil is hot, add asparagus tips and cook for about 4 minutes.

2 Add the shrimp, garlic, pepper flakes, lemon juice, wine, and salt. Cover and cook for 3 minutes.

3 Uncover and mix in the butter. Remove from heat and mix in the parsley.

PER SERVING: *Calories 200 (From Fat 60); Fat 7g (Saturated 2g); Cholesterol 175mg; Sodium 320mg; Carbohydrate 5g (Dietary Fiber 1g); Protein 24g; Sugar 1g.*

NOTE: Even though shrimp and asparagus can sometimes cause food sticking, using smaller shrimp and only the tips of the asparagus reduce the chances.

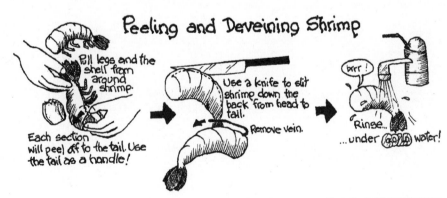

FIGURE 12-1:
How to peel and devein shrimp.

Illustration by Elizabeth Kurtzman

Shrimp Louie

STAGE: REGULAR FOODS | PREP TIME: 10 MIN | YIELD: 2 SERVINGS

INGREDIENTS

¼ cup light mayonnaise

1 tablespoon purchased chili sauce

1½ teaspoons dry mustard

1½ tablespoons fresh lemon juice

¼ teaspoon black pepper

2 cups mixed baby greens

¼ avocado, peeled and chopped

6 ounces cooked bay (cold-water) shrimp

1 green onion, finely chopped

DIRECTIONS

1 To make the dressing, combine mayonnaise, chili sauce, mustard, lemon juice, and pepper in a small bowl and blend.

2 Arrange greens on 2 plates and top with avocado and shrimp. Spoon on dressing and sprinkle with green onion.

PER SERVING: *Calories 260 (From Fat 130); Fat 15g (Saturated 1g); Cholesterol 175mg; Sodium 700mg; Carbohydrate 14g (Dietary Fiber 4g); Protein 20g; Sugar 4g.*

Taking Shortcuts with Canned Fish and Seafood

If you've checked out the canned fish section at the grocery store lately, you know there's much more than canned tuna available. You can find a variety of fish, plain or already seasoned. Keeping a selection in your pantry makes for quick meals without having to worry about keeping perishable fresh seafood on hand.

You may have noticed that you can buy chunk (flaked) or solid tuna. Chunk is flaked, separated pieces of the fillet, and solid is part of the whole fillet. Flake tends to be a bit more moist.

In addition, you can choose between cans and pouches of fish and seafood. Pouches contain less liquid and more food than cans, and the taste is better. Pouches tend to cost a little more, but the taste difference is worth it.

Black-Eyed Dill Tuna

STAGE: REGULAR FOODS	PREP TIME: 15 MIN	YIELD: 4 SERVINGS

INGREDIENTS

One 15-ounce can black-eyed peas, drained and rinsed

1 medium red pepper, finely diced

One 6-ounce can water-packed chunk light tuna, drained and flaked

2 hard-boiled eggs, chopped fine

¼ cup finely chopped onion

2 tablespoons lemon juice

1½ tablespoons olive oil

2 teaspoons chopped fresh dill

DIRECTIONS

Place all ingredients in a medium bowl and stir to combine.

PER SERVING: *Calories 150 (From Fat 70); Fat 8g (Saturated 2g); Cholesterol 120mg; Sodium 420mg; Carbohydrate 7g (Dietary Fiber 3g); Protein 15g; Sugar 2g.*

TIP: To hard-boil eggs, place eggs into a medium-sized pot and cover with water. Place on the stove and bring to a boil, then turn off the heat and let the eggs sit in the hot water for 12 to 15 minutes. Refrigerate eggs until you're ready to use them.

Crab Salad Melts

STAGE: REGULAR FOODS	PREP TIME: 10 MIN	COOK TIME: 3 MIN	YIELD: 2 SERVINGS

INGREDIENTS

One 6.5-ounce can crab meat, drained

¼ cup finely chopped celery

¼ cup finely chopped red pepper

1 tablespoon chopped green onion

1 teaspoon finely chopped fresh cilantro

4 teaspoons lemon juice

2 tablespoons light mayonnaise

¼ teaspoon Old Bay seasoning

4 plain brown rice cakes

½ cup shredded lowfat cheddar cheese

DIRECTIONS

1 Preheat the broiler on high heat. In a medium bowl, combine the crab, celery, red pepper, green onion, cilantro, lemon juice, mayonnaise, and Old Bay seasoning.

2 Place the rice cakes on a baking sheet. Spread ¼ cup crab mixture on each. Sprinkle each with 2 tablespoons of shredded cheese. Broil until the cheese melts, about 3 minutes.

PER SERVING: *Calories 240 (From Fat 70); Fat 8g (Saturated 2g); Cholesterol 65mg; Sodium 650mg; Carbohydrate 20g (Dietary Fiber 1g); Protein 22g; Sugar 2g.*

VARY IT! You can substitute fresh crab for the canned, but don't substitute with imitation crab. It's usually made with Alaskan pollock and contains no crab whatsoever, and because it's highly processed, it's much higher in sodium than real crab meat.

VARY IT! If you don't like cilantro, simply switch to fresh parsley.

TIP: Old Bay seasoning can be found in the grocery store in the spice section. It's a blend of herbs and spices typically used to season seafood but you can use it on chicken, beef, or vegetables as well. The blend contains salt so you don't need to add additional salt when using Old Bay.

Salmon Patties

STAGE: REGULAR FOODS	PREP TIME: 10 MIN	COOK TIME: 6 MIN	YIELD: 4 SERVINGS

INGREDIENTS

2 eggs, beaten

¼ cup nonfat milk

¼ cup chopped green onion

¼ cup finely chopped celery

¼ teaspoon Old Bay seasoning

Two 6-ounce cans salmon, without bones and skin, drained and flaked

¼ cup bread crumbs

2 teaspoons canola oil

Honey Mustard Sauce (see the following recipe)

DIRECTIONS

1 Combine eggs, milk, green onion, celery, and Old Bay seasoning in a medium bowl. Add the salmon and bread crumbs and mix well. Form into four equal, thin patties.

2 Heat oil in a large sauté pan over medium heat. Cook patties for about 3 minutes, and turn and cook another 3 minutes or until browned. Serve with Honey Mustard Sauce.

Honey Mustard Sauce

¼ cup light mayonnaise

1 teaspoon Dijon mustard

1 teaspoon honey

Combine all ingredients is a small bowl. Serve with patties.

PER SERVING: *Calories 246 (From Fat 144); Fat 16g (Saturated 3g); Cholesterol 157mg; Sodium 559mg; Carbohydrate 9g (Dietary Fiber 1g); Protein 18g; Sugar 3g.*

Chapter **13**

Viva la Vegetarian

Some people choose to eat vegetarian after weight loss surgery because they have difficulty tolerating meat. Sometimes this difficulty lessens as time goes on, but for others, intolerance is long term. Whatever your reason for eating vegetarian, you can still meet your protein goals and enjoy delicious food. This chapter provides you with tasty meatless recipes that are sure to please even the most devoted carnivore.

REMEMBER

If you omit high-protein animal foods on a regular basis, you have to do some careful planning to make sure you meet your protein goals. Taking your vitamin and mineral supplements after surgery is always critical, but if you regularly eat vegetarian, you may need extra. To monitor your health, keep all your follow-up appointments and get your lab work done as directed by your surgeon.

Developing Delicious Dinner Salads

A dinner salad can be so much more than lettuce and tomatoes. It can be part of dinner, or it can be satisfying enough to be a complete meal. You can save prep time by shopping in the produce department for packaged veggies that are cleaned, cut, and ready to go. They may cost more, but your time is valuable, too. Plus there is no waste because you can buy smaller quantities.

REMEMBER

Most salads are accompanied by a salad dressing. A key ingredient in regular packaged dressing is fat, and even one tablespoon of fat carries a lot of calories. Light and fat-free versions are better choices then full-fat salad dressings, because obviously you don't want to add extra calories to your healthy salads.

GETTING TO KNOW TOFU

Tofu has been around for over 2,000 years, but maybe you never tried it because you aren't sure what it is or how to use it.

Tofu is made from soybeans, an excellent source of protein. By itself, tofu is bland, but that's part of what makes it great because it can go well in a wide variety of dishes and pick up the flavors of the other ingredients. Although all tofu is smooth in texture, it comes in different forms:

- Silken tofu has a softer texture and works best in sauces, salad dressings, and desserts. It doesn't have to be refrigerated until it's opened, so you can probably find it on the shelf.

- Regular tofu comes in different textures such as soft, firm, and extra firm. Recipes usually tell you which kind you need. This tofu is usually found in a refrigerator case near the produce or dairy department. After opening, put any leftovers in a container, cover with water, and put a cover on the container. It will keep for about a week.

Lots of commercially prepared tofu foods are available at the grocery. You can find tofu cheese, yogurt, ice cream, and smoothies. Remember to check the nutrition labels for sugar and fat content — just because it's made from tofu doesn't mean it meets your weight loss surgery dietary guidelines.

Fresh Spinach Salad with Roasted Corn

STAGE: REGULAR FOODS	PREP TIME: 15 MIN	COOK TIME: 5 MIN	YIELD: 4 SERVINGS

INGREDIENTS

2 cups fresh spinach, rinsed and stems removed

½ cup frozen shelled edamame

¾ cup roasted corn (buy and thaw frozen preroasted corn, or see the following Tip)

¼ cup chopped red onion

¼ cup chopped tomatoes

¼ cup chopped fresh strawberries

¼ cup lowfat raspberry vinaigrette

DIRECTIONS

1 Bring a small pot of water to a boil and add edamame. Cook for 2 to 3 minutes until bright green; then drain and rinse under running cold water to stop cooking. Drain.

2 Place all ingredients into a medium mixing bowl and toss.

PER SERVING: *Calories 80 (From Fat 20); Fat 2g (Saturated 0g); Cholesterol 0mg; Sodium 50mg; Carbohydrate 14g (Dietary Fiber 3g); Protein 4g; Sugar 6g.*

TIP: To roast corn, preheat the oven to 350 degrees. Husk and clean fibers from fresh corn on the cob, place cobs directly on rack in the center of oven, and roast for 15 minutes. Let cool and slice the roasted corn from cob with a knife.

TIP: This salad can be made a day in advance, just don't add the salad dressing until ready to serve.

A VEGETARIAN BY ANY OTHER NAME

Not all people who refrain from eating meat follow the same diet. Following are the different kinds of vegetarians:

- A *lacto-ovo vegetarian* consumes dairy products and eggs but doesn't eat meat, poultry, fish, or seafood.

- A *lacto-vegetarian* consumes dairy products but doesn't eat eggs, meat, poultry, fish, or seafood.

- A *vegan* omits dairy products, eggs, meat, poultry, fish, and seafood — all animal-based foods.

Quinoa Salad with Cashews and Greens

STAGE: SOFT OR REGULAR FOODS	PREP TIME: 5 MIN	COOK TIME: 20–25 MIN	YIELD: 4 SERVINGS

INGREDIENTS

1 cup dry quinoa, rinsed

2 cups vegetable stock or water with ½ teaspoon salt

3 cups mixed winter greens, such as Swiss chard, beet or turnip greens, or kale

1 tablespoon olive oil

¼ cup raw cashews, chopped

½ teaspoon salt

½ teaspoon pepper

½ teaspoon turmeric

DIRECTIONS

1 In a medium saucepan, mix the rinsed quinoa and stock. Bring to a boil, lower to a low heat, and cover for 15 minutes until most of the liquid is absorbed.

2 Add the greens, stir, and then cover the saucepan and let sit for 2 to 3 minutes, until wilted.

3 Add the oil, cashews, salt, pepper, and turmeric. Adjust the seasonings to taste. Enjoy hot or room temperature for lunch.

PER SERVING: *Calories 292 (From Fat 103); Fat 11g (Saturated 2g); Cholesterol 4mg; Sodium 482mg; Carbohydrate 37g (Dietary Fiber 5g); Protein 11g; Sugar 3g.*

Tabbouleh with Avocado

STAGE: REGULAR FOODS	PREP TIME: 15 MIN	COOK TIME: 20 MIN	CHILL TIME: 4 HR	YIELD: 4 SERVINGS

INGREDIENTS

½ cup boiling water

½ cup fine cracked wheat

½ cup minced fresh parsley leaves

¼ cup minced fresh mint leaves

¼ cup finely chopped yellow onion

1 clove garlic, minced

1 cup diced tomato

1 cup peeled, seeded, and diced cucumbers

1 tablespoon olive oil

1 tablespoon lemon juice, or to taste

½ teaspoon salt

½ avocado, peeled, seeded, and cut into small cubes

DIRECTIONS

1 In a large mixing bowl, pour the boiling water over the cracked wheat, cover, and let stand about 20 minutes until the wheat is tender and water is absorbed.

2 Add the chopped herbs, onion, garlic, tomato, and cucumber and toss with the wheat.

3 Combine the oil, lemon juice, and salt in a separate bowl. Add to wheat mixture and mix well.

4 Chill for 4 hours and serve. Add avocado to top of salad just before you serve.

PER SERVING: *Calories 149 (From Fat 64); Fat 7g (Saturated 1g); Cholesterol 0mg; Sodium 305mg; Carbohydrate 21g (Dietary Fiber 7g); Protein 4g; Sugar 2g.*

Corn Tomato Basil Salad

STAGE: REGULAR FOODS	PREP TIME: 10 MIN	COOK TIME: 15 MIN	YIELD: 4 SERVINGS

INGREDIENTS

2 ears large sweet corn, cooked and chilled

1 pint grape tomatoes

¼ cup olive oil

⅓ cup balsamic vinegar

¼ teaspoon sea salt

¼ teaspoon fresh ground pepper

2 to 4 tablespoons fresh basil, chopped or 3 teaspoons dried basil

4 ounces lowfat mozzarella, cubed

DIRECTIONS

1 Cut the corn from the cob and add to a medium bowl.

2 Halve the tomatoes and add to the corn.

3 In a 1-cup glass measurement, mix the oil, vinegar, salt, pepper, and basil with a fork or whisk.

4 Pour over the corn and tomatoes.

5 Fold in the mozzarella.

PER SERVING: *Calories 285 (From Fat 172); Fat 19g (Saturated 5g); Cholesterol 18mg; Sodium 340mg; Carbohydrate 21g (Dietary Fiber 2g); Protein 10g; Sugar 10g.*

TIP: Enjoy over a bed of greens or as a side with chicken, lean pork, or fish.

Lentil, Eggplant, and Mushroom Curry

STAGE: SOFT OR REGULAR FOODS	PREP TIME: 5 MIN	COOK TIME: 35 MIN	YIELD: 4 SERVINGS

INGREDIENTS

1 cup lentils

2 cups water or vegetable stock

½ large sweet onion, minced

1 tablespoon canola or light olive oil

½ medium eggplant, cubed

4 cups mixed winter greens, such as kale, Swiss chard, or spinach

1 cup chopped mushrooms

1 tablespoon curry powder

½ teaspoon salt

½ cup water

½ cup plain nonfat yogurt

2 cups cooked brown rice

DIRECTIONS

1 In a medium saucepan, simmer the lentils in the water or stock. Bring to a boil, lower the heat to simmer, and cover until the lentils are soft, about 20 minutes.

2 Meanwhile, in a large skillet, sauté the onion in the oil until soft.

3 Add the eggplant and stir-fry until soft, about 5 minutes.

4 Add the greens and mushrooms. Stir fry for 2 to 3 minutes.

5 Stir in the curry powder, salt, and water. Simmer for 5 minutes.

6 Remove from the heat and add the yogurt and the lentils.

7 Serve over ½ cup cooked brown rice per serving.

PER SERVING: *Calories 397 (From Fat 52); Fat 6g (Saturated 1g); Cholesterol 1mg; Sodium 357mg; Carbohydrate 69g (Dietary Fiber 21g); Protein 21g; Sugar 8g.*

Caprese: Tomato, Basil, and Mozzarella Pasta

STAGE: SOFT OR REGULAR FOODS	PREP TIME: 10 MIN	COOK TIME: 12 MIN	YIELD: 2 SERVINGS

INGREDIENTS

2 teaspoons olive oil

2 ounces dried or fresh linguine pasta

1 pint grape tomatoes, quartered

¼ teaspoon salt

¼ teaspoon pepper

2 tablespoons extra-virgin olive oil

1 tablespoon balsamic vinegar

¼ cup fresh basil, julienned

2 ounces part-skim mozzarella, cubed

DIRECTIONS

1 Bring a medium saucepan of water to a boil. Add the olive oil and the pasta.

2 If you're using fresh pasta, cook according to package directions, and then drain and cool.

3 Add the tomatoes, salt, pepper, olive oil, and vinegar.

4 When the pasta is cooled (about 15 minutes), add the basil and mozzarella.

PER SERVING: *Calories 371 (From Fat 209); Fat 23g (Saturated 5g); Cholesterol 18mg; Sodium 478mg; Carbohydrate 29g (Dietary Fiber 3g); Protein 12g; Sugar 6g.*

Seared Tofu with Peanut Sauce

STAGE: SOFT OR REGULAR FOODS	PREP TIME: 10 MIN	COOK TIME: 15 MIN	YIELD: 4 SERVINGS

INGREDIENTS

2 teaspoons canola or peanut oil

One 8-ounce package extra-firm tofu, drained and pressed in kitchen or paper towels to remove excess liquid

Peanut Sauce (see the following recipe)

DIRECTIONS

1 In a medium skillet, heat the oil.

2 Slice the tofu into ¼-inch-thick slices and cook on each side in the pan until browned, about 3 to 4 minutes.

3 While the tofu is cooking, make the Peanut Sauce.

4 When the tofu is turned to brown side up cook for 2 minutes, pour the sauce over the tofu and simmer 2 minutes.

Peanut Sauce

3 tablespoons smooth peanut butter

2 tablespoons rice wine vinegar

3 tablespoons soy sauce

2 tablespoons brown sugar

2 cloves garlic, minced

¼ teaspoon grated fresh ginger or ginger powder

½ cup water

In a small bowl, combine the ingredients and whisk until blended.

PER SERVING: *Calories 178 (From Fat 105); Fat 12g (Saturated 2g); Cholesterol 0mg; Sodium 816mg; Carbohydrate 11g (Dietary Fiber 1g); Protein 10g; Sugar 8g.*

VARY IT! If you prefer, you can use 3 tablespoons Hoison sauce in place of the soy sauce and brown sugar in the Peanut Sauce recipe. You can also use 1 teaspoon garlic powder in place of the 2 cloves of garlic in the same recipe.

Vegetable-Tofu Stir-Fry

| STAGE: REGULAR FOODS | PREP TIME: 15 MIN | COOK TIME: 15 MIN | YIELD: 2 SERVINGS |

INGREDIENTS

2 teaspoons refined sesame or canola oil

6 ounces extra-firm tofu, cubed

2 teaspoons sesame (high-heat) or canola oil

½ large sweet onion, chopped

½ large eggplant, chopped

½ cup quartered baby carrots

1 large tomato, chopped

1-2 cloves garlic, minced

2 cups fresh spinach

1 cup water

1 teaspoon each salt, turmeric, cumin, Chinese 5 spice

1 cup cooked brown rice

DIRECTIONS

1 In a large skillet, heat the oil until slightly smoking and add tofu. Cook on each side 2 to 3 minutes. Removed from pan.

2 Heat the remaining 2 teaspoons oil and add the onion and eggplant. Sauté 5 minutes until browned. Add carrots, garlic and tomato. Sauté another 2 to 3 minutes.

3 Combine the water and spices in a 1 cup glass measuring cup and pour over vegetables. Simmer 2 to 3 minutes and add spinach. Stir until wilted.

4 Add tofu back; simmer 2 minutes and remove from heat.

5 Enjoy with ½ cup cooked brown rice per serving.

PER SERVING: *Calories 356 (From Fat 139); Fat 15g (Saturated 1g); Cholesterol 0mg; Sodium 1,234mg; Carbohydrate 45g (Dietary Fiber 9g); Protein 15g; Sugar 12g.*

Blackened Tofu

STAGE: REGULAR FOODS	PREP TIME: 5 MIN	COOK TIME: 15 MIN	YIELD: 4 SERVINGS

INGREDIENTS

One 16-ounce package extra-firm tofu

1 tablespoon canola oil

2 tablespoons steak seasoning

DIRECTIONS

1 Using a kitchen towel or paper towel, press the liquid out of ½-inch-thick slices of tofu.

2 Rub the oil over the slabs of tofu and sprinkle steak seasoning on each side.

3 Preheat a grill pan on medium-high heat for 5 minutes and spray with oil.

4 Grill the tofu for 7 to 8 minutes on each side. Only turn once to avoid crumbling.

5 Remove from the heat and serve.

PER SERVING: *Calories 141 (From Fat 92); Fat 10g (Saturated 1g); Cholesterol 0mg; Sodium 10mg; Carbohydrate 4g (Dietary Fiber 1g); Protein 11g; Sugar 1g.*

TIP: Add the tofu to stir-fry vegetables or a salad, or serve on a whole-grain bun.

Tofu Vegetable—Non-Spicy Curry

STAGE: REGULAR FOODS	PREP TIME: 10 MIN	COOK TIME: 20 MIN	YIELD: 2 SERVINGS

INGREDIENTS

8 ounces cubed, firm tofu, drained

½ teaspoon salt

½ teaspoon pepper

1 tablespoon canola or peanut oil

½ cup diced onion

¼ cup diced carrot

1 clove garlic, minced

1 cup cabbage, shredded

1 cup fresh spinach

¼ cup frozen or fresh peas

1 cup vegetable broth

1 teaspoon turmeric

¼ teaspoon cumin

1 cup cooked brown rice

DIRECTIONS

1 Using a kitchen towel or paper towel, press the liquid out of the tofu and season with salt and pepper.

2 In a large skillet, heat the oil. Add the tofu to the skillet and cook until browned on each side. Remove from the heat and add the onion and carrot. Stir-fry for 2 minutes until slightly softened.

3 Add the garlic, cabbage, spinach, peas, broth, turmeric, and cumin. Stir-fry until mixed together, another 2 to 3 minutes.

4 Pour over the brown rice and serve.

PER SERVING: *Calories 304 (From Fat 103); Fat 11g (Saturated 1g); Cholesterol 0mg; Sodium 1,128mg; Carbohydrate 38g (Dietary Fiber 5g); Protein 14g; Sugar 9g.*

Making "Meaty" Baked Dishes

Even the meat-and-potatoes type may be convinced to go meatless after giving some tasty vegetarian dishes a try. Meatless meals can be just as filling as those with meat because they tend to be high in fiber, which is filling.

You can find meat-substitute products that are tasty and lower in fat in the freezer section of the grocery store. These products are also softer and more moist than meat products, so are less likely to cause food-sticking problems.

Smoked Gouda–Stuffed Peppers

STAGE: REGULAR FOODS	PREP TIME: 10 MIN	COOK TIME: 20 MIN	YIELD: 4 SERVINGS

INGREDIENTS

2 large green bell peppers, cut in half lengthwise and seeded

Water

6 ounces Morningstar Farm Sausage Style Recipe Crumbles

¾ cup low-sodium vegetable broth

1 large chopped plum tomato

⅔ cup instant brown rice

⅓ cup chopped fresh basil

⅓ cup finely shredded smoked Gouda cheese

DIRECTIONS

1 Preheat the oven to 350 degrees.

2 Place peppers cut-side down in a large, microwave-safe dish. Fill the dish with ½ inch water, cover, and microwave on high until the peppers are tender crisp, 7 to 10 minutes. Drain the water and transfer the peppers to a roasting pan.

3 While peppers are in the microwave, heat a medium sauté pan. When hot, add breakfast crumbles, broth, tomato, and rice. Bring to a simmer, cover, reduce heat to medium low, and simmer until the rice is softened but still moist, about 10 minutes.

4 Stir the basil and half the cheese into the rice mixture. Divide the filling into the peppers, then top with the remaining cheese. Bake until the cheese is melted, approximately 10 minutes.

PER SERVING: *Calories 190 (From Fat 50); Fat 6g (Saturated 2g); Cholesterol 10mg; Sodium 440mg; Carbohydrate 21g (Dietary Fiber 5g); Protein 13g; Sugar 3g.*

Easy Cheesy Navy Bean Bake

STAGE: REGULAR FOODS	PREP TIME: 15 MIN	COOK TIME: 36 MIN	YIELD: 6 SERVINGS

INGREDIENTS

1 teaspoon olive oil

2 cloves fresh garlic, chopped fine

½ cup diced onion

¼ cup diced green pepper

1 cup diced tomato

1 teaspoon dried thyme

One 14.5-ounce can navy beans, rinsed and drained

One 14.5-ounce can low-sodium pinto beans, rinsed and drained

½ cup low-sodium vegetable broth

1 cup shredded lowfat cheddar cheese

DIRECTIONS

1 Preheat the oven to 325 degrees. Coat an 8-x-8-inch oven-proof pan with nonstick cooking spray.

2 Add oil to a medium sauté pan over medium-high heat. Add the garlic, onion, green pepper, tomato, and thyme and sauté for 3 minutes. Add the beans and broth and bring to a simmer for 3 minutes.

3 Pour the bean mixture into the pan. Top with cheese and bake for 30 minutes, or until cheese is bubbly. Let stand to thicken slightly and serve.

PER SERVING: *Calories 180 (From Fat 30); Fat 3g (Saturated 1g); Cholesterol 5mg; Sodium 430mg; Carbohydrate 26g (Dietary Fiber 7g); Protein 13g; Sugar 2g.*

TIP: If you want a fast meal, you can mix up the dish ahead of time and store it in refrigerator. Just pop the pan into the oven when you get home, and 30 minutes later, dinner is done!

Hearty Moussaka with Beans

STAGE: REGULAR FOODS	PREP TIME: 15 MIN	REST TIME: 30 MIN	COOK TIME: 1 HR 15 MIN	YIELD: 6 SERVINGS

INGREDIENTS

1 eggplant, peeled and sliced into ¼-inch rounds

1 teaspoon salt

1 teaspoon vegetable oil

1 medium onion, roughly chopped

1 garlic clove, minced

One 14-ounce can no-salt-added diced tomatoes

One 7-ounce can no-salt-added navy beans, drained and chopped

½ cup low-sodium vegetable broth

1 teaspoon dried oregano

1 medium zucchini, sliced into ¼-inch rounds

1 cup crumbled reduced-fat feta cheese

Topping Sauce (see the following recipe)

¼ cup fresh grated Parmesan cheese

DIRECTIONS

1 Sprinkle the slices of eggplant with salt and let sit for at least 30 minutes. Rinse off the salt.

2 Preheat the oven to 350 degrees and coat a 9-x-11-inch casserole dish with nonstick cooking spray.

3 Heat the oil in a medium sauté pan over medium-high heat. Sauté onion and garlic until browned, about 3 minutes. Add tomatoes, navy beans, vegetable broth, and oregano. Cover and simmer on medium low for about 15 minutes.

4 Using ⅓ of each, layer eggplant, zucchini, and feta, and pour ⅓ of the tomato and bean mixture over the top. Repeat all the layers 2 more times. Bake for about 25 minutes. While baking, make the Topping Sauce.

5 Remove the vegetable casserole from the oven and pour the Topping Sauce over it. Top with Parmesan cheese and continue to bake for another 30 minutes.

Topping Sauce

2 tablespoons butter

2 tablespoons all-purpose flour

1¼ cups nonfat milk

⅛ teaspoon nutmeg

1 egg, beaten

Mix together butter, flour, and milk. While whisking, bring to a boil. When it's thick and smooth, add nutmeg. Remove from heat and let the mixture cool for about 5 minutes. Mix in the beaten egg.

PER SERVING: *Calories 210 (From Fat 80); Fat 9g (Saturated 5g); Cholesterol 50mg; Sodium 510mg; Carbohydrate 21g (Dietary Fiber 7g); Protein 13g; Sugar 8g.*

Cooking Full-Flavor Vegetarian Burgers

Americans love their burgers! They eat an average of one to three burgers a week, making it the most popular sandwich sold in the country. *Burger* is the name given to a ground meat, fish, poultry, or vegetarian product that's made into a patty and typically served on a bun with condiments. The possible combinations are endless, and no beef is needed to make a "meaty" burger that can satisfy your burger desire.

To grill or not to grill? It depends on the recipe. Grilling veggie burgers lends grilled flavor to the burger. However, if the grill is too hot, your veggie burger will quickly dry out, so low heat is the key. Coat the grill grates with nonstick cooking spray to keep your veggie burger from sticking to them. Cooking time varies depending on grill and patty thickness, but in general it's close to the time stated in each recipe.

Potato and Zucchini Veggie Burger

STAGE: REGULAR FOODS	PREP TIME: 15 MIN	COOK TIME: 15 MIN	YIELD: 2 SERVINGS

INGREDIENTS

1 large Russet potato, baked and mashed with skin on

2 eggs, whisked

1 cup minced mushrooms

½ cup shredded zucchini

½ cup minced onion

1½ tablespoons multipurpose seasoning with salt

1 tablespoon canola or peanut oil

DIRECTIONS

1 In a medium bowl, mash together the potato, eggs, mushrooms, zucchini, onion, and seasoning. Form into 4 patties.

2 In a medium skillet, heat the oil and add the patties. Cook for 7 to 8 minutes each side until golden.

PER SERVING: *Calories 267 (From Fat 66); Fat 7g (Saturated 1g); Cholesterol 0mg; Sodium 407mg; Carbohydrate 43g (Dietary Fiber 6g); Protein 10g; Sugar 8g.*

TIP: Enjoy with a bed of salad greens and your favorite lowfat salad dressing.

Portobello Burger

STAGE: REGULAR FOODS	PREP TIME: 5 MIN	MARINATE TIME: 20 MIN	COOK TIME: 8 MIN	YIELD: 4 SERVINGS

INGREDIENTS

4 large portobello mushrooms, stems removed

1 tablespoon olive oil

1 teaspoon garlic powder

1 teaspoon onion powder

¼ teaspoon salt

1 tablespoon balsamic vinegar

4 whole-wheat hamburger buns

Four 1-ounce slices lowfat cheddar cheese

4 tomato slices

4 romaine lettuce leaves

DIRECTIONS

1 In a medium mixing bowl combine whole mushrooms caps, olive oil, garlic powder, onion powder, salt, and balsamic vinegar and let marinate for 20 minutes.

2 Preheat the oven broiler on high. Remove mushrooms from the marinade and place on an ungreased cookie sheet. Broil on the middle rack for 4 minutes. Turn mushrooms over and broil an additional 4 minutes.

3 Place each cooked portobello on a whole-wheat bun and top with 1 slice of cheddar cheese, 1 slice of tomato, and 1 leaf of lettuce.

PER SERVING: *Calories 240 (From Fat 70); Fat 8g (Saturated 2g); Cholesterol 5mg; Sodium 530mg; Carbohydrate 30g (Dietary Fiber 5g); Protein 13g; Sugar 7g.*

3
Simple Recipes to Enjoy Any Time

IN THIS PART . . .

Find a great collection of soups, salads, and savory stews.

Get recipes for snacks, appetizers, and side dishes for those times you really need to have a little something to tide you over until the next meal.

Draw on healthy and delicious smoothie and dessert recipes.

Discover a special selection of recipes that can be made if you're cooking for one or two.

» Blending fruit into fabulous smoothies

» Spicing up smoothies with spices and flavorings

» Whipping up dessert-worthy chocolate and peanut butter smoothies

Chapter **14**

Scrumptious Smoothies

RECIPES IN THIS CHAPTER

- Banana Berry
- Strawberry Cheesecake
- Mango Twister
- Coconut Kiwi
- Peaches and Cream
- Orangalicious
- Honeydew Mint
- Spiced Apple Pie
- Smooth Peanut Banana
- Chocolate-Covered Berries

Smoothies just seem to work well for people who had weight loss surgery. They're easy to make, portable, and taste good. You don't have to remember to chew them, the varieties are endless, and they can give you a good shot of protein. What's not to love?

Because all the smoothies in this chapter are made in the blender, they work great for Stage 3, smooth foods, in your postoperative diet progression. If you had AGB surgery, these recipes work perfectly when you get a fill, or adjustment, and must follow the smooth food diet stage for a day or two.

If you're still in the stages of the diet progression, take careful note of the yield for each recipe, because it's probably more than you can or should eat. Either split it into two portions to share with someone else or halve the recipe for yourself. If you're months or years out from surgery, you know your portion sizes have increased over time. You may want to double the recipe if you use it for a meal; otherwise it can be a snack.

REMEMBER

Note that sugar occurs naturally in milk, as lactose, and in fruit, as fructose. These sugars do not cause dumping syndrome unless they're concentrated, like in fruit juice. We use sugar substitutes in our recipes, so the sugar content is not from added sugars.

Smoothie-Making Tips

A smoothie may seem like the easiest thing to make. You just throw it in the blender, right? Well, you can, but the following tips can improve the final product. You'll get tasty smoothies that are grit- and lump-free and not too foamy in addition to discovering how to incorporate them into your new diet.

>> **Take advantage of smoothies as a great opportunity to get some much-needed protein.** Our recipes are made without supplemental protein powders, but you can easily add your favorite flavored or unflavored protein powder to increase the protein in any smoothie. Choose a good-quality protein powder made from whey protein isolates or soy.

>> **Feel free to use either nonfat milk, lactose-free milk, or light, unsweetened soy milk depending on your tolerance, regardless of what we specify in the recipe.** We also include nonfat dry powdered milk in some of the recipes to add some protein and calcium. If you're lactose intolerant, omit the powdered milk.

>> **Use a blender instead of a food processor.** It's all about the blades! The blender blades make an *X* and are pointed toward the bottom, which draws the ingredients down into the blender to blend evenly. A food processor's blades are arranged differently and will never get your drink smooth enough.

>> **Use small pieces of ice if you can.** Using small cubes allows your smoothie to mix quicker and stay creamy instead of frothy.

>> **Check out the spice section at your supermarket for smoothie flavorings.** Extract flavorings can change the taste from ho-hum to yum. These little bottles of flavor are sugar-free and zero calories. However, you want to use them sparingly because they're very concentrated.

Healthy Fruity Smoothies

Nothing beats fresh fruit, unless it's frozen! When the fresh fruit isn't in season, it can be pretty expensive. You can buy frozen fruit instead, but make sure to get it with no added sugar. When using frozen fruit, you can omit the ice because the frozen fruit will thicken your smoothie like ice. You may prefer to add a little more of the liquid of your choice to thin it so it blends easily.

Banana Berry

INGREDIENTS

½ cup nonfat milk

2 tablespoons nonfat dry powdered milk

¼ cup blueberries, fresh or frozen

¼ cup raspberries, fresh or frozen

¼ cup sliced banana

⅛ teaspoon vanilla extract

¼ cup ice

1 packet sugar substitute, or to taste

DIRECTIONS

Stir the powdered milk into the nonfat milk and let stand for 2 to 3 minutes. Then place all ingredients in a blender and blend well.

PER SERVING: *Calories 140 (From Fat 0); Fat 0g (Saturated 0g); Cholesterol 5mg; Sodium 100mg; Carbohydrate 29g (Dietary Fiber 2g); Protein 8g; Sugar 19g.*

Strawberry Cheesecake

STAGE: SMOOTH FOODS	PREP TIME: 5 MIN	YIELD: 1 SERVING

INGREDIENTS

½ cup nonfat milk

½ cup sliced fresh strawberries

¼ teaspoon lemon extract

¼ cup part-skim ricotta cheese

¼ cup ice

1 packet sugar substitute, or to taste

DIRECTIONS

Place all ingredients in a blender and blend well.

PER SERVING: *Calories 160 (From Fat 45); Fat 5g (Saturated 3g); Cholesterol 20mg; Sodium 130mg; Carbohydrate 16g (Dietary Fiber 2g); Protein 12g; Sugar 10g.*

TIP: Look for lemon extract in the spice section at the grocery alongside vanilla extract.

Mango Twister

STAGE: SMOOTH FOODS | PREP TIME: 5 MIN | YIELD: 1 SERVING

INGREDIENTS

¼ cup plain calcium-enriched soy milk

2 tablespoons nonfat dry powdered milk

½ cup peeled, seeded, and chopped fresh mango

¼ cup orange juice

¼ cup ice

1 packet sugar substitute, or to taste

DIRECTIONS

Stir the powdered milk into the soy milk and let stand for 1 to 2 minutes. Then place all ingredients in a blender and blend well.

PER SERVING: *Calories 140 (From Fat 10); Fat 1g (Saturated 0g); Cholesterol 0mg; Sodium 70mg; Carbohydrate 29g (Dietary Fiber 2g); Protein 5g; Sugar 19g.*

TIP: If you don't want try your hand at cutting up a mango (see Chapter 19 for an illustration), you can buy precut frozen slices.

Coconut Kiwi

STAGE: SMOOTH FOODS	PREP TIME: 5 MIN	YIELD: 1 SERVING

INGREDIENTS

¼ cup nonfat milk

¼ cup peeled and chopped kiwi

¼ cup canned crushed pineapple in its own juice, drained

¼ teaspoon coconut extract

¼ cup silken soft tofu

¼ cup ice

¼ cup water

1 packet sugar substitute, or to taste

DIRECTIONS

Place all ingredients in a blender and blend well.

PER SERVING: *Calories 100 (From Fat 20); Fat 2g (Saturated 0g); Cholesterol 0mg; Sodium 30mg; Carbohydrate 18g (Dietary Fiber 2g); Protein 5g; Sugar 14g.*

Peaches and Cream

STAGE: SMOOTH FOODS	PREP TIME: 5 MIN	YIELD: 1 SERVING

INGREDIENTS

¼ cup nonfat milk

2 tablespoons nonfat dry powdered milk

½ cup canned no-sugar-added peaches, drained

¼ teaspoon vanilla extract

¼ cup plain nonfat yogurt

¼ cup ice

1 packet sugar substitute, or to taste

DIRECTIONS

Stir the powdered milk into the nonfat milk and let stand for 2 to 3 minutes. Then place all ingredients in a blender and blend well.

PER SERVING: *Calories 110 (From Fat 0); Fat 0g (Saturated 0g); Cholesterol 5mg; Sodium 110mg; Carbohydrate 20g (Dietary Fiber 2g); Protein 8g; Sugar 17g.*

Orangalicious

| STAGE: SMOOTH FOODS | PREP TIME: 5 MIN | YIELD: 1 SERVING |

INGREDIENTS

½ cup orange juice

⅓ cup nonfat dry powdered milk

¼ cup mandarin oranges

⅛ teaspoon lemon extract

⅓ cup ice

DIRECTIONS

Stir the powdered milk into the orange juice and let stand for 2 to 3 minutes. Then place all ingredients in a blender and blend well.

PER SERVING: *Calories 150 (From Fat 0); Fat 0g (Saturated 0g); Cholesterol 5mg; Sodium 130mg; Carbohydrate 29g (Dietary Fiber 1g); Protein 9g; Sugar 16g.*

Honeydew Mint

STAGE: SOFT OR REGULAR FOODS	PREP TIME: 10–15 MIN	YIELD: 1 SERVING

INGREDIENTS

1 cup fresh spinach

1 cup ripe honeydew melon, cubed

½ cup plain nonfat Greek yogurt

½ cup green grapes

3 large fresh mint leaves

Zest and juice of half a lemon

1 cup ice

1 packet stevia or other non-nutritive sweetener, if desired

DIRECTIONS

Blend all ingredients in a high-speed blender and enjoy!

PER SERVING: *Calories 188 (From Fat 5); Fat 1g (Saturated 2g); Cholesterol 8mg; Sodium 106mg; Carbohydrate 34g (Dietary Fiber 3g); Protein 16g; Sugar 24g.*

Spice-It-Up Delights

You can experiment with your smoothies by adding different flavorings. Look in your spice pantry to see what you have available. If you would add it to a dessert, you can add it to a smoothie. For example, cinnamon makes a great addition to many drinks. Try the smoothies with spice blends in this section until you're brave enough to invent your own.

Spiced Apple Pie

| STAGE: SMOOTH FOODS | PREP TIME: 5 MIN | YIELD: 1 SERVING |

INGREDIENTS

¼ cup nonfat milk

¼ cup unsweetened applesauce

¼ teaspoon apple pie spice

⅛ teaspoon vanilla extract

½ cup plain nonfat yogurt

¼ cup ice

2 packets sugar substitute, or to taste

DIRECTIONS

Place all ingredients in a blender and blend well.

PER SERVING: *Calories 100 (From Fat 0); Fat 0g (Saturated 0g); Cholesterol 5mg; Sodium 95mg; Carbohydrate 19g (Dietary Fiber 1g); Protein 7g; Sugar 15g.*

TIP: If you can't find apple pie spice at the supermarket, you can make your own by blending together ½ teaspoon ground cinnamon, ¼ teaspoon ground nutmeg, ⅛ teaspoon ground allspice, and ⅛ teaspoon ground cardamom.

Peanut Butter and Chocolate Temptations

Peanut butter and chocolate are at the top of the list when it comes to favorite flavors. Chocolate is made from cocoa beans, the most eaten bean in the world. After it's dried and pounded into cocoa powder, this taste sensation is used in innumerable desserts and dishes. For smoothies, sugar-free chocolate syrup works the best. It gives you that chocolatey flavor but none of the calories.

TIP

If you have a peanut allergy, or just want some more variety, try almond, cashew, or walnut butter. They all have about 100 calories and 3 grams of protein per tablespoon. Because they're high in calories, watch your portion size!

Smooth Peanut Banana

STAGE: SMOOTH FOODS	PREP TIME: 5 MIN	YIELD: 1 SERVING

INGREDIENTS

¼ cup plain calcium-enriched soy milk

1 tablespoon creamy natural peanut butter

¼ cup sliced bananas

½ cup plain nonfat yogurt

¼ cup ice

1 packet sugar substitute, or to taste

DIRECTIONS

Place all ingredients in a blender and blend well.

PER SERVING: *Calories 210 (From Fat 80); Fat 9g (Saturated 1g); Cholesterol 5mg; Sodium 150mg; Carbohydrate 26g (Dietary Fiber 2g); Protein 10g; Sugar 15g.*

NOTE: Not all peanut butters are the same. Some have sugar and hydrogenated oils added, so look for natural peanut butter that contains only peanuts and a dash of salt.

Chocolate-Covered Berries

STAGE: SMOOTH FOODS	PREP TIME: 5 MIN	YIELD: 1 SERVING

INGREDIENTS

¼ cup nonfat milk

2 tablespoons nonfat dry powdered milk

¼ cup raspberries

¼ cup sliced strawberries

1 tablespoon sugar-free chocolate syrup

¼ cup plain nonfat yogurt

¼ cup ice

1 packet sugar substitute, or to taste

DIRECTIONS

Stir the powdered milk into the nonfat milk and let stand for 2 to 3 minutes. Then place all ingredients in a blender and blend well.

PER SERVING: *Calories 110 (From Fat 0); Fat 0g (Saturated 0g); Cholesterol 5mg; Sodium 170mg; Carbohydrate 22g (Dietary Fiber 1g); Protein 8g; Sugar 13g.*

TIP: You can find sugar-free chocolate syrup with the other ice cream toppings or flavored milk mixes at the grocery.

Chapter **15**

Alluring Appetizers

ppetizers have a new meaning after weight loss surgery. Before surgery, who would have thought that appetizer portions would be enough to fill you up? Now, they can easily be a meal.

If you're at a party or restaurant and appetizers are available, choose wisely. Many of them are high-calorie, high-fat foods that don't help you meet your goals. And if you had GBP surgery and are prone to dumping syndrome, many traditional appetizers may cause you problems.

Of course, to get around these problems, your best bet is to make and serve your own appetizers, starting with the recipes in this chapter.

The portion sizes in our recipes have been adjusted to an appetizer amount for someone who has had weight loss surgery. If you plan to serve these to guests who have not had weight loss surgery, you may choose to double the portion size. If you had weight loss surgery and are serving appetizers as part of a meal, plan on two servings of appetizers. If you're only serving appetizers, plan on four servings. For diners who have not had weight loss surgery, that means four appetizer servings with a meal, and eight as the meal.

Making Tasty Morsels

The great thing about appetizers is that many of them can be made ahead of time so you're not in the kitchen the entire time your guests are visiting. If appetizers are served hot, you can still make them up early in the day and keep them refrigerated until it's time to heat and serve.

REMEMBER

You want to serve a balance of tastes and textures. Make sure to have some sweet, spicy, soft, and crunchy. Color is important, too, so pick foods containing a variety of colors. If all your appetizers are brown, they won't look too appetizing.

Grilled Shrimp

STAGE: REGULAR FOODS	PREP TIME: 10 MIN	MARINATE TIME: 30 MIN	COOK TIME: 4 MIN	YIELD: 8 SERVINGS

INGREDIENTS

1 pound raw medium-sized shrimp

1 large tomato, seeded and chopped (see Figure 15-1)

2 tablespoons fresh chopped tarragon

2 tablespoons lemon juice

3 cloves garlic, chopped

1 teaspoon horseradish

½ teaspoon salt

¼ teaspoon black pepper

DIRECTIONS

1 Peel and devein the shrimp, keeping tails intact. Rinse shrimp, pat dry with paper towels, and set aside.

2 In a food processor, combine tomato, tarragon, lemon juice, garlic, horseradish, salt, and pepper. Cover and pulse until nearly smooth.

3 Combine the shrimp and tomato mixture in a large resealable bag. Marinate in the refrigerator for 30 to 45 minutes.

4 Preheat the grill to medium. When hot, remove shrimp from marinade and place on grill. Cook for 2 minutes each side or until shrimp are opaque, turning once.

PER SERVING: *Calories 60 (From Fat 10); Fat 1g (Saturated 0g); Cholesterol 85mg; Sodium 120mg; Carbohydrate 1g (Dietary Fiber 0g); Protein 12g; Sugar 0g.*

HOW TO SEED AND DICE TOMATOES

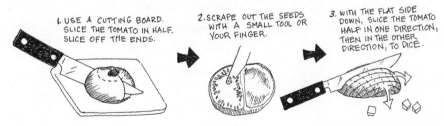

1. USE A CUTTING BOARD. SLICE THE TOMATO IN HALF. SLICE OFF THE ENDS.

2. SCRAPE OUT THE SEEDS WITH A SMALL TOOL OR YOUR FINGER.

3. WITH THE FLAT SIDE DOWN, SLICE THE TOMATO HALF IN ONE DIRECTION, THEN IN THE OTHER DIRECTION, TO DICE.

FIGURE 15-1: How to seed and dice a tomato.

Illustration by Elizabeth Kurtzman

Scallops with Spicy Tomato Chutney

STAGE: REGULAR FOODS	PREP TIME: 10 MIN	COOK TIME: 6 MIN	CHILL TIME: 1 HR	YIELD: 8 SERVINGS

INGREDIENTS

1 teaspoon olive oil

1 pound medium-sized sea scallops

½ teaspoon salt

½ teaspoon black pepper

Spicy Tomato Chutney (see the following recipe)

DIRECTIONS

1 Heat olive oil in a large sauté pan over medium–high heat. Salt and pepper the scallops.

2 Cook the scallops in hot oil for 2 minutes on one side; then turn scallops over and cook an additional 2 minutes. Turn back to the first side and cook 1 minute; then turn once more and cook 1 minute. Scallops will be opaque in color when done. Depending on their thickness, you may need to cook longer.

3 Place scallops in the refrigerator and let chill for 1 hour. While scallops are cooling, make Spicy Tomato Chutney. Top each scallop with 1 teaspoon of chutney to serve.

Spicy Tomato Chutney

1 cup diced tomatoes

¼ cup finely diced onion

1 teaspoon curry powder

1 teaspoon olive oil

1 teaspoon chopped parsley

1 clove garlic, minced

¼ teaspoon cayenne pepper (optional)

Combine all ingredients in a medium bowl, mix well, and chill until ready to serve. Bring to room temperature before serving.

PER SERVING: *Calories 60 (From Fat 10); Fat 1g (Saturated 0g); Cholesterol 20mg; Sodium 240mg; Carbohydrate 1g (Dietary Fiber 0g); Protein 10g; Sugar 0g.*

VARY IT! You can substitute bay scallops, which are small (ranging from the size of a nickel to a quarter) and come up to 20 per pound. Sea scallops are larger (ranging from the size of a quarter to a half dollar) and come 10 to 12 per pound.

TIP: This recipe prepares more chutney than you need. Refrigerate the extra and use it as a condiment on other dishes. It tastes great on eggs in the morning!

Crab-Stuffed Deviled Eggs

STAGE: SOFT FOODS	PREP TIME: 10 MIN	YIELD: 16 SERVINGS

INGREDIENTS

8 large eggs, hard-boiled and peeled

4 tablespoons light mayonnaise

1½ tablespoons chopped fresh tarragon

1 tablespoon minced shallot

2 teaspoons lemon juice

⅛ teaspoon black pepper

¼ teaspoon hot sauce

One 6.5-ounce can crabmeat, drained

DIRECTIONS

1 Cut eggs in half lengthwise. Scoop yolks into a medium bowl and mash with a fork.

2 Mix in mayonnaise, tarragon, shallot, lemon juice, black pepper, and hot sauce. Mix in crab.

3 Divide the crab mixture into 16 equal portions and spoon into the cavity of each half egg white.

PER SERVING: *Calories 130 (From Fat 70); Fat 8g (Saturated 2g); Cholesterol 240mg; Sodium 220mg; Carbohydrate 2g (Dietary Fiber 0g); Protein 12g; Sugar 1g.*

TIP: To hard-boil eggs, place eggs into a medium-sized pot and cover with water. Place on the stove and bring to a boil, then turn off the heat and let the eggs sit in the hot water for 12 to 15 minutes. Refrigerate eggs until you're ready to use them.

Mini Sweet Peppers Baked with Cheese and Herbs

STAGE: REGULAR FOODS	PREP TIME: 15 MIN	COOK TIME: 20 MIN	YIELD: 5 SERVINGS

INGREDIENTS

1 pound package of mini sweet peppers, sliced in half and seeded

One 3- to 4-ounce container garlic and herb soft cheese

4 ounces nonfat cream cheese, room temperature

1 tablespoon chopped chives

2 tablespoons chopped basil

2 tablespoons chopped mint

Zest of 1 lemon

3 tablespoons grated Parmesan cheese, divided

DIRECTIONS

1 Preheat the oven to 400 degrees.

2 In a small bowl, blend the garlic and herb cheese with the cream cheese, chives, basil, mint, lemon zest, and half of the parmesan cheese with a rubber spatula or a spoon.

3 Spoon the cheese mixture into each half of the peppers and place them on a baking sheet.

4 Sprinkle the remaining Parmesan cheese over the peppers and bake for 20 minutes until golden and bubbly.

PER SERVING: *Calories 105 (From Fat 55); Fat 6g (Saturated 4g); Cholesterol 21mg; Sodium 322mg; Carbohydrate 7g (Dietary Fiber 2g); Protein 7g; Sugar 4g.*

Thai Chicken Wraps

STAGE: REGULAR FOODS	PREP TIME: 10 MIN	COOK TIME: 4–8 MIN	YIELD: 8 SERVINGS

INGREDIENTS

1 pound boneless, skinless chicken breast, diced small

¼ cup shredded carrots

¼ cup finely chopped green onion

1 clove garlic, minced

1 teaspoon low-sodium soy sauce

½ teaspoon red pepper flakes

1 teaspoon sesame oil

8 large lettuce leaves

DIRECTIONS

1 In a medium bowl combine the chicken, carrots, green onion, garlic, soy sauce, pepper flakes, and oil. Mix well.

2 Heat a nonstick medium sauté pan over medium–high heat. Add the chicken mixture and sauté for 4 to 8 minutes or until chicken is done.

3 Place in a serving bowl. To make wraps, fill eat lettuce leaf with ⅛ of the chicken mixture and fold the leaf around it.

PER SERVING: *Calories 70 (From Fat 20); Fat 2g (Saturated 0g); Cholesterol 35mg; Sodium 60mg; Carbohydrate 1g (Dietary Fiber 0g); Protein 13g; Sugar 0g.*

No Double Dipping! Stirring Up Salsas and Dips

Dips are easy to prepare and can be made up to a day or two in advance. Commercially prepared dips are typically made with regular-fat mayonnaise or sour cream and are very high calorie. You can make your own healthier version that tastes just as good and may help you avoid the dreaded dumping syndrome. Just pair your homemade dips with a platter of fresh vegetables or whole-grain crackers for dipping.

White Albacore Tuna Dip

STAGE: SMOOTH FOODS	PREP TIME: 5 MIN	YIELD: 6 SERVINGS

INGREDIENTS

Two 6-ounce pouches white albacore tuna

4 tablespoons chopped fresh dill weed

2 teaspoons hot sauce

2 teaspoons minced garlic

2 tablespoons fresh lemon juice

½ cup light sour cream

½ cup light mayonnaise

DIRECTIONS

Place the tuna, dill, hot sauce, garlic, and lemon juice in a food processor and purée for 20 seconds. Scrape down the sides of the bowl with a rubber spatula, add sour cream and mayonnaise, and purée for another 30 seconds.

PER SERVING: *Calories 90 (From Fat 45); Fat 5g (Saturated 1g); Cholesterol 20mg; Sodium 105mg; Carbohydrate 2g (Dietary Fiber 0g); Protein 8g; Sugar 1g.*

TIP: Stored in an airtight container, this keeps fresh for two days.

Chunky Salsa

| STAGE: REGULAR FOODS | PREP TIME: 10 MIN | CHILL TIME: 1 HR | YIELD: 8 SERVINGS |

INGREDIENTS

2 large tomatoes, chopped

¼ large jalapeño pepper, seeded and chopped

3 cloves garlic, chopped

2 tablespoons lime juice

2 tablespoons chopped fresh cilantro

½ small onion, chopped

½ teaspoon salt

1 teaspoon cumin

DIRECTIONS

Place all ingredients in a small bowl and mix. Refrigerate for at least 1 hour to let flavors blend.

PER SERVING: *Calories 14 (From Fat 0); Fat 0g (Saturated 0g); Cholesterol 0mg; Sodium 150mg; Carbohydrate 3g (Dietary Fiber 1g); Protein 1g; Sugar 2g.*

VARY IT! If you want a smoother salsa, you can make this in a food processor. Pulse until it reaches your desired consistency.

The Best Hummus

STAGE: REGULAR FOODS   PREP TIME: 10 MIN   YIELD: 10 SERVINGS

INGREDIENTS

2 cups canned low-sodium garbanzo beans, drained and rinsed

2 tablespoons fresh lemon juice

2 cloves garlic, chopped

1 dash cayenne pepper

¼ cup tahini

2 tablespoons olive oil

¼ cup fresh chopped parsley

DIRECTIONS

Place all ingredients in a food processor and blend well. If hummus is too thick, add 1 tablespoon water at a time until it reaches your desired consistency.

TIP: Use leftover tahini on bread or crackers like you would use peanut butter. Keep it refrigerated after opening.

PER SERVING: *Calories 70 (From Fat 35); Fat 4g (Saturated 1g); Cholesterol 0mg; Sodium 10mg; Carbohydrate 7g (Dietary Fiber 1g); Protein 2g; Sugar 0g.*

Putting Snacks on a Stick

When serving appetizers, you want every bite to be packed with flavor, but you also want these morsels to be easy and attractive to eat. Putting foods on a stick makes food easy to handle and helps keep portions sizes down.

Chicken Satay

STAGE: REGULAR FOODS	PREP TIME: 5 MIN	MARINATE TIME: 20 MIN	COOK TIME: 15 MIN	YIELD: 12 SERVINGS

INGREDIENTS

1 pound boneless skinless chicken breast, cut into 12 long thin strips

2 tablespoon low-sodium teriyaki sauce

½ teaspoon sesame oil

½ teaspoon onion powder

12 large blackberries

Twelve 6-inch wooden skewers soaked in water

DIRECTIONS

1 In a medium mixing bowl combine the chicken, teriyaki sauce, oil, and onion powder. Let marinate for 20 minutes.

2 Preheat the oven to 350 degrees. Thread 1 piece of chicken onto a skewer and place on an ungreased cookie sheet. Repeat until all skewers are used.

3 Bake in the oven for 15 minutes or until the chicken is done (cut a small slit in a piece to check the inside). Place one blackberry on each stick just before serving.

PER SERVING: Calories 50 (From Fat 10); Fat 1g (Saturated 0g); Cholesterol 20mg; Sodium 45mg; Carbohydrate 1g (Dietary Fiber 1g); Protein 9g; Sugar 1g.

Pork Ginger Kebabs

STAGE: REGULAR FOODS	PREP TIME: 10 MIN	MARINATE TIME: 30 MIN	COOK TIME: 20 MIN	YIELD: 12 SERVINGS

INGREDIENTS

1 pound pork tenderloin, cut into twenty-four ½-inch cubes

12 cherry tomatoes

Twelve 1-inch cubes of fresh peeled and cored pineapple

1 teaspoon fresh grated ginger

1 tablespoon canola oil

2 tablespoons fresh lemon juice

½ teaspoon salt

½ teaspoon garlic powder

½ teaspoon paprika

Twelve 6-inch wooden skewers soaked in water

DIRECTIONS

1 Place all ingredients except for skewers into a medium bowl, mix well, and marinate for 30 minutes.

2 Preheat the oven to 350 degrees. Thread a piece of pork, a cherry tomato, another piece of pork, and a pineapple chunk onto each skewer. Repeat until all skewers are used.

3 Place pork skewers on an ungreased cookie sheet and bake for 20 minutes or until the pork is fully cooked (it will no longer be pink in the middle when done). Serve hot.

PER SERVING: *Calories 60 (From Fat 20); Fat 2g (Saturated 0g); Cholesterol 25mg; Sodium 70mg; Carbohydrate 4g (Dietary Fiber 1g); Protein 8g; Sugar 3g.*

Chapter **16**

Sumptuous Soups and Stews

When you want a comforting meal, a cup of hot soup or stew really hits the spot. It warms you up from the top of your head to the tips of your toes. They're easy to make, and when you prepare them yourself, you can control the ingredients to make sure you get enough nutrients.

Salad and soup combinations are endless and can please everyone. Making them is a cinch and doesn't require a whole lot of cooking skills. If you can chop, you can make salads and soups. Pair any of the soup or stew recipes in this chapter with a salad for an easy, satisfying meal.

Serving Up Satisfying Soups

We're believers in homemade soup, which allows you to control the ingredients. In the case of commercially prepared soups, not all soups are created equal. Canned soups are high in sodium unless you buy the low-sodium versions. We use low-sodium broth in our recipes, so you can rest assured these soups have less sodium than most canned. Some soups, both canned and prepacked in the deli section of the supermarket, are high in fat. If you had GBP surgery, some of them have enough fat to give you dumping syndrome. If you had AGB, you still want to avoid these soups because the fat makes them very high in calories.

Soups aren't usually a great source of protein unless you choose bean or lentil soups. We put more meat in our soup recipes than you find in those found in stores, because if the soup is your meal, you need to get in your protein!

Broccoli Cheese Soup

STAGE: SOFT OR REGULAR FOODS	PREP TIME: 10 MIN	COOK TIME: 20 MIN	YIELD: 4 SERVINGS

INGREDIENTS

1 large shallot, minced

1 tablespoon butter

1 large head broccoli or 1 pound fresh or frozen broccoli, chopped into 1- inch pieces

2 cups vegetable or chicken stock

¼ teaspoon salt

1 large Russet potato, cubed

½ cup nonfat milk

½ cup shredded lowfat cheddar cheese

DIRECTIONS

1 In a large soup pot, add the shallot and butter on medium heat. Stir until softened.

2 Add the broccoli, stock, salt, and potato. Simmer 15 minutes or so until broccoli softens.

3 Turn off the heat and add the milk. With a handheld blender, blend until smooth.

4 Stir in the cheese with a wooden spoon or spatula until melted.

PER SERVING: *Calories 150 (From Fat 41); Fat 5g (Saturated 3g); Cholesterol 11mg; Sodium 773mg; Carbohydrate 20g (Dietary Fiber 4g); Protein 10g; Sugar 4g.*

Mexi Turkey Tortilla Soup

STAGE: REGULAR FOODS	PREP TIME: 15 MIN	COOK TIME: 25 MIN	YIELD: 8 SERVINGS

INGREDIENTS

1 tablespoon olive oil

1 cup chopped onion

2 tablespoons minced garlic

Three 6-inch corn tortillas, cut into 1-inch pieces

One 14.5-ounce can diced tomatoes

2 tablespoons chopped green chili pepper

4 cups low-sodium chicken broth

1 teaspoon ground cumin

1 teaspoon ground coriander

1 teaspoon dried oregano

12 ounces cooked ground or shredded turkey breast

1 cup frozen corn kernels

½ cup fat-free half-and-half

1 cup shredded Monterey Jack cheese

2 tablespoons fresh lime juice

¼ cup chopped fresh cilantro (optional)

½ cup fat-free sour cream (optional)

Black Bean Salsa (optional) (see Chapter 10)

DIRECTIONS

1 Heat oil in a large saucepan over medium-high heat. Add the onion and garlic and sauté for 3 minutes. Stir in the tortilla pieces and sauté until they are crisp.

2 Add the tomatoes, green chili peppers, broth, and spices and bring to a boil. Remove from the heat and let cool for 5 minutes.

3 Purée the soup in small batches in a blender and return to the saucepan. Add the turkey, corn, and half-and-half. Bring to a boil and simmer for 5 minutes, or until the soup begins to thicken.

4 Reduce heat to medium, sprinkle in the cheese, and stir until melted. Add lime juice. Serve in bowls, topped with cilantro, sour cream, and Black Bean Salsa if desired.

PER SERVING: *Calories 220 (From Fat 70); Fat 8g (Saturated 4g); Cholesterol 50mg; Sodium 300 mg; Carbohydrate 16g (Dietary Fiber 1g); Protein 20g; Sugar 3g.*

TIP: To prevent the soup from leaking out the top of the blender, purée in small batches.

TIP: You can buy precooked turkey at most delis. When purchasing, ask for the amount you need to be weighed and sliced thick so that you can cube or shred it.

TIP: Be sure to use corn tortillas, not flour, because they're lower in sodium and won't make the soup cloudy. Then to top off this fiesta of a soup, head over to Chapter 10 and make the Black Bean Salsa.

Chunky Chicken Noodle Soup

STAGE: REGULAR FOODS	PREP TIME: 10 MIN	COOK TIME: 35 MIN	YIELD: 8 SERVINGS

INGREDIENTS

1 tablespoon butter

1 pound boneless skinless chicken breast cut into ½-inch pieces

1 large celery stalk, thinly sliced

1 large carrot, thinly sliced

½ cup chopped onion

½ teaspoon dried basil

¼ teaspoon dried rosemary

¼ teaspoon black pepper

½ teaspoon salt

2 teaspoons all-purpose flour

6 cups low-sodium chicken broth

1 cup water

2 ounces thin egg noodles

DIRECTIONS

1 Melt the butter in a large pot. Add the chicken, celery, carrot, onion, basil, rosemary, pepper, and salt and sauté for 3 minutes.

2 Add flour and sauté an additional 2 minutes; then stir in chicken broth and water and bring to a simmer. Simmer for 30 minutes, adding egg noodles for the last 10 minutes.

PER SERVING: Calories 140 (From Fat 35); Fat 4g (Saturated 2g); Cholesterol 45mg; Sodium 270mg; Carbohydrate 10g (Dietary Fiber 1g); Protein 18g; Sugar 2g.

FRESH VERSUS DRIED HERBS

Fresh and dried herbs are great for fresh preparations and cooking, but knowing when to use them makes all the difference in the way your meals taste. Use dried herbs for dishes that cook more than 30 minutes. Use fresh herbs in fresh salad preparations and when cooking less than 30 minutes. If you cook fresh herbs too long, they become bitter and black, and can also burn in high-heat preparations, such as sautéing, grilling, and broiling. Use your best judgment when preparing your favorite recipes.

Pork and Sauerkraut Soup

STAGE: REGULAR FOODS	PREP TIME: 5 MIN	COOK TIME: 2 HR 20 MIN	YIELD: 8 SERVINGS

INGREDIENTS

1 pound pork loin, trimmed

1 cup chopped onion

1 teaspoon dried basil

1 teaspoon dried thyme

1 teaspoon garlic powder

6 cups low-sodium chicken broth

One 14.5-ounce can sauerkraut, drained

2 cups mashed potatoes

DIRECTIONS

1 Put the pork, onion, basil, thyme, garlic powder, and broth in a medium pot. Bring to a light simmer, cover, and continue to simmer lightly for 2 hours.

2 Remove the pork from the broth, and using 2 forks, pull it apart into small pieces. Return the pork to the pot. Add the sauerkraut and bring back to a simmer.

3 Let simmer for 5 minutes. Serve 1 cup of soup over ¼ cup warmed mashed potatoes.

TIP: To make prep easier, you can use the mashed potatoes from the refrigerator section or the deli at the grocery, or make them from mashed potato flakes.

TIP: Sauerkraut can be found on the shelf canned or jarred, or in a refrigerated jar. If you're watching your sodium intake, check the labels. The sauerkraut in the refrigerated section, while still high in sodium, may be lower than the shelf products.

PER SERVING: *Calories 170 (From Fat 45); Fat 5g (Saturated 2g); Cholesterol 45mg; Sodium 590mg; Carbohydrate 15g (Dietary Fiber 3g); Protein 17g; Sugar 3g.*

Savoring Home-Style Stews

Stews are meals by themselves. They can be made ahead of time and even work well in a slow cooker. In addition, stews are packed with flavor and can combine most of the food groups in one dish.

Smoky Chicken Stew

| STAGE: REGULAR FOODS | PREP TIME: 10 MIN | COOK TIME: 40 MIN | YIELD: 8 SERVINGS |

INGREDIENTS

¼ cup plus 2 teaspoons olive oil

1 pound boneless, skinless chicken breast, cut into 1-inch pieces

6 ounces turkey kielbasa, sliced in to ¼-inch slices and cut into small pieces

¼ cup all-purpose flour

¾ cup diced green pepper

¾ cup diced onion

¾ cup minced celery

3 garlic cloves, minced

1 teaspoon black pepper

1 teaspoon cayenne pepper

One 14.5-ounce can diced tomatoes

4 cups low-sodium chicken broth

¼ cup chopped fresh parsley

2 tablespoons fresh chopped tarragon

DIRECTIONS

1 Heat 2 teaspoons of the olive oil in a large pot over medium heat. Add the chicken and sausage and cook, turning occasionally, until browned on all sides, about 5 minutes. Remove the meats from the pot and set aside.

2 Combine the ¼ cup olive oil and flour in the same pot the meat was browned in. Cook, stirring constantly, until it's the consistency and color of peanut butter, about 3 minutes.

3 Add the green pepper, onion, celery, garlic, black pepper, and cayenne pepper. Cook about 5 minutes or until vegetables are soft. Stir in the tomatoes, broth, parsley, and tarragon. Simmer 10 to 15 minutes. Add the meat and simmer another 5 minutes.

PER SERVING: *Calories 220 (From Fat 110); Fat 12g (Saturated 2g); Cholesterol 45mg; Sodium 410mg; Carbohydrate 10g (Dietary Fiber 1g); Protein 20g; Sugar 3g.*

VARY IT! For a heartier meal, try serving the soup over brown rice.

TIP: This stew tastes even better the next day and freezes well for up to 60 days.

Meaty Lentil Stew

STAGE: REGULAR FOODS	PREP TIME: 15 MIN	COOK TIME: 1 HR 15 MIN	YIELD: 8 SERVINGS

INGREDIENTS

2 tablespoons olive oil

2 cloves garlic, finely chopped

1 medium onion, finely chopped

4 ounces fully cooked ham, diced

2 ounces Genoa salami, diced

1 bay leaf

4 cups water

2 cups low-sodium chicken broth

½ teaspoon black pepper

1½ cups dried lentils, sorted and rinsed

DIRECTIONS

1 Heat oil in a medium pot over medium-high heat. Add the garlic and onion and sauté 5 minutes, stirring frequently, until onion is tender. Stir in the ham and salami and cook over medium heat for 5 minutes, stirring frequently.

2 Stir in the bay leaf, water, broth, pepper, and lentils. Heat to boiling; then reduce heat, cover, and simmer for 1 hour, stirring occasionally, until lentils are tender. Remove the bay leaf and serve.

PER SERVING: *Calories 210 (From Fat 70); Fat 8g (Saturated 2g); Cholesterol 15mg; Sodium 340mg; Carbohydrate 24g (Dietary Fiber 4g); Protein 14g; Sugar 1g.*

TIP: Bags of lentils may have little stones from the milling process, so make sure to sift through them and sort out any stones before cooking.

Chapter **17**

Completing the Meal: Vegetables and Side Dishes

red Astaire was a great dancer, but when he was paired with Ginger Rogers, they were unbeatable on the dance floor. The best part of the meal isn't always the entrée; sometimes it's what's sitting next to it. Though you may focus on preparing a wonderful protein-based entrée, the food you use to complement it can take the meal from ho-hum to yahoo.

A side dish is a smaller portion size than the entrée. Your side dish can be hot or cold, smooth or crunchy, sweet or sour. Typically side dishes are vegetables, salads, or starches, such as potatoes, rice, pasta, or bread. Because your meals are smaller after weight loss surgery, you may only have room in your pouch for one side dish to accompany your entrée. If you aren't far out from surgery, a side dish may be enough for your entire meal.

Here are some things to think about when picking a side dish for your meal:

>> **Prep time:** If your entrée is going to take you some time to prepare, pick a side dish that requires little preparation or one that can be made ahead of time.

>> **Tastes good together:** Make sure your dishes go together, but don't go overboard. You don't want everything to taste salty or sweet.

>> **Looks good together:** Baked fish with cauliflower looks boring, but baked fish with sautéed broccoli and red peppers is a pretty sight, which makes meals far more appealing.

Packing Flavor into Potato Dishes

Potatoes have gotten a bad rap because they're a high-carbohydrate food. However, potatoes are a good source of vitamins C and B6, potassium, and fiber. They're naturally low in fat, but the way they are often prepared or the toppings added can turn them into a high-calorie, high-fat nightmare. If you want to add a potato to your meal, just make sure you choose a preparation method that doesn't add a lot of fat or load it up with high-calorie toppings after cooking.

As you prepare potatoes, you may notice black or green spots. Black spots are caused by bruising the potato. As firm as a potato feels, it bruises as easily as an apple or a banana. Simply cut away any black spots before using. Green spots are caused by long exposure light. Like with black spots, simply cut away the discolored part before using.

Potatoes are tubers, which means they grow underground as part of a root system. Most root vegetables grow as a single root directly below where they're planted, like a carrot, but a potato plant can have 5 to 8 potatoes (tubers).

Asiago Carrot and Potato Au Gratin

STAGE: SMOOTH FOODS	PREP TIME: 10 MIN	COOK TIME: 17 MIN	YIELD: 4 SERVINGS

INGREDIENTS

2 medium carrots, cut into quarters

2 medium red potatoes, cut into quarters

1 egg

¼ cup grated Asiago cheese, divided

1 tablespoon butter

1 tablespoon fat-free sour cream

¼ teaspoon Dijon mustard

½ teaspoon salt

⅛ teaspoon cayenne pepper

DIRECTIONS

1 Place quartered carrots and potatoes into a large pot and cover with cold water. Bring to a boil and cook until tender, about 15 minutes depending on their size. Drain.

2 Preheat the broiler to high. Spray an 8-x-8-inch baking dish with nonstick cooking spray.

3 Put the carrots and potatoes in a food processor (a blender won't work). Add the egg, 3 tablespoons Asiago cheese, butter, sour cream, mustard, salt, and cayenne and purée until smooth.

4 Spoon the mixture into the baking dish and sprinkle with the remaining 1 tablespoon of Asiago cheese. Broil 3 to 6 minutes or until golden brown.

PER SERVING: *Calories 160 (From Fat 55); Fat 6g (Saturated 4g); Cholesterol 60mg; Sodium 440mg; Carbohydrate 21g (Dietary Fiber 3g); Protein 6g; Sugar 3g.*

Sweet Potato Bake

STAGE: SMOOTH FOODS	PREP TIME: 5 MIN	COOK TIME: 20 MIN	YIELD: 4 SERVINGS

INGREDIENTS

2 cups canned sweet potatoes, drained

1 egg

1 tablespoon brown sugar

1 teaspoon vanilla extract

¼ cup fat-free cream cheese

½ teaspoon cinnamon

⅛ teaspoon nutmeg

⅛ teaspoon ground clove

DIRECTIONS

1 Preheat the oven to 350 degrees. Coat an 8-x-8-inch baking dish with nonstick cooking spray.

2 Place all ingredients into a food processor and purée until well mixed. Pour the mixture into the dish and bake for 20 minutes.

PER SERVING: *Calories 140 (From Fat 20); Fat 2g (Saturated 1g); Cholesterol 55mg; Sodium 160mg; Carbohydrate 27g (Dietary Fiber 3g); Protein 5g; Sugar 7g.*

SWEET POTATOES VERSUS YAMS

Sweet potatoes and yams are not the same thing. Most of the "yams" you see in the grocery store are really sweet potatoes. The USDA requires that anything called a yam also be labeled "sweet potato," but they come from different botanical families. Sweet potatoes are about the size of regular potatoes, yams can grow up to 70 pounds! Yams are not as moist or as sweet as sweet potatoes and contain less beta-carotene.

Making a Little Go a Long Way: Pasta Side Dishes

Pasta doesn't have to be a food you left behind after weight loss surgery. Granted, some pastas work better than others, and chances are you won't be able to eat a whole bowl like you did before. Being restricted to a smaller portion size is just part of the reason. The type of flour makes the difference in how well it sets in the pouch.

REMEMBER

Pasta made with white flour typically doesn't work well because it sticks together and forms big lumps. If you've ever cooked pasta, put it in the drainer without rinsing, and left it for a few minutes, you know that you ended up with a big clump of noodles all stuck together. That's what happens to it in your pouch, too, and you won't feel good. Whole-wheat pasta has a lot more fiber and doesn't clump together after cooking, so it won't lump up in your pouch as much, either.

Pasta can be served as a main dish or a side dish. What's the difference? If the recipe contains a protein food like chicken or seafood, consider it a main dish. If there isn't a protein food in the recipe, consider it a side dish and pair it with a protein food. Pasta is an especially good side dish when paired with lots of vegetables.

TIP

Here are a few tips for cooking pasta:

>> When cooked correctly, pasta is *al dente:* soft to the touch with a slight firmness in the center. However, pasta will probably set better in the pouch if you cook it until it's soft all the way through. No two packaged pastas are the same, so be sure to read the directions before cooking. Contrary to popular belief, throwing the pasta in the air and having it stick the ceiling is not an accurate way to test doneness.

>> Don't add oil to the water when cooking pasta. The oil coats the pasta and keeps sauces and other foods from clinging to it.

>> Add salt to the water when cooking pasta. Salt adds flavor to the pasta, and if it's not added to the water it is difficult to make your pasta flavorful after cooking. Use 1 teaspoon of salt for every gallon of water used.

Creamy Romano Asparagus Pasta

STAGE: REGULAR FOODS	PREP TIME: 10 MIN	COOK TIME: 15 MIN	YIELD: 6 SERVINGS

INGREDIENTS

2 ounces dry whole-wheat rigatoni pasta

2 cups asparagus pieces (peel and cut the top half into ¾-inch pieces)

¾ cup fat-free half-and-half

2 teaspoons whole-grain mustard

2 teaspoons all-purpose flour

¼ teaspoon black pepper

1 teaspoon olive oil

2 teaspoons minced garlic

1 teaspoon minced fresh tarragon

1 teaspoon lemon juice

½ cup fresh grated Romano cheese, divided

DIRECTIONS

1 Cook pasta according to the package directions, adding the asparagus and stirring occasionally for the last three minutes. Drain and return to the pot.

2 Meanwhile, whisk half-and-half, mustard, flour, and pepper in a medium bowl.

3 Heat oil in a small saucepan over medium-high heat. Add garlic and cook, stirring constantly, for 30 seconds. Whisk in the half-and-half mixture. Bring to a simmer, stirring constantly, and cook until thickened, 2 minutes. Stir in tarragon and lemon juice.

4 Stir the cooked pasta and asparagus into the sauce and cook over medium-high heat, stirring constantly, until the sauce is thick, creamy, and coats the pasta.

5 Stir ¼ cup Romano cheese into the pasta until combined. Serve the pasta topped with the remaining ¼ cup Romano cheese.

PER SERVING: *Calories 110 (From Fat 40); Fat 4g (Saturated 2g); Cholesterol 5mg; Sodium 200mg; Carbohydrate 13g (Dietary Fiber 2g); Protein 6g; Sugar 3g.*

Tuscan Pasta Sauté

STAGE: REGULAR FOODS	PREP TIME: 10 MIN	COOK TIME: 15 MIN	YIELD: 4 SERVINGS

INGREDIENTS

2 ounces dry whole-wheat angel hair pasta

1 tablespoon olive oil

2 cloves fresh garlic, minced

½ cup chopped plum tomatoes

½ cup peeled and thin sliced carrots

½ cup thin strips green bell peppers

½ cup chopped zucchini

¼ cup chopped fresh basil

½ teaspoon salt

¼ teaspoon red pepper flakes

DIRECTIONS

1 Cook pasta according to the package directions and set aside.

2 Heat oil in a large sauté pan over medium-high heat. Add garlic and sauté for 30 seconds. Add tomatoes, carrots, peppers, and zucchini, and sauté for 3 minutes.

3 Mix in the cooked pasta and sauté for 2 minutes. Toss with fresh basil, salt, and red pepper flakes.

PER SERVING: *Calories 100 (From Fat 40); Fat 4g (Saturated 1g); Cholesterol 0mg; Sodium 310mg; Carbohydrate 15g (Dietary Fiber 3g); Protein 3g; Sugar 3g.*

Putting Veggies and Side Salads in the Spotlight

Whether eaten cooked or raw, vegetables are a must at every meal. They're low in calories, fat, and sodium, and add flavor, color, and texture to most of your favorite dishes. In this section we provide you with some cooked veggie recipes as well as some delicious side salads.

Rinse and scrub fresh vegetables to remove any dirt or chemicals that may remain from the farm. Try to avoid cutting vegetables in advance — they begin to lose quality and nutrients and go bad in two to three days.

When cooking vegetables, the variety and size of the vegetables matter greatly. You want to use pieces of vegetables that take the same amount of cook time. Hard vegetables like potatoes and carrots should be cut smaller and faster-cooking veggies like broccoli and squash should be cut into larger pieces so when they're all cooked together they finish cooking at the same time.

For best results, store vegetables in a cool, dark place. The best spot is in your refrigerator crisper drawer. The exception here is tomatoes; store these at room temperature. If you're not sure of the best way to store your veggies, look at how they're displayed at the store. You won't find tomatoes in the cooler and you won't find lettuce in unchilled cases.

Roasted Vegetables with Tahini Sauce

STAGE: REGULAR FOODS	PREP TIME: 10 MIN	COOK TIME: 20 MIN	YIELD: 4 SERVINGS

INGREDIENTS

½ large eggplant, sliced into rounds and then sliced into ½-inch sticks

1 cup baby carrots

1 zucchini, sliced into ½-inch sticks

1 tablespoon olive oil

1 teaspoon dried Herbs de Provence or ½ teaspoon dried thyme and ¼ teaspoon dried basil and ¼ teaspoon dried oregano

½ teaspoon sea salt

Tahini Sauce (see the following recipe)

DIRECTIONS

1 Preheat the oven to 400 degrees.

2 Place the eggplant, carrots, and zucchini on a baking sheet lined with foil.

3 Drizzle the vegetables with the oil, herbs, and salt.

4 Bake for 20 minutes.

5 Dip the vegetables into the Tahini Sauce, room temperature or chilled.

Tahini Sauce

¼ cup tahini

2 tablespoons fresh lemon juice

¼ cup plain yogurt

¼ teaspoon cumin

⅛ teaspoon salt

⅛ teaspoon pepper

In a small bowl, whisk all the ingredients. Adjust the seasoning to taste.

PER SERVING: *Calories 159 (From Fat 107); Fat 12g (Saturated 2g); Cholesterol 0mg; Sodium 334mg; Carbohydrate 11g (Dietary Fiber 5g); Protein 5g; Sugar 5g.*

Three Bean Salad

STAGE: REGULAR FOODS	PREP TIME: 10 MIN	YIELD: 6 SERVINGS

INGREDIENTS

½ cup garbanzo beans, drained and rinsed

1 cup no-salt-added kidney beans, drained and rinsed

1 cup no-salt-added black beans, drained and rinsed

½ small onion, chopped fine

¼ cup thinly sliced green olives

One 4-ounce can mushrooms, drained

¼ cup finely chopped fresh dill

3 cloves garlic, minced

1 tablespoon olive oil

¼ cup fresh lemon juice

DIRECTIONS

Place all ingredients into a large mixing bowl and mix well.

PER SERVING: *Calories 90 (From Fat 30); Fat 3g (Saturated 0g); Cholesterol 0mg; Sodium 320mg; Carbohydrate 13g (Dietary Fiber 4g); Protein 4g; Sugar 2g.*

VARY IT! To turn this into a main dish, add shrimp or cooked chicken.

Southern-Style Green Beans

STAGE: REGULAR FOODS	PREP TIME: 10 MIN	COOK TIME: 45 MIN	YIELD: 8 SERVINGS

INGREDIENTS

4 slices chopped bacon

1 large onion, chopped

2 teaspoons chopped garlic

1½ pounds fresh green beans, cleaned and ends removed

¼ cup chopped fresh dill

1 teaspoon black pepper

Water

DIRECTIONS

1 In a medium pot over medium-high heat, add bacon and sauté until bacon is well done. Do not drain fat. Add onion and garlic to pan and sauté for 3 minutes.

2 Add fresh green beans, dill, and pepper to the pot, and fill pot with just enough water to cover the beans. Simmer on low for 30 minutes or until beans become soft. Drain.

PER SERVING: *Calories 60 (From Fat 15); Fat 2g (Saturated 1g); Cholesterol 5mg; Sodium 100mg; Carbohydrate 8g (Dietary Fiber 3g); Protein 3g; Sugar 2g.*

NOTE: Southern green beans are meant to be soft and cooked longer. This gives the green beans a chance absorb more flavor.

Cucumber Cheese Salad

STAGE: REGULAR FOODS	PREP TIME: 10 MIN	CHILL TIME: 30 MIN	YIELD: 4 SERVINGS

INGREDIENTS

1 medium cucumber, peeled and thinly sliced

½ cup julienne cut red bell pepper

¼ cup sliced green onion

¼ cup finely diced celery

2 ounces Monterey Jack cheese, cut into small cubes

¼ cup plain nonfat yogurt

1½ teaspoons white wine vinegar

½ teaspoon Dijon mustard

¼ teaspoon Worcestershire sauce

⅛ teaspoon salt

⅛ teaspoon black pepper

DIRECTIONS

1 Combine the cucumber, red pepper, green onion, celery, and cheese in a medium bowl.

2 Combine yogurt, white wine vinegar, mustard, Worcestershire sauce, salt, and pepper in a small bowl.

3 Pour the dressing over the vegetables and cheese. Mix well and refrigerate for 30 to 60 minutes before serving.

PER SERVING: *Calories 80 (From Fat 45); Fat 5g (Saturated 3g); Cholesterol 15mg; Sodium 230mg; Carbohydrate 5g (Dietary Fiber 1g); Protein 5g; Sugar 3g.*

Avocado, Tomato, and Feta Salad

STAGE: REGULAR FOODS	PREP TIME: 10 MIN	CHILL TIME: 1 HR	YIELD: 4 SERVINGS

INGREDIENTS

½ medium cucumber, peeled, seeded, and chopped

2 chopped Roma tomatoes

2 tablespoons finely chopped green onions

1 clove garlic, minced

1 tablespoons minced fresh parsley

1 teaspoon chopped fresh dill

2 ounces crumbled reduced-fat feta cheese

1 teaspoon fresh lemon juice

1 tablespoon olive oil

½ avocado, sliced into 8 slices

DIRECTIONS

1 Combine the cucumber, tomato, green onions, garlic, parsley, dill, feta cheese, lemon juice, and olive oil in a bowl and refrigerate for 1 hour.

2 Divide salad mixture evenly on four plates and top each with 2 slices of avocado.

PER SERVING: *Calories 110 (From Fat 80); Fat 9g (Saturated 3g); Cholesterol 5mg; Sodium 200mg; Carbohydrate 5g (Dietary Fiber 3g); Protein 4g; Sugar 1g.*

TIP: Be sure to allow enough time for chilling to blend the flavors.

Edamame Salad

STAGE: REGULAR FOODS | **PREP TIME: 15 MIN** | **YIELD: 4 SERVINGS**

INGREDIENTS

8 ounces frozen shelled edamame

1½ cups frozen petite corn kernels

½ red bell pepper, chopped

½ cup sliced green onion

¼ cup finely chopped red onion

¼ cup chopped fresh flat-leaf parsley

1 tablespoon chopped fresh oregano or basil

Dressing (see the following recipe)

DIRECTIONS

1 Prepare the edamame according to package directions. Drain, rinse with cold water, and drain again thoroughly.

2 Combine edamame, corn, red bell pepper, green onion, red onion, parsley, and oregano or basil in a large bowl. Pour dressing over veggies and toss to coat.

Dressing

¼ cup fresh lemon juice

1 tablespoon Dijon mustard

1 tablespoon olive oil

¼ teaspoon salt

¼ teaspoon fresh ground black pepper

In a small bowl, whisk together all ingredients.

PER SERVING: *Calories 180 (From Fat 60); Fat 7g (Saturated 1g); Cholesterol 0mg; Sodium 240mg; Carbohydrate 22g (Dietary Fiber 4g); Protein 9g; Sugar 7g.*

Waldorf Salad

STAGE: REGULAR FOODS	PREP TIME: 15 MIN	CHILL TIME: 2 HR	YIELD: 6 SERVINGS

INGREDIENTS

2 cups peeled and chopped Granny Smith apples

1 tablespoon lemon juice

3 tablespoons light mayonnaise

⅓ cup nonfat plain Greek yogurt

½ cup halved grapes

3 tablespoons chopped walnuts

2 tablespoons sugar substitute

DIRECTIONS

Place all ingredients into a medium mixing bowl and mix well. Refrigerate before serving.

PER SERVING: *Calories 90 (From Fat 45); Fat 5g (Saturated 1g); Cholesterol 5mg; Sodium 70mg; Carbohydrate 10g (Dietary Fiber 1g); Protein 2g; Sugar 7g.*

Oriental Slaw

STAGE: REGULAR FOODS	PREP TIME: 15 MIN	CHILL TIME: 2 HR	YIELD: 6 SERVINGS

INGREDIENTS

¼ cup green onion, sliced

2 cups finely shredded cabbage

1 cup shredded carrots

¼ cup water chestnuts, drained and cut into thin strips

¼ cup julienne cut red bell pepper

¼ cup unsalted sunflower seeds

¼ cup sliced almonds

3 tablespoons sugar substitute

1 tablespoon sesame oil

¾ teaspoon salt

1 teaspoon black pepper

4 tablespoons cider vinegar

DIRECTIONS

Place all ingredients into a medium bowl and mix well. Refrigerate before serving.

TIP: No time to shred cabbage and carrots? Buy it already shredded and bagged in the produce section of the supermarket.

PER SERVING: Calories 100 (From Fat 60); Fat 1g (Saturated 6g); Cholesterol 0mg; Sodium 310mg; Carbohydrate 7g (Dietary Fiber 2g); Protein 3g; Sugar 2g.

Lentils with Greens, Lemon, and Smoked Paprika

STAGE: REGULAR FOODS	PREP TIME: 5 MIN	COOK TIME: 30 MIN	YIELD: 4 SERVINGS

INGREDIENTS

1 cup raw brown lentils

4 cups water

2 teaspoons canola or olive oil

3 cups winter greens (kale, spinach, beet or turnip greens, or Swiss chard)

½ teaspoon salt

½ lemon, chopped (with the rind, but without the white pith)

1 cup regular vegetable stock (not a low-sodium variety)

1 teaspoon smoked paprika

DIRECTIONS

1 In a large saucepan, bring the lentils and water to a boil. Lower the heat and simmer for 20 minutes.

2 Drain the lentils and transfer to a medium bowl.

3 In the same saucepan over medium heat, add the oil and greens. Cover for 2 to 3 minutes until wilted. Add the lemon and cover for another 2 to 3 minutes until the lemon softens.

4 Add all to the lentils, stir, and serve.

PER SERVING: *Calories 226 (From Fat 33); Fat 4g (Saturated 1g); Cholesterol 2mg; Sodium 396mg; Carbohydrate 35g (Dietary Fiber 16g); Protein 15g; Sugar 2g.*

Chapter **18**

Smart Snacking

Everyone has that time of day when the urge to snack hits you. Snacks are okay, but grazing is not. What's the difference? A snack is eating a set amount of food at one time, but grazing is that nibbling and picking that goes on all day and leads to weight regain. Although your pouch may not hold a lot of food at one time, if you eat every hour it will hold a lot of food throughout the day. That's why planning your snacks is just as important as planning your meals.

Your surgeon may have recommendations for you about snacking. If you had GBP, you may find that you feel better if you eat about every three hours, keeping your blood sugar stable. If you had AGB and go too long between eating, you may find yourself getting too hungry and then wanting to eat too much and too fast.

If you have had weight loss surgery a few weeks or months ago, your surgeon or dietitian may advise you to choose protein supplement-type snacks, such as shakes or bars, so that you can meet your protein goals before choosing snacks that have a lower protein content.

What makes a good snack? The same rules apply for snacks as for meals. Include some protein, carbs, and fat. A snack with some fiber keeps you feeling fuller longer than a snack of a dry, crumbly, high-carb food like pretzels. If you want to eat some crackers, make them whole grain and add a protein-based food to them. The snack recipes in this chapter are sure to keep your hunger at bay and help you meet your nutritional needs.

STORING YOUR FRUIT

Storing your favorite fruits a dark, cool space is best. If left out of the refrigerator, fruit ripens faster and doesn't last as long than if refrigerated. When refrigerated the fruit takes longer to go bad and in some cases may never ripen to its fullest potential. Bananas are a perfect example of when that's a good thing: When picked, they're green and need to ripen, so leaving them on the counter for two to three days makes them perfect for eating. If refrigerated they can take up a week to ripen and some cases never reach their full ripening potential.

TIP

When you make your snack, put away all the ingredients and clean up right away. You'll be less tempted to have more if you have to start the process all over again. Also, eat your snack mindfully so you know what you're eating and when you feel satisfied. Eating in front of the TV or at the computer is unconscious eating and usually leads to overeating.

Finding Not-So-Ordinary Fruit Snacks

Fruit is a good source of fiber, vitamins, and minerals. It's a great snack and even better when combined with some protein. You may be inclined to avoid fruit because of the sugar content; however, the sugar is naturally occurring and doesn't cause a dumping problem like added sugars.

TIP

Some folks have problems with fruit peels getting stuck, so if in doubt, peel it.

Apple with Honey Almond Butter

STAGE: REGULAR FOODS	PREP TIME: 5 MIN	YIELD: 1 SERVING

INGREDIENTS

2 teaspoons almond butter

½ teaspoon honey

⅛ teaspoon cinnamon

1 small apple, cored, peeled and cut into 8 slices

DIRECTIONS

In a small bowl combine almond butter, honey, and cinnamon and mix well. Serve with apple slices for dipping.

PER SERVING: *Calories 150 (From Fat 60); Fat 6g (Saturated 1g); Cholesterol 0mg; Sodium 50mg; Carbohydrate 26g (Dietary Fiber 2g); Protein 2g; Sugar 19g.*

NOTE: 16 grams of sugar in this recipe come from the apple. We've added just a touch of honey, so it won't be a problem if you are prone to dumping syndrome. Eating too much honey at one time can give you dumping because it is a concentrated sugar.

Pineapple with Ricotta

STAGE: REGULAR FOODS	PREP TIME: 5 MIN	YIELD: 1 SERVING

INGREDIENTS

¼ cup crushed pineapple, packed in juice, drained

¼ cup part-skim ricotta cheese

½ teaspoon lemon juice

1 teaspoon sugar substitute

4 lowfat graham cracker squares

DIRECTIONS

In a small bowl mix pineapple, ricotta, lemon juice, and sugar substitute. Serve with graham crackers.

PER SERVING: *Calories 170 (From Fat 55); Fat 6g (Saturated 3g); Cholesterol 20mg; Sodium 150mg; Carbohydrate 22g (Dietary Fiber 1g); Protein 8g; Sugar 11g.*

Quelling Cravings for Crunchy Bites

Sometimes you just gotta have something crunchy. Dry, high-carbohydrate foods are crunchy but won't fill you up and aren't great in the nutrition department, either. Pass on the chips and pretzels and crunch into something that does your body good.

Fresh fruits and vegetables are perfect for those crisp and crunchy cravings. The crunch of a fresh, juicy apple is unsurpassed by greasy potato chips. In addition, bell pepper, carrot, or celery sticks dipped in your favorite low-calorie dip are not only great tasting, but also give your body plenty of added nutrition.

Whole-Wheat Cheddar Pita

STAGE: REGULAR FOODS	PREP TIME: 3 MIN	COOK TIME: 2 MIN	YIELD: 1 SERVING

INGREDIENTS

1 small whole-wheat pita

¼ cup shredded lowfat cheddar cheese

⅛ teaspoon garlic powder

⅛ teaspoon chili powder

DIRECTIONS

1 Preheat the oven broiler. While broiler is preheating, top the pita with cheddar cheese, garlic, and chili powder.

2 Place under broiler for 1 to 2 minutes or until cheese is melted and bubbly. Let cool for 2 minutes and cut into pieces.

PER SERVING: *Calories 130 (From Fat 30); Fat 3g (Saturated 2g); Cholesterol 5mg; Sodium 330mg; Carbohydrate 16g (Dietary Fiber 2g); Protein 10g; Sugar 0g.*

Parmesan Popcorn Delight

STAGE: REGULAR FOODS	PREP TIME: 2 MIN	COOK TIME: 5 MIN	YIELD: 1 SERVING

INGREDIENTS

2 cups popped light-butter microwave popcorn

2 teaspoons grated Parmesan cheese

⅛ teaspoon black pepper

DIRECTIONS

Pop the popcorn according to directions. As soon as the popcorn is done, place 2 cups in a small bowl, add Parmesan cheese and pepper, and toss.

PER SERVING: *Calories 80 (From Fat 30); Fat 3g (Saturated 1g); Cholesterol 5mg; Sodium 190mg; Carbohydrate 12g (Dietary Fiber 2g); Protein 3g; Sugar 0g.*

NOTE: Be sure to check your surgeon's recommendations for popcorn before including it in your diet. This is one of those foods that you may have to wait several months before eating.

Spicy Almonds

STAGE: REGULAR FOODS	PREP TIME: 3 MIN	COOK TIME: 5 MIN	YIELD: 1 SERVING

INGREDIENTS

¼ cup whole raw almonds

¼ teaspoon olive oil

A dash of salt

⅛ teaspoon onion powder

⅛ teaspoon red pepper flakes

DIRECTIONS

1 Preheat the oven to 350 degrees. In a small bowl add all the ingredients and mix well.

2 Place the mix on a ungreased cookie sheet and roast for 5 minutes, turning the almonds once. Let cool.

PER SERVING: *Calories 220 (From Fat 170); Fat 19g (Saturated 2g); Cholesterol 0mg; Sodium 160mg; Carbohydrate 8g (Dietary Fiber 4g); Protein 7g; Sugar 2g.*

Peanut Butter Honey over Rice Cakes

STAGE: REGULAR FOODS	PREP TIME: 3 MIN	YIELD: 1 SERVING

INGREDIENTS

1 tablespoon natural creamy peanut butter

½ teaspoon honey

¼ teaspoon vanilla extract

2 brown rice cakes

DIRECTIONS

Place peanut butter, honey, and vanilla extract into a small bowl and mix well. Spread over rice cakes.

PER SERVING: *Calories 180 (From Fat 80); Fat 9g (Saturated 1g); Cholesterol 0mg; Sodium 120mg; Carbohydrate 21g (Dietary Fiber 2g); Protein 5g; Sugar 4g.*

NOTE: Remember to check the ingredient label on your peanut butter: You want "natural" peanut butter that's just made up of peanuts and salt.

Making Everything Better with Cheese

Moooove over for cheese, a favorite food for a lot of folks. Creamy or hard, sharp or mild; a type of cheese exists for even the pickiest of eaters.

Keep in mind that because of its high fat content, cheese is not a low-calorie food. Cheese is labeled with different levels of fat: regular, reduced fat, and fat free. Regular cheese is the highest in fat and calories. Reduced fat cheese has less fat but is not a lowfat food. It's made with 2 percent milk and has 25 percent less fat than regular cheese. Reduced fat cheese melts and can be used in cooking. Fat-free cheeses have a rubbery texture and do not melt. They only work if you eat a slice on a cold sandwich or sprinkle some on a salad.

Pears and Gorgonzola

STAGE: REGULAR FOODS	PREP TIME: 3 MIN	YIELD: 1 SERVING

INGREDIENTS

2 teaspoons Gorgonzola crumbles

1 teaspoon fat-free cream cheese, softened

⅛ teaspoon black pepper

1 small pear, peeled, cored, and cut into 6 sections

DIRECTIONS

In a small bowl combine gorgonzola, cream cheese, and pepper and mix well. Serve with pear slices.

PER SERVING: *Calories 110 (From Fat 20); Fat 2g (Saturated 1g); Cholesterol 5mg; Sodium 100mg; Carbohydrate 24g (Dietary Fiber 3g); Protein 2g; Sugar 15g.*

NOTE: Some pears have a thin skin and may not cause you sticking problems. We peel ours just to be save. Prevention is the best remedy for food sticking.

TIP: Store pears loose in the refrigerator and ripen them on the counter. Keep them away from strong-smelling foods because they absorb odors easily.

Mexi Cheese Cubes

STAGE: SOFT FOODS	PREP TIME: 3 MIN	YIELD: 1 SERVING

INGREDIENTS

½ cup small cubes reduced-fat Monterey Jack cheese

¼ teaspoon chili powder

¼ teaspoon cumin powder

¼ teaspoon garlic powder

¼ teaspoon onion powder

DIRECTIONS

In a small bowl add all ingredients and mix well. (The seasoning sticks to the outside of the cheese.) Keep cold until ready to serve.

PER SERVING: *Calories 170 (From Fat 110); Fat 12g (Saturated 7g); Cholesterol 40mg; Sodium 490mg; Carbohydrate 4g (Dietary Fiber 1g); Protein 15g; Sugar 0g.*

Chapter **19**

Divine Desserts

Desserts take on a new meaning after weight loss surgery. You may have had a sweet tooth before and now you notice your desire for sweets has changed. This can be from the surgery itself (if you had GBP) or simply because you eat less sugar as a part of your new lifestyle and therefore crave it less often. After weight loss surgery you can still enjoy desserts, but keep a few guidelines top of mind.

Avoid filling your pouch with foods that don't provide good nutrition, and choose your desserts wisely. Look for desserts that include some protein, fruit, or whole-grain carbs. Making your own sweets is healthier than buying foods from the supermarket because packaged foods usually contain high-fructose corn syrup or trans fats. "Sugar-free" desserts are usually made with sugar alcohols, which doesn't mean they're calorie-free. Some folks have a problem tolerating sugar alcohols, as they can cause gastric discomfort, so be mindful of the portion size if you choose to eat these foods.

Some folks decide to have GBP surgery rather than AGB because they want the possibility of getting dumping syndrome. This miserable reaction to high-sugar and/or high-fat foods helps keep people on the straight and narrow. Over time the severity of dumping syndrome usually lessens, and some people are tempted to push the envelope to see just how much they can eat before getting sick. If you let sweets start creeping into your diet with more frequency, before you know it, your sweet tooth could return. By limiting sweets and sticking with healthier desserts like the recipes in this chapter, you can keep your sugar cravings at bay and maintain your weight loss.

Enjoying Sweet Fruits without Added Calories

Sweet and good for you, fruit makes a fantastic dessert. Fruits provide vitamins, minerals, phytonutrients (healthy compounds found in fruits and vegetables), and fiber; plus they're naturally low in fat and sodium. Some people have problems with skins getting stuck, so if you're in doubt about a certain fruit or your own pouch, peel the fruit to be safe.

REMEMBER

If you had GBP, your surgeon probably provided recommendations about how much sugar you can safely eat at one time. These recommendations, typically ranging from 8 to 15 grams of sugar, are for *added* sugars, not the naturally occurring sugars found in fruits and dairy foods. It's the added sugars that will cause you problems. Unfortunately, the nutrition facts on food labels don't tell you if the sugars are natural or added. When shopping for packaged fruit or dairy foods, check the list of ingredients for added sugars, keeping in mind that sugar travels under a lot of names.

Several different kinds of sugar substitutes are available on the market and the choice is yours. If you use a sugar substitute in a recipe that requires baking or cooking, be sure to use one that is heat-stable, like Splenda.

Peach Parfait

STAGE: REGULAR FOODS	PREP TIME: 10 MIN	CHILL TIME: 2 HR	YIELD: 4 SERVINGS

INGREDIENTS

½ cup plain nonfat Greek yogurt

¼ cup fat-free cream cheese, softened

¼ cup part-skim ricotta cheese

¼ teaspoon vanilla extract

2 tablespoons sugar substitute

2 medium peaches, peeled and sliced

DIRECTIONS

1 In a medium bowl add the yogurt, cream cheese, ricotta, vanilla, and sugar substitute and blend with an electric mixer for 2 minutes or until smooth.

2 Place ¼ peach in the bottom of an 8-ounce glass and top with 2 tablespoons of the cream mixture. Top with another ¼ peach and 2 more tablespoons of the cream mixture. Repeat for three additional glasses. Refrigerate for 2 hours before serving.

PER SERVING: *Calories 80 (From Fat 20); Fat 2g (Saturated 2g); Cholesterol 5mg; Sodium 130mg; Carbohydrate 11g (Dietary Fiber 1g); Protein 7g; Sugar 8g.*

TIP: Store fresh peaches at room temperature, because keeping them in the refrigerator decreases the flavor of the fruit.

NOTE: If fresh peaches aren't available, you can substitute canned peach slices packed in juice or unsweetened frozen peaches.

Fruit with Dark Chocolate Sauce

STAGE: SOFT OR REGULAR FOODS	PREP TIME: 5 MIN	COOK TIME: 10 MIN	YIELD: 8 SERVINGS

INGREDIENTS

1 cup cold coffee

½ cup unsweetened cocoa

½ cup sugar

2 tablespoons cornstarch

¼ to ½ teaspoon almond extract or spearmint extract

1 teaspoon vanilla extract

2 cups fresh cherries, sliced bananas, strawberries, or ripe pear or apple

DIRECTIONS

1 In a medium saucepan, whisk the coffee, cocoa, sugar, and cornstarch until thickened with bubbles starting to form.

2 Remove from the heat and add the extracts.

3 Dip the fruit into warm or chilled sauce.

PER SERVING: *Calories 79 (From Fat 8); Fat 1g (Saturated 0g); Cholesterol 0mg; Sodium 2mg; Carbohydrate 20g (Dietary Fiber 3g); Protein 3g; Sugar 14g.*

Poached Pears in Red Wine Sauce

STAGE: REGULAR FOODS	PREP TIME: 10 MIN	COOK TIME: 30–45 MIN	YIELD: 2 SERVINGS

INGREDIENTS

2 Bosc pears, peeled, cored and halved

1 cup red wine or grape juice

2 cups water

2 or 3 cinnamon sticks

½ teaspoon cloves

½ teaspoon black peppercorns

1½ tablespoons sugar or honey

Strips of lemon and orange zest from one of each

DIRECTIONS

1 In a skillet with high sides, combine all the ingredients, making sure that the pears can lie in the liquid and not rest on top of one another.

2 Bring to a boil, reduce the heat to medium low, and simmer until the pears are soft.

3 Remove from the heat and enjoy warm or chill.

PER SERVING: *Calories 218 (From Fat 2); Fat 0g (Saturated 0g); Cholesterol 0mg; Sodium 6mg; Carbohydrate 34g (Dietary Fiber 5g); Protein 1g; Sugar 24g.*

Savoring Creamy and Chewy Tasty Treats

Sometimes you just want the comforting texture of a smooth food. In the old days before weight loss surgery you may have headed to the freezer for the ice cream, but ice cream, frozen yogurt, and sherbet are foods to eat with caution. If you had AGB, these foods melt and slide right through the band with no problem, meaning you can eat a lot of calories and never feel full. If you had GBP, either the sugar or the fat can cause dumping.

TIP

Pudding can be a great substitute for ice cream and provide extra protein. The small prepackaged cups in the supermarket are convenient but not a good source of protein. You can increase your protein intake by making your own pudding using the packaged dry sugar-free, fat-free mix and whipping it up with nonfat milk. You can add even more protein by including nonfat dry powdered milk or unflavored protein powder to the mixing bowl. Other creamy foods, like ricotta cheese, puréed sweet potatoes, and pumpkin, can also satisfy your cravings in a more healthful way.

Bars, unlike cookies, can be baked all in single pan and then cut into different shapes. Bars are typically rectangular, but you can create a variety of different shapes to make your bars more fun and bring added attention to your dessert.

TIP

Always use the middle rack when baking bars to make sure they bake evenly. The bars are most likely done when the edges brown and pull away from the pan. Most importantly, allow the pan to cool at least a little before cutting. Some bars may require you to cut them while warm, and others may need to cool completely first. Recipes instruct you on which method is preferred.

Berries with Cannoli Cream

STAGE: SOFT FOODS	PREP TIME: 5 MIN	YIELD: 1 SERVING

INGREDIENTS

1 cup plain, nonfat Greek yogurt or ¾ cup yogurt and ¼ cup skim ricotta cheese

2 tablespoons sugar-free or no-sugar-added orange marmalade (adjust to taste with a few drops stevia as needed)

⅛ teaspoon almond extract

¼ teaspoon unsweetened cocoa powder

½ cup fresh blueberries or strawberries

1 In a blender, combine the yogurt, marmalade, almond extract, and cocoa powder.

2 Place the berries in a small bowl and pour the cream over them.

PER SERVING: *Calories 161 (From Fat 3); Fat 0g (Saturated 0g); Cholesterol 10mg; Sodium 66mg; Carbohydrate 28g (Dietary Fiber 2g); Protein 19g; Sugar 15g.*

Dark Fudge Brownies

STAGE: REGULAR FOODS	PREP TIME: 10 MIN	COOK TIME: 20 MIN	YIELD: 9 SERVINGS

INGREDIENTS

One 15- to 16-ounce can black beans, drained

2 eggs

½ cup semisweet chocolate chips

¼ cup unsweetened cocoa

1 tablespoon butter or oil

1 cup sugar

½ cup sugar substitute blend or stevia blend

¼ cup whole-grain flour

¼ cup room-temperature coffee

DIRECTIONS

1 Preheat the oven to 350 degrees.

2 In a blender or food processor, blend the beans, eggs, chocolate chips, cocoa, oil, and sugar.

3 When combined, add the sweetener, flour, and coffee and mix with a spatula.

4 Pour the mixture into a 9-inch square baking pan and bake for 30 minutes.

PER SERVING: *Calories 203 (From Fat 46); Fat 5g (Saturated 2g); Cholesterol 0mg; Sodium 159mg; Carbohydrate 39g (Dietary Fiber 4g); Protein 4g; Sugar 28g.*

Sweet Potato Pie

STAGE: REGULAR FOODS	PREP TIME: 20 MIN	COOK TIME: 1 HR 25 MIN	YIELD: 10 SERVINGS

INGREDIENTS

1 pound sweet potatoes, peeled and cubed

¼ cup butter, softened

⅓ cup sugar substitute

4 eggs

1 teaspoon cinnamon

½ teaspoon nutmeg

¼ teaspoon cloves

½ teaspoon salt

7 ounces evaporated nonfat milk

One 9-inch pie crust shell, unbaked

DIRECTIONS

1 Boil sweet potatoes in water until easily pierced by fork, about 20 minutes. Cool slightly.

2 Preheat the oven and a cookie sheet to 375 degrees.

3 Place cooked potatoes in large mixing bowl and beat with an electric mixer until smooth. Stir in butter and sugar substitute.

4 Beat in eggs one at a time. Mix in the spices and evaporated milk, and then pour the mixture into an unbaked pie crust.

5 Bake on the preheated cookie sheet near the center of the oven for 70 minutes or until knife inserted in center comes out clean.

PER SERVING: *Calories 220 (From Fat 100); Fat 11g (Saturated 5g); Cholesterol 85mg; Sodium 300mg; Carbohydrate 24g (Dietary Fiber 2g); Protein 6g; Sugar 6g.*

TIP: Be certain to use a sugar substitute that's good for baking.

Ricotta Lemon Curd

STAGE: SMOOTH FOODS	PREP TIME: 5 MIN	CHILL TIME: 2 HR	YIELD: 4 SERVINGS

INGREDIENTS

1½ cups part-skim ricotta cheese

½ cup plain nonfat Greek Yogurt

¼ cup lemon juice

¼ cup sugar substitute

½ teaspoon butter extract

1 teaspoon lemon zest

DIRECTIONS

Place all ingredients into a medium mixing bowl and whip for two minutes with a mixer on medium speed. Refrigerate for 2 hours before serving.

PER SERVING: *Calories 140 (From Fat 65); Fat 7g (Saturated 5g); Cholesterol 30mg; Sodium 115mg; Carbohydrate 8g (Dietary Fiber 0g); Protein 11g; Sugar 1g.*

Chocolate and Strawberry Layered Pudding

STAGE: REGULAR FOODS	PREP TIME: 15 MIN	CHILL TIME: 1 HR	YIELD: 4 SERVINGS

INGREDIENTS

2 cups nonfat milk

One 1-ounce package sugar-free, fat-free instant chocolate pudding mix

1 teaspoon almond extract

8 whole strawberries, stems removed, rinsed, and cut in half

1 cup light whipped topping

DIRECTIONS

1 Pour the milk into a large bowl. Add the pudding mix and almond extract and beat with a wire whisk for 2 minutes or until well blended. Let stand 5 minutes.

2 Layer an 8-ounce glass with ¼ cup of pudding. Add 2 strawberry halves. Repeat both layers and top with ¼ cup whipped topping. Repeat the layers for three additional glasses. Refrigerate for 1 hour before serving.

PER SERVING: *Calories 118 (From Fat 20); Fat 2g (Saturated 2g); Cholesterol 3mg; Sodium 142mg; Carbohydrate 18g (Dietary Fiber 1g); Protein 5g; Sugar 10g.*

VARY IT! For a change, you can use sliced bananas instead of strawberries. Either way, we bet you'll make this recipe again and again.

Pumpkin Custard

STAGE: SMOOTH FOODS	PREP TIME: 10 MIN	CHILL TIME: 1 HR	YIELD: 4 SERVINGS

INGREDIENTS

1 cup pumpkin purée

¼ teaspoon nutmeg

1 teaspoon cinnamon, divided

¼ teaspoon ginger

2 tablespoons brown sugar

¼ cup sugar substitute

1 cup nonfat plain Greek yogurt

2 tablespoon orange zest

DIRECTIONS

1 In a large bowl combine pumpkin, nutmeg, ½ teaspoon cinnamon, ginger, brown sugar, and sugar substitute. Mix well and set aside.

2 In another large bowl mix the yogurt and orange zest.

3 In a glass add ⅛ cup of the pumpkin mixture and layer ⅛ cup of yogurt on top. Repeat both layers; then do the same for three additional glasses. Dust the tops with the remaining ½ teaspoon cinnamon and refrigerate for 1 hour before serving.

PER SERVING: *Calories 80 (From Fat 0); Fat 0g (Saturated 0g); Cholesterol 0mg; Sodium 25mg; Carbohydrate 13g (Dietary Fiber 3g); Protein 6g; Sugar 9g.*

Mango Cream

STAGE: SMOOTH FOODS	PREP TIME: 3 MIN	CHILL TIME: 2 HR	YIELD: 4 SERVINGS

INGREDIENTS

2 cups peeled and cubed mango (see Figure 19-1 for tips on cubing mango)

2 tablespoons fresh lime juice

DIRECTIONS

1 Place mango into a resealable plastic bag and place in freezer for 2 hours.

2 Place the frozen cubed mango and lime juice in a food processor and pulse just until the mango is creamy. (Overblending causes it to defrost and become liquid.)

PER SERVING: *Calories 60 (From Fat 0); Fat 0g (Saturated 0g); Cholesterol 0mg; Sodium 0mg; Carbohydrate 17g (Dietary Fiber 2g); Protein 1g; Sugar 14g.*

TIP: Don't substitute a blender for the food processor. Because of the blade shape, a blender requires more liquid to mix than this recipe includes.

TIP: Store fresh mango at room temperature until ripe. When ripened, mangoes can be stored in the refrigerator for up to five days.

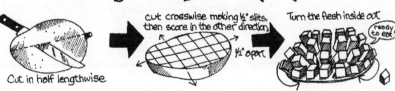

Cutting a Mango the Easy Way

cut crosswise making ½" slits, then score in the other direction

Turn the flesh inside out

ready to eat!

½" apart

Cut in half lengthwise

FIGURE 19-1: How to chop a mango.

Illustration by Elizabeth Kurtzman

Not Your Grandma's Chocolate Cake

STAGE: REGULAR FOODS	PREP TIME: 10 MIN	COOK TIME: 12–40 MIN	YIELD: 8 SERVINGS

INGREDIENTS

1½ cups whole-wheat flour

1½ cups all-purpose flour

1½ cups sugar

¾ teaspoon salt

½ cup unsweetened cocoa

1 teaspoons baking soda

2 tablespoons balsamic vinegar

⅔ cup canola oil

1 teaspoon vanilla extract

1 teaspoon almond extract

2 cups cold coffee

Powdered sugar, for serving

DIRECTIONS

1 Preheat the oven to 350 degrees. Spray with cooking spray a 24-cup mini cupcake pan, a 12-cup muffin pan, or a 9-x-13-inch baking pan.

2 In a large mixing bowl, sift the flours, sugar, salt, cocoa, and baking soda together.

3 In a 4-cup glass measuring cup, whisk the vinegar, oil, extracts, and coffee.

4 Pour the wet ingredients over the dry ingredients and whisk until incorporated, 2 or 3 minutes.

5 Pour the mixture into the prepared pan and bake until a toothpick inserted in the center comes out clean (12 minutes if you're using a mini cupcake pan, 20 minutes if you're using a 12-cup muffin pan, or 35 to 40 minutes if you're using a 9-x-13-inch pan).

6 Cool and dust with powdered sugar.

PER SERVING: *Calories 486 (From Fat 179); Fat 20g (Saturated 2g); Cholesterol 0mg; Sodium 379mg; Carbohydrate 75g (Dietary Fiber 5g); Protein 7g; Sugar 38g.*

Oatmeal Bars

STAGE: REGULAR FOODS	PREP TIME: 10 MIN	COOK TIME: 20 MIN	YIELD: 16 SERVINGS

INGREDIENTS

1 cup quick-cooking oats

1 cup bran cereal

¼ cup whole-wheat flour

½ cup walnut pieces

½ cup nonfat powdered milk

½ teaspoon ground cinnamon

¼ teaspoon ground ginger

¼ cup honey

2 large eggs

DIRECTIONS

1 Preheat the oven to 350 degrees. Coat a 9-x-13-inch baking pan with nonstick spray.

2 Place oats, cereal, flour, walnuts, powdered milk, cinnamon, and ginger in a food processor and coarsely chop and mix. Add the honey and eggs and pulse until the mixture is well combined.

3 Place the mixture in the pan and spread evenly. Bake until lightly browned around the edges, about 20 minutes.

4 Let cool for 20 minutes; then cut into 16 bars.

PER SERVING: *Calories 90 (From Fat 35); Fat 4g (Saturated 0g); Cholesterol 25mg; Sodium 30mg; Carbohydrate 14g (Dietary Fiber 2g); Protein 4g; Sugar 6g.*

TIP: If stored in an airtight container, these bars keep for up to a week.

Chapter **20**

Super Simple Cooking for One . . . or Two

People who have had weight loss surgery often ask us how to cook for one or two. Making small meals is a challenge. Your portions are a lot smaller, so traditional recipe servings are way more than you need or can eat. Even if you don't want to be a short order cook and prepare more than one meal, sometimes you just can't eat what the rest of the family is eating. If you live alone you don't want to spend a lot of time in the kitchen and eat the same leftover meal for the next week.

Food at the supermarket isn't usually packaged for one or two people. If you go to the fresh meat and seafood counter where the food is in cases, you can ask for just the amount you need. If the meat, fish, or poultry is already packaged, you can ask the butcher to break down the package to the size you need. The same goes for the produce department. You don't have to buy bags of apples, oranges, or potatoes. Buy just what you need for less waste. Yes, it's usually a little more expensive to buy smaller quantities, but not having to throw out spoiled food you couldn't eat in time may actually save money.

We're happy to help you with your small meals dilemma! In this chapter we provide you with plenty of quick and delicious recipes that are meant to be enjoyed by one or two people. If you do happen to want leftovers or have a few additional mouths to feed, you can always double or triple the recipes to suit your needs. Enjoy!

Wasting Nothing with Recipes for One

You can't just always take a recipe for four to six servings or more and cut it down to one or two servings. When cooking smaller portions, take into consideration pan size, the temperature that you're cooking your food, and how the food will hold before serving. Without measuring, most people tend to make too much food when cooking for one or two, which can make your food costs go higher.

REMEMBER

Pots and pans need to be smaller when cooking for one. If the pots and pans are too big, the food will likely overcook and become dry, and then it's more likely to cause problems with sticking. Using small pots and pans cooks the food evenly and keep it moist and tender. For small meals, a good sized sauté pan is 6 inches and a 1-quart pot is plenty large enough. Not all cookware sets come with these small sizes. Invest in a good-quality small pots and pans because you'll get a lot of use out of them. And both the small size and good quality make clean up easier!

TIP

If you're eating alone, set the table for yourself. Use your good dishes. Use a placemat and cloth napkin. Turn off the TV. Treat yourself like a guest. Focus on the food, chewing, and eating slowly. Food tastes better when it is savored.

Chicken Mexi Pita

STAGE: REGULAR FOODS	PREP TIME: 7 MIN	COOK TIME: 5 MIN	YIELD: 1 SERVING

½ teaspoon canola oil

4 ounces boneless skinless chicken breast, cut into ¼-inch cubes

1 tablespoon chopped onion

1 tablespoon chopped bell pepper

½ teaspoon hot sauce

¼ teaspoon chili powder

¼ teaspoon garlic powder

⅛ teaspoon black pepper

One 4-inch whole-wheat pita

2 tablespoons shredded lowfat cheddar cheese

1 In a small sauté pan over medium–high heat, add oil. When oil is hot, add chicken, onion, bell pepper, hot sauce, chili powder, garlic powder, and pepper. Sauté for 5 minutes or until chicken is done.

2 Stuff the chicken mixture into the pita and sprinkle cheese on top.

PER SERVING: *Calories 250 (From Fat 55); Fat 6g (Saturated 2g); Cholesterol 70mg; Sodium 380mg; Carbohydrate 18g (Dietary Fiber 3g); Protein 33g; Sugar 1g.*

Zesty Egg Salad

STAGE: REGULAR FOODS	PREP TIME: 10 MIN	YIELD: 1 SERVING

2 hard-boiled eggs, chopped fine

1½ teaspoon light mayonnaise

⅛ teaspoon red pepper flakes

1 teaspoon feta cheese

½ teaspoon chopped black olives

4 reduced-fat whole-wheat crackers

Place eggs, mayonnaise, pepper flakes, feta cheese, and olives into a small bowl and mix well. Serve with crackers.

PER SERVING: *Calories 260 (From Fat 140); Fat 16g (Saturated 4g); Cholesterol 430mg; Sodium 330 mg; Carbohydrate 14g (Dietary Fiber 2g); Protein 15g; Sugar 1g.*

TIP: To hard-boil eggs, place eggs into a medium-sized pot and cover with water. Place on the stove and bring to a boil, then turn off the heat and let the eggs sit in the hot water for 12 to 15 minutes. Refrigerate eggs until you're ready to use them.

Shrimp Cocktail

STAGE: REGULAR FOODS	PREP TIME: 5 MIN	YIELD: 1 SERVING

2 tablespoons low-sodium ketchup

½ teaspoon prepared horseradish

½ teaspoon fresh lemon juice

4 ounces peeled and deveined cooked shrimp

½ teaspoon Old Bay seasoning

1 lemon wedge

1 For the cocktail sauce, combine ketchup, horseradish, and lemon juice in a small bowl.

2 Sprinkle Old Bay seasoning over shrimp and squeeze the lemon wedge to sprinkle juice over the top. Serve with cocktail sauce.

PER SERVING: *Calories 170 (From Fat 20); Fat 2g (Saturated 0g); Cholesterol 230mg; Sodium 660mg; Carbohydrate 8g (Dietary Fiber 0g); Protein 29g; Sugar 7g.*

TIP: You can buy peeled, deveined, cooked shrimp at the seafood counter at your grocery.

Bean Tostada

STAGE: REGULAR FOODS	PREP TIME: 5 MIN	COOK TIME: 3 MIN	YIELD: 1 SERVING

½ cup canned no-salt-added black beans, drained and rinsed

¼ teaspoon diced jalapeño peppers

2 teaspoon shredded carrots

¼ teaspoon chili powder

¼ teaspoon garlic powder

¼ teaspoon onion powder

⅛ teaspoon cumin

One 6-inch whole-wheat tortilla

1 tablespoon shredded lowfat cheddar cheese

1 In a small bowl, slightly mash beans with a fork. Add jalapeño, carrots, chili powder, garlic powder, onion powder, and cumin. Mix well.

2 Coat a 9- or 10-inch nonstick skillet with nonstick spray and place over medium heat. Place the tortilla in the center of the pan.

3 Spread bean mixture over the tortilla, leaving 1 inch of space around the edge. Sprinkle cheese on the top and cook for 2 minutes or until the cheese melts.

PER SERVING: *Calories 230 (From Fat 35); Fat 4g (Saturated 0g); Cholesterol 0mg; Sodium 480mg; Carbohydrate 41g (Dietary Fiber 9g); Protein 11g; Sugar 3g.*

Cottage Veggie Salad

STAGE: REGULAR FOODS	PREP TIME: 5 MIN	YIELD: 1 SERVING

¾ cup lowfat cottage cheese

1 teaspoon chopped chives

¼ teaspoon chili powder

6 peeled cucumber slices

4 halved cherry tomatoes

In a small bowl mix cottage cheese, chives, and chili powder. Serve with cucumber slices and cherry tomatoes.

PER SERVING: *Calories 170 (From Fat 45); Fat 5g (Saturated 2g); Cholesterol 15mg; Sodium 570mg; Carbohydrate 10g (Dietary Fiber 1g); Protein 21g; Sugar 9g.*

TIP: You can mix up the cottage cheese and pack your veggies the night before and store in the fridge. Then in the morning you really have a grab-and-go meal. Now that's fast food!

Preparing Quick and Easy Dishes for Two

Cooking for two can be both harder and easier than cooking just for yourself. Although you should always consider the other person's tastes and keep in mind if he has allergies, your options are wider when cooking for two. Most recipes can be made for two, and when you buy a larger quantity of ingredients, you may save money.

REMEMBER

When cooking for two, medium-sized pots and pans work well. Use an 8- to 10-inch skillet and a 2-quart pot. If the pans are too small, the food may take longer to cook and become chewy. If they're too big, the food can be overcooked and dry. As a rule of thumb, you want your protein to have at least ½ inch of space between pieces. When sautéing veggies, your pan should be no more than ⅔ full to keep food from spilling out.

We made the following recipes for two people, but you can make them for one and then have the leftovers at another meal to save you kitchen time.

Vegetable Soup

STAGE: SOFT FOODS | **PREP TIME: 15 MIN** | **COOK TIME: 30 MIN** | **YIELD: 2 SERVINGS**

1 cup vegetable broth

½ cup canned navy beans, drained and rinsed

¼ cup fresh green beans cut in 1-inch pieces

¼ cup thinly sliced fresh carrots

¼ cup finely chopped cabbage

½ cup chopped tomatoes

1 clove garlic, minced

¼ teaspoon black pepper

¼ teaspoon dried thyme

¼ teaspoon dried basil

In a small pot add all ingredients and bring to a simmer. Cover and continue to simmer for 25 minutes.

PER SERVING: *Calories 100 (From Fat 0); Fat 0g (Saturated 0g); Cholesterol 0mg; Sodium 570mg; Carbohydrate 20g (Dietary Fiber 6g); Protein 6g; Sugar 3g.*

TIP: This soup reheats well so you can make a bigger batch and have leftovers. If you want to increase the protein and calories, you can add some cooked chicken or beef.

Tangy Mustard Baked Chicken

STAGE: REGULAR FOODS	PREP TIME: 10 MIN	MARINATE TIME: 30 MIN	COOK TIME: 20–30 MIN	YIELD: 2 SERVINGS

2 tablespoons fresh lime juice

2 tablespoons fresh lemon juice

1 tablespoon spicy ground mustard

8 ounces boneless, skinless chicken breast

A dash white pepper

⅛ teaspoon curry powder

1 teaspoon lemon zest

⅓ cup fine panko bread crumbs

2 teaspoons melted butter

1 In a small bowl combine the lime juice, lemon juice, and mustard. Brush over the chicken; cover and refrigerate for about 30 minutes.

2 Preheat the oven to 400 degrees. Coat a cooking sheet with nonstick spray.

3 Remove the chicken from the marinade mixture and roll in the bread crumbs, coating both sides. In a small dish combine the pepper, curry powder, and lemon zest, and then sprinkle the mixture over both sides of the chicken.

4 Place chicken on the cooking sheet and drizzle melted butter over the top. Bake for 20 to 30 minutes or until juices run clear.

PER SERVING: *Calories 240 (From Fat 55); Fat 6g (Saturated 3g); Cholesterol 75mg; Sodium 300mg; Carbohydrate 15g (Dietary Fiber 1g); Protein 29g; Sugar 2g.*

NOTE: Panko bread crumbs are also referred to as Japanese bread crumbs. The crumbs are light yet bigger then tradition bread crumbs, which makes the cooked food crispier. You can find them in most supermarkets next to regular bread crumbs.

Creamed Spinach

STAGE: SOFT FOODS | PREP TIME: 15 MIN | COOK TIME: 35 MIN | YIELD: 2 SERVINGS

1 cup water

One 6-ounce bag fresh baby spinach, stems removed

2 tablespoons light cream cheese

1 teaspoon softened butter

A dash of nutmeg

1 tablespoon grated Parmesan cheese

1 Preheat the oven to 350 degrees. Coat an 8-x-8-inch pan with nonstick spray and set aside.

2 Pour 1 cup of water into a 2-quart pot and bring to a boil. Add spinach and cover with a tight lid. Remove from heat and let sit for 3 minutes; then drain the spinach.

3 Combine the cream cheese, butter, and nutmeg and stir well. Stir in the spinach and gently spoon the mixture into the pan. Sprinkle with the Parmesan cheese, cover, and bake for 30 minutes.

PER SERVING: Calories 90 (From Fat 45); Fat 5g (Saturated 3g); Cholesterol 15mg; Sodium 260mg; Carbohydrate 10g (Dietary Fiber 4g); Protein 4g; Sugar 1g.

Balsamic Strawberries

STAGE: REGULAR FOODS	PREP TIME: 5 MIN	REST TIME: 20 MIN	YIELD: 2 SERVINGS

2 cups sliced fresh strawberries

1 teaspoon sugar substitute

1 teaspoon balsamic vinegar

Toss the strawberries, sugar substitute, and balsamic vinegar in a bowl. Let stand 20 minutes before serving.

PER SERVING: *Calories 60 (From Fat 0); Fat 0g (Saturated 0g); Cholesterol 0mg; Sodium 0mg; Carbohydrate 13g (Dietary Fiber 3g); Protein 1g; Sugar 9g.*

NOTE: The longer balsamic vinegar is aged, the sweeter and thicker it gets. The downside is the older the vintage, the more the balsamic vinegar costs. Like a lot of things, you get what you pay for. Store the opened bottle in a cool, dark place and it will keep for a long time.

Peaches and Creamy Wheat

STAGE: SOFT FOODS | PREP TIME: 3 MIN | COOK TIME: 3–7 MIN | YIELD: 2 SERVINGS

6 tablespoons dry Cream of Wheat or 2 packets unflavored Cream of Wheat

1½ cups nonfat milk

½ cup diced canned peaches in light syrup

3 teaspoons sugar substitute

Add all ingredients to a small bowl if microwaving or a small pot if cooking on the stove top. Cook according to package directions.

PER SERVING: *Calories 200 (From Fat 0); Fat 0g (Saturated 0g); Cholesterol 5mg; Sodium 80mg; Carbohydrate 38g (Dietary Fiber 2g); Protein 9g; Sugar 12g.*

TIP: To add 2 grams of protein per serving, stir 2 tablespoons nonfat dry powdered milk into the Cream of Wheat.

VARY IT! If you want to try some different flavors, add 2 to 3 drops of lemon extract, vanilla extract, or almond extract.

Cherry Shrimp Salad

STAGE: REGULAR FOODS	PREP TIME: 10 MIN	CHILL TIME: 1 HR	YIELD: 2 SERVINGS

6 ounces canned shrimp, drained

3 tablespoons dried tart cherries, plumped

½ cup halved cherry tomatoes

2 green onions, chopped

2 tablespoons light mayonnaise

2 tablespoons nonfat plain yogurt

1 tablespoon fresh lemon juice

½ teaspoon chopped fresh oregano

Black pepper to taste

2 cups chopped Bibb lettuce

1 In a large bowl, combine shrimp, cherries, tomatoes, and green onions and mix well.

2 Combine mayonnaise, yogurt, lemon juice, oregano, and pepper in a small bowl and pour over the shrimp mixture. Mix together gently, cover, and refrigerate for one to two hours.

3 Place one cup chopped lettuce on a salad plate. Top each with half of the shrimp salad.

PER SERVING: *Calories 110 (From Fat 35); Fat 4g (Saturated 0g); Cholesterol 90mg; Sodium 190mg; Carbohydrate 8g (Dietary Fiber 2g); Protein 12g; Sugar 4g.*

NOTE: Using canned shrimp makes this salad easy to prepare, but you can use fresh shrimp if you prefer.

TIP: To plump dried cherries, pour ½ cup boiling water over dried cherries and let sit for 5 minutes. Drain before using.

4

The Part of Tens

Chapter **21**

Ten Tips for Long-Term Success

Your weight loss surgery is just the beginning. You have embarked on a life-long journey, and you're going to have to embrace permanent changes in order to enable not only long-term weight loss, but also your overall health. The whole process can be overwhelming, but if you take it step by step and one day at a time, these adjustments will become second nature.

In this chapter, we highlight the top tried-and-true tips to keep you on the path to good health and permanent weight loss. *Remember:* Just as each surgeon is different (and you should always abide by what yours recommends), each weight loss patient is also different. Follow these tips while figuring out what works for you, and remember that your journey may be nothing like your friend or coworker's experience.

Eat on a Schedule

No longer is it possible for you to eat everything you want, any time you want. By having the surgery, you have made an investment in your lifelong health. But the surgery is just a tool. Success will hinge on effort, grit, and deliberate practice on your part.

By eating on a schedule, you will avoid grazing, which leads to weight gain. You may not experience hunger in the early days after surgery, but a point may come when you will. This decreased hunger will actually help you stay on your meal plan. By forming good habits now, it will be easier to avoid weight gain down the road.

Put Good-Quality Foods First

Each meal and snack is an opportunity to fuel your body optimally. Because you can't eat as much as before surgery, be sure you get the most nutritional bang for your calorie buck. Focus on nutrient-rich foods that are loaded with vitamins and minerals and tend to be lower in calories. Keep healthy foods in the house and junk food out!

Choose foods that are as close to their natural state as possible, focusing on

>> Proteins — remember to eat these first!

>> Fruits

>> Vegetables

>> 100 percent whole grains

>> Healthy fats

>> Lowfat or fat-free dairy

Chew, Chew, Chew

One of the most important habits to adopt after weight loss surgery is to take very small bites (the size of a pencil eraser) and chew food thoroughly. This helps you to avoid nausea, vomiting, and food getting stuck. Trust us, none of those are pleasant!

Chew each bite 20 to 30 times until it's a smooth consistency. Put your utensils down between bites. The longer you take to eat, the fuller you feel with less food. After all, that's the goal, isn't it?

Watch Your Portion Sizes

Portion size is key to weight loss. It is estimated that people tend to underestimate the calories they consume by 25 percent. This can really add up in terms of calories consumed.

Weigh and measure everything you eat. Alternatively, eat 1 cup of cereal (or other food) out of a 1 cup container to make sure you don't exceed that amount. If you aren't careful, you may experience "portion creep," in which you make portions larger as time goes by because you forget what they should look like. Measuring your portions keeps you honest and helps move you toward your goals.

Stop Eating When Your Pouch Is Full

Think back to the last holiday meal you had before surgery. You may have eaten a lot very quickly. You probably went from hungry to stuffed in a matter of a few minutes. Stuffed is not going to cut it anymore!

You now have the advantage of having a smaller capacity to store food. In order for you to achieve your weight loss goals and not experience nausea and vomiting, stop eating when your hunger is satisfied. By eating slower, it will be easier to realize when you have had enough. Pay attention to the pouch!

Don't Drink Beverages with Meals

If your pouch is full of liquids, you won't be able to eat, and drinking too soon after a meal may overfill the pouch, causing nausea. You certainly don't want to fill up on liquids and not be able to eat, do you? So be sure you stop drinking 5 to 10 minutes before you eat a meal, and don't begin drinking again for 30 minutes after you finish.

Stay Hydrated

Keep something with you at all times (except at meals) and sip, sip, sip. You can't hold as much liquid as you could before, so if you get dehydrated it will be difficult for your body to catch up. Check the color of your urine to monitor your hydration status. It should be pale yellow or clear, not dark yellow.

Don't wait until you're thirsty to drink. By the time you're thirsty, you are already dehydrated. Your goal is about 64 ounces a day of decaffeinated, sugar-free liquids, and more on hot or humid days and if you're sweating excessively.

Take Your Supplements

Taking supplements is a requirement, not a recommendation. Because you can't eat as much as you could before surgery, you won't be getting everything your body needs through food. Consider your supplements an insurance policy to ensure you get all the vitamins and minerals you need to stay healthy.

Remember, supplements are just that. They're not meant to take the place of food, but to supplement what you get from the foods you eat.

Add Physical Activity

Calories in minus calories out equals weight loss, right? Physical activity is half of the equation for weight loss success.

Find activities you *enjoy* and make them part of your lifestyle. You do not have to go to a gym for hours each day. Break physical activity up into smaller pieces. Get out and walk for 10 minutes three times a day if you can't find 30 minutes to exercise.

Any extra movement is good. Remember, physical activity increases your metabolism, improves energy, and boosts your mood. Incorporate movement into your day by

>> Parking further away from your office

>> Taking the stairs instead of the elevator

>> Marching or doing squats while talking on the phone

>> Exercising during commercials

>> Going outside and playing with your kids

Continue to Follow Up with Your Surgeon

Have a lifelong friendship with your surgeon. You made a lifelong commitment to yourself, and he or she is an important partner you can trust to guide you long term.

Your surgeon should require you return to his or her office for a series of postoperative visits (no, not just one) during the first year, and then annually after that. It's important to keep these appointments, even if you think you're doing fine. You need to have ongoing monitoring of your weight loss, lab values (to detect possible vitamin or mineral deficiencies), nutritional status, and other medical concerns you or your surgeon may have.

Chapter **22**

Ten Easy-to-Prepare Meals Your Family Will Love

I n this chapter you find some quick and easy meal ideas that are pleasing to adults and kids alike. Each meal utilizes at least one recipe from this book, and we provide guidelines for serving sizes for everyone.

TIP

If meal planning and eating together as a family is something new for you, check out Part 1.

Caprese: Tomato Basil Mozzarella Pasta

When tomatoes and basil are fresh, enjoy this flavorful, family–friendly meal. It's also great in a lunch box, cold or warm. Serve with a side of sliced fruit and you have a complete meal.

Menu:

>> Caprese: Tomato Basil Mozzarella Pasta (Chapter 13)

>> Slice of fruit

See the following table for serving sizes:

	WLS Patient	Kids Age 2 to 8	Older Kids and Adults
Caprese Pasta	½ to 1 cup	½ to 1 cup	1 to 2 cups
Sliced fresh melon	2 to 4 tablespoons	¼ to ½ cup	½ to 1 cup

Starting with the Slow Cooker: Pork and Sauerkraut Soup

You family will love this traditional Polish meal. If your family has never eaten sauerkraut, this a great recipe to start with. Kids may need to try a food several times before they accept it, so don't give up on sauerkraut (or any other food) after one or two attempts.

Slow-cooked Pork and Sauerkraut Soup, found in Chapter 16, is easy to make. During the last hour of cooking the soup, have the kids help prepare the mashed potatoes. The kids can peel the potatoes and you can cut them up. After the potatoes are cooked, have the kids help put in the butter and milk and whip them up using the mixer.

Menu:

>> Pork and Sauerkraut Soup (Chapter 16)

>> Mashed potatoes

>> Fresh apple slices sprinkled with cinnamon

See the following table for serving sizes:

	WLS Patient	Kids Age 2 to 8	Older Kids and Adults
Pork and Sauerkraut Soup	½ to 1 cup	½ cup	1 cup
Mashed Potatoes	2 to 4 tablespoons	¼ to ½ cup	½ to 1 cup
Fresh Apple Slices	2 to 4 slices	2 to 4 slices	8 slices
Milk	No beverages with meals!	½ to ¾ cup	1 cup

Mixing Up a Home-Style Meatloaf Meal

Meatloaf has been around for many years, but it's still a welcome addition to anyone's menu. This meatloaf recipe from Chapter 10 still has the beloved ketchup in it, but we top it with tomato gravy, too. Kids love to work with their hands, and making meatloaf is the perfect opportunity. After having your kids wash their hands, place all the ingredients for the meatloaf into a large bowl and let them mix away. This is a perfect way to introduce different ingredients to your kids, and since they helped, they'll love to eat it. The leftovers make great sandwiches the next day.

Menu:

» Home-Style Meatloaf with Tomato Gravy (Chapter 10)

» Corn on the cob

» Fresh strawberries

See the following table for serving sizes:

	WLS Patient	Kids Age 2 to 8	Older Kids and Adults
Meatloaf with Tomato Gravy	2 to 3 ounces	1 to 2 ounces	3 ounces
Corn on the Cob	¼ medium ear	¼ to ½ medium ear	1 medium ear
Fresh Strawberries	2 to 4 berries	2 to 4 berries	4 to 8 berries
Milk	No beverages with meals!	½ to ¾ cup	1 cup

Keeping It Light with Crab Salad Melts

Need a quick dinner after a busy day, or a light weekend lunch? Tuna sandwiches are great, but easy-to-make crab melts are even better. Your family may be surprised by this change in a melt, but we bet they'll like it. Have the kids find the Crab Salad Melts recipe in Chapter 12, help assemble all the ingredients, and mix up the crab salad. Each person can make her own sandwich (but make sure an adult cooks them up).

Menu:

>> Crab Salad Melts (Chapter 12)

>> Baked potato chips

>> Fresh chopped mango

See the following table for serving sizes:

	WLS Patient	Kids Age 2 to 8	Older Kids and Adults
Crab Salad Melt	1 sandwich melt	½ to 1 sandwich melt	2 sandwich melts
Baked Potato Chips	¼ cup	¼ to ½ cup	1 cup
Fresh Chopped Mango	2 to 4 tablespoons	¼ to ½ cup	½ to 1 cup
Milk	No beverages with meals!	½ to ¾ cup	1 cup

Bison Sliders

What kid doesn't love a juicy hamburger? The problem with most burgers is that they're super-sized and loaded with saturated fat. Bring on bison or buffalo mini burgers from Chapter 10 for the perfect lean protein and size for anyone! Kids who grow up eating meals low in saturated fat are less likely to develop chronic heart disease. Enjoy these flavorful burgers with a side salad of lettuce, grape tomatoes, and sliced cucumbers and a nutritious dessert of Dark Chocolate Sauce with Fruit (Chapter 19).

Menu:

- ➤ Bison Burgers (Chapter 10)
- ➤ Nonfat or lowfat milk
- ➤ Dark Chocolate Sauce with Fruit (Chapter 19)

See the following table for serving sizes:

	WLS Patient	Kids Age 2 to 8	Older Kids and Adults
Bison burger	1 ounce or 1 to 2 tablespoons chopped	1 to 2 ounces cooked	3 to 4 ounces cooked
Whole-grain dinner roll	½ of a roll	1 roll	1 roll
Nonfat or lowfat Milk	No beverages with meals!	½ to ¾ cup	1 cup
Dark Chocolate Sauce with Fruit	1 tablespoon sauce, ¼ cup fruit	2 tablespoons sauce, ¼ cup fruit	¼ cup sauce, ¼ to ½ cup fruit

Partying Down with an Enchilada Fiesta

Kids love tacos, so why not introduce them to enchiladas? Chapter 8's Cheesy Chicken Enchiladas are the perfect dish to put on the table for brunch or dinner. After making the chicken mixture, have your kids fill and roll the enchiladas. When baked to perfection, let them cool slightly and serve with Black Bean Salsa from Chapter 10's Spanish Steak recipe.

Menu:

- ➤ Cheesy Chicken Enchiladas (Chapter 8)
- ➤ Black Bean Salsa (Chapter 10)
- ➤ Brown rice

See the following table for serving sizes:

	WLS Patient	Kids Age 2 to 8	Older Kids and Adults
Cheesy Chicken Enchiladas	½ to 1 enchilada	½ to 1 enchilada	1 to 2 enchiladas
Black Bean Salsa	2 to 4 tablespoons	¼ to ½ cup	½ to 1 cup
Brown Rice	1 to 2 tablespoons	¼ to ½ cup	½ cup
Milk	No beverages with meals!	½ to ¾ cup	1 cup

Broccoli Cheese Soup

This soup from Chapter 16 is a crowd pleaser and a good fit for most ages and tastes. Make a double batch and enjoy for a few meals throughout the week.

Menu:

>> Broccoli Cheese Soup (Chapter 16)

>> Whole-grain crackers

>> Sliced apples with cinnamon

See the following table for serving sizes:

	WLS Patient	Kids Age 2 to 8	Older Kids and Adults
Broccoli-Cheese Soup	½ to 1 cup	½ to 1 cup	1 to 2 cups
Whole-grain crackers	½ ounce, crushed	1 ounce serving	1 to 2 ounces
Sliced apples with cinnamon	¼ cup	¼ to ½ cup	1 cup
Milk	No beverages with meals!	½ to ¾ cup	1 cup

Having Your Quiche and Eating , Too

Eggs are great, but adding veggies and seafood makes them irresistible. This crustless quiche found in Chapter 8 is perfect for breakfast, brunch, or a light dinner. Have the kids mix all the ingredients and pour it into a prepared casserole pan. While the quiche is baking, start preparing your fresh fruit salad and set the table for a family meal.

Menu:

» Crustless Seafood Quiche (Chapter 8)

» Fresh fruit salad

» Whole-wheat toast

See the following table for serving sizes:

	WLS Patient	Kids Age 2 to 8	Older Kids and Adults
Crustless Seafood Quiche	½ cup	¼ to ½ cup	1 cup
Fresh Fruit Salad	2 to 4 tablespoons	¼ to ½ cup	½ to 1 cup
Whole-Wheat Toast	½ to 1 slice	½ to 1 slice	1 to 2 slices
Milk	No beverages with meals!	½ to ¾ cup	1 cup

Making It Meatless: Veggie Lasagna

Not every meal needs meat, and a great vegetarian dish, Vegetable Lasagna, can be found in Chapter 8. You may get the kids to love their vegetables when you prepare them with cheese. After all the vegetables are cut, have the kids layer the cheese and vegetables while you make the sauce. Be sure to let cool for about 10 minutes after baking so the lasagna sets up nice and firm. For dessert, check out Chapter 19. We recommend Chocolate and Strawberry Layered Pudding.

Menu:

» Vegetable Lasagna (Chapter 8)

» Garlic breadsticks

» Chocolate and Strawberry Layered Pudding (Chapter 19)

See the following table for serving sizes:

	WLS Patient	Kids Age 2 to 8	Older Kids and Adults
Vegetable Lasagna	½ to 1 cup	¼ to ½ cup	1 to 2 cups
Garlic Breadsticks	¼ to ½ breadstick	½ to 1 breadstick	1 to 2 breadsticks
Chocolate and Strawberry Layered Pudding	¼ to ½ cup	¼ to ½ cup	½ to 1 cup
Milk	No beverages with meals!	½ to ¾ cup	1 cup

Cookin' a Quick Chicken Dinner

Tender and moist Chicken with Tomato–Mushroom Sauce, found in Chapter 9, has a hint of white wine, tastes great, and looks great with the colorful vegetables in it. Don't worry about serving this to kids with wine in the sauce. Very little wine is used, and the alcohol cooks out. However, if you like, the wine can be substituted with chicken broth. The dish takes about 20 minutes to cook, just enough time to make the pasta.

Menu:

» Chicken with Tomato-Mushroom Sauce (Chapter 9)

» Whole-wheat pasta tossed with olive oil and shredded Parmesan cheese

» Fresh cut watermelon

See the following table for serving sizes:

	WLS Patient	Kids Age 2 to 8	Older Kids and Adults
Chicken with Tomato-Mushroom Sauce	2 to 3 ounces	1 to 2 ounces	3 ounces
Whole-Wheat Pasta	2 to 4 tablespoons	¼ to ½ cup	½ cup
Fresh Cut Watermelon	¼ cup	¼ to ½ cup	1 cup
Milk	No beverages with meals!	½ to ¾ cup	1 cup

Index

About the Authors

Brian K. Davidson: Brian is the coauthor of *Weight Loss Surgery For Dummies.* He has been featured on television, spoken at various industry events, and consulted with hundreds of leading industry professionals and patients. He is a passionate advocate of improving obesity awareness and increasing public education for this devastating disease. Brian lives in Connecticut and is the proud father of his daughter, Grace, and son, Riley. You may contact him at bk311d@gmail.com.

Sarah Krieger, MPH, RDN, LDN: Sarah is a registered dietitian nutritionist and is an immediate past media spokesperson for the Academy of Nutrition and Dietetics. She has interviewed with local and national television, radio, print and podcasts in a variety of venues, covering the topics of childhood obesity, food safety, pregnancy, and pediatric nutrition, as well as all things culinary.

Sarah is a graduate of Central Michigan University and earned a master's degree in public health from the University of South Florida. She is wife to Kevin, the IT department for SarahRD.tv, and mother to three children and four to six chickens in St. Petersburg, Florida.

Dedication

This book is dedicated to all who are or have been afflicted with the disease of severe obesity. To those who have tried to diet and failed time and time again. To those who provide support, guidance, and motivation for all to continue on this journey for a healthier and happier life.

Authors' Acknowledgments

From Brian: A heartfelt thanks to the many people who have made this book possible. I'm grateful to the thousands of patients and professionals who have shared their experiences and inspirational stories and were generous with their time. A special thanks to Chef Dave Fouts — you would not be holding this book without his participation and culinary mastery. Thanks also to the amazing team at Wiley, including Tracy Boggier, for her unwavering belief in this book; Elizabeth Kuball, for her important additions, comments, and guidance along the last mile, which is definitely the longest; and Rachel Nix, technical reviewer and nutrition analyst, and Emily Nolan, recipe tester. Finally, thank you to my parents for a lifetime of encouragement; my two brothers; and my children, Grace and Riley, who inspire me every day with the beauty of their spirit, compassion, and love.

From Sarah: I owe the past spokespeople of the Academy of Nutrition and Dietetics accolades for inspiring me to contribute to this book. I love counseling anyone on the journey of weight loss surgery, so it's an honor to contribute my tasty, nutritious recipes to my clients and anyone on this new path. A special thanks to the team of the first edition of *Weight Loss Surgery Cookbook For Dummies.* You paved the path of tasty meals and I am honored to assist in the update. Yes, it is possible to enjoy meals no matter what life brings. Thank you for letting me share some of my simple, yet tasty recipes.

Publisher's Acknowledgments

Senior Acquisitions Editor: Tracy Boggier

Project Editor: Elizabeth Kuball

Copy Editor: Elizabeth Kuball

Technical Editor: Rachel Nix, RDN

Recipe Tester: Emily Nolan

Nutrition Analyst: Rachel Nix, RDN

Production Editor: Vasanth Koilraj

Photographer: TJ Hine Photography, Inc.

Food Stylist: Lisa Bishop

Cover Photos: © Nataliya Arzamasova/ Shutterstock